NAVIGATING COMPLEXITY IN OUR WORLD

PUBLIC THEOLOGIES FOR EVERYDAY LIFE

Editors

Gregg Okesson and Amanda Allen

First Fruits Press
Wilmore, Kentucky
c2021

ISBN: 9781648170119

Navigating complexity in our world : public theologies for everyday life
Editors: Gregg Okesson and Amanda Allen..
Published in the U.S.A. by First Fruits Press, ©2020.
Digital version at https://place.asburyseminary.edu/academicbooks/37/

First Fruits Press is a digital imprint of the Asbury Theological Seminary, B.L. Fisher Library. Asbury Theological Seminary is the legal owner of the material previously published by the Pentecostal Publishing Co. and reserves the right to release new editions of this material as well as new material produced by Asbury Theological Seminary. Its publications are available for noncommercial and educational uses, such as research, teaching and private study. First Fruits Press has licensed the digital version of this work under the Creative Commons Attribution Noncommercial 3.0 United States License. To view a copy of this license, visit http://creativecommons.org/licenses/by-nc/3.0/us/.

For all other uses, contact:

First Fruits Press
B.L. Fisher Library
Asbury Theological Seminary
204 N. Lexington Ave.
Wilmore, KY 40390
http://place.asburyseminary.edu/firstfruits

Navigating complexity in our world : public theologies for everyday life / ǂc editors, Gregg Okesson and Amanda Allen.. – Wilmore, Kentucky : First Fruits Press, ©2020.

    285 pages ; cm.

    ISBN: 9781648170119 (paperback)
    ISBN: 9781648170126 (uPDF)
    ISBN: 9781648170133 (Mobi)
    OCLC: 1200760636

    1. Public theology. 2. Christianity and culture. I. Title. II. Okesson, Gregg A., editor. III. Allen, Amanda L, editor.

BT83.63.N39 2020   230

Cover design by Amanda Kessinger

First Fruits Press
The Academic Open Press of Asbury Theological Seminary
204 N. Lexington Ave., Wilmore, KY 40390
859-858-2236
first.fruits@asburyseminary.edu
asbury.to/firstfruits

TABLE OF CONTENTS

Introduction: *Gregg Okesson* 1

Chapter 1: A Public Theology for Privacy in the
    Technological Age 13
        Jacob E. Tenney

Chapter 2: From Heaven to the Food Desert: How the
    Incarnation Speaks to Issues of Poverty and Obesity
    in the United States 45
        Sadie V. Sasser

Chapter 3: Food as Other: The Manifestation of Hospitality in Food
    and Place During the Global Age 69
        Graham Hoppstock-Mattson

Chapter 4: The Pursuit of Public Theology toward Women Under
    Confucian Society 99
        Kyeo Re Lee

Chapter 5: Love Thy Ecological Neighbor: Christian Love as the
    Healing Balm for Our Broken World 123
        Benjamin D. Foss

Chapter 6: Who Owns the Land? Zimbabwean Traditional
    Leaders' Use of African Traditional Customs and Religion
    Contrasted with Biblical Approaches 151
        Dwight S. M. Mutonono

Chapter 7: A Theological Response to Growing "Vaccine Hesitancy" in American Evangelical Churches 185
Samuel J. Hood

Chapter 8: "I Was Suicidal and You Welcomed Me": Framing Suicide Prevention in Mongolia Through the Lens of Christian Hospitality 205
Michael S. Bennett

Chapter 9: Toward a Public Ecclesiology for the Evangelical Church: Embodying Our Biblical Identity 243
Michael Schlatt

Conclusion: *Amanda Allen* 273

Introduction

Gregg Okesson

This book began, at least in seminal form, back in May 2010. I was sitting in my office at Kijabe Hospital, Kenya, when I received an email letting me know I was accepted as a new faculty member at Asbury Theological Seminary, USA.

I had been teaching at a theological institution in Kenya for nearly a decade. My African seminary posted me to Kijabe hospital in order to help integrate theology within a medical curriculum. While in the West this might appear a curious union; there it made complete sense. In Africa (and elsewhere around the world) health represents a significant theological category due in large part to the larger cosmology found on the continent, with more fluid interaction between spiritual and material realities. "Health" involves negotiating the different ways people become sick as well as how they appropriate resources within the spiritual realm for becoming healthy. Furthermore, health is not just vertical in terms of how people relate to the divine, but also horizontal. People are sick together; they also heal together. Working at the hospital allowed me to engage health as a rich, multifaceted theological concept.

I had been moving theologically in "public" directions for years, led first by living in a rural Tanzanian village for two years, then subsequently teaching theology at the African theological institution for almost a decade. At our seminary, students would naturally bring public realities into the classroom. They wrestled with topics such as poverty and tribalism and politics. Our theological institution had a farm in the middle of campus. In addition to crops, we raised cows, chickens, and fish. This was not merely for economic reasons. It was central to how we taught theology and trained leaders. John Mbiti asks something similar of Western education: "Will theological education in the West ever get out into the streets without an umbrella, get wet and hear the birds singing? … Much theological activity is taking place on the ground and in the streets, in the fields where people are, where the church is."[1]

My office at Kijabe hospital, as I recall it, was six foot by six foot, located outside the hospital morgue. Family members would congregate at various times of the day to receive the bodies of loved ones. Sometimes they would wail uncontrollably. Other times churches would join them and sing beautiful songs of worship. The sound of ambulances echoed regularly across the hills of the Great Rift Valley, while the stench of decaying bodies wafted into my study on a hot day. The location of my office was a sobering reminder of frailty and death; as well as a wonderful venue for contemplating intersections of doxology and life.

I was sitting in my office when I received the email from Asbury. The following day I was sitting in the same office when the dean asked me to send him the syllabus for a new course proposal. He gave me three days to submit the syllabus (which subsequently needed to get approved by different committees). My new faculty position related to teaching international development. As a theologian and missiologist, I wanted to help future pastors, missionaries, and church leaders not only think about such topics as health, land, economics, and justice in global spaces but more importantly connect theology with everyday realities such as disease, deforestation, poverty, and the marginalization of people. As I sat at my desk and watched people outside my door wrestle with death, while listening to choir groups sing songs of doxology and hope in the face of loss, the new course took shape in my mind.

I have now been teaching the course for almost a decade. Like most courses it has morphed over time. It is called, "Public Theology for Global Development" and introduces students to the complex realities of poverty, injustice, disease, environmental decay, migration, globalization, and wayward forms of politics humans experience in the world. The goal of the course is to enable students to enter into these convoluted global realities through the rich resources of theology. The course is missiological in the sense of foregrounding the centrality of

---

[1] John Mbiti, "When the Bull is in a Strange Land, It Does Not Bellow," In *God and Globalization: Christ and the Dominions of Civilization*, Max L. Stackhouse and Diane B. Obenchain (eds.) (Harrisburg, PA: Trinity, 2002), 170.

the gospel of Jesus Christ; along with highlighting the importance of the church as the "hermeneutic of the gospel;"[2] while grappling with the socioreligious complexity of highly dynamic, global spaces.

This past academic year I had an exceptional group of students in this course. Half of them were PhD students while the other half were enrolled in MA or MDiv degrees. We had students from throughout the U.S, along with the countries of Kenya, Nigeria, Taiwan, Zimbabwe, and India. Amanda Allen, one of my doctoral students, served as the teaching intern for the course and we decided, based upon the exceptional quality of the final papers submitted for the course, to ask the students to revise the papers for publishing in this edited volume. The nine chapters included in this volume represent well the breadth of issues covered in this course, as well as the thoughtful, nuanced theological engagement of the individual students.

What is Public Theology?

The course itself and the chapters found in this volume represent examples of public theology. There is no definite definition for public theology.[3] The phrase itself was first coined by Martin Marty in the 1970s within the context of discussion regarding civil religion. In the ensuing years a number of theologians and Christian ethicists employed the term to grapple with Christian faith in the context of Western secularism. Public theology has subsequently broadened its scope within a widening array of disciplines, including missiology, biblical studies, and church history, while moving into non-Western contexts where the discipline continues to morph. Scholars define it as: *"theologically informed descriptive and normative public discourse about public issues, institutions, and interactions, addressed to the church or other religious body as well as the larger public or publics, and argued in ways that can be evaluated*

---

[2] Lesslie Newbigin used this phrase in *The Gospel in a Pluralist Society* (Grand Rapids, MI: Eerdmans, 1989), Chapter Eighteen.

[3] Dirkie Smit says, "In short, the notion of public is used in so many meanings and discourses that it defies any unequivocal and technical definition. It should not be surprising, therefore, that the expression 'public theology' can be used in many different ways and discourses as well." "Notions of the Public and Doing Theology," *International Journal of Public Theology* 1 (2007), 431–454: 443.

and judged by publicly available warrants and criteria."[4] Let me use this working definition to unpack some of its contemporary meaning and lay a framework for the essays found in this volume.

First, public theology can be *descriptive,* as in studying empirically what is happening in a particular society at a given time, or *normative,* where the focus rests upon articulating a compelling vision and praxis for how theology should impact society. Scholars move fluidly between descriptive and normative poles. Sometimes they begin descriptively in order to posit a normative appeal. The particular point of emphasis may depend on what discipline they use in order to engage public theology. Historians and social scientists tend to be more descriptive, while ethicists, systematic theologians, and biblical scholars are more normative. Due to its interdisciplinary foundation, missiologists often move readily between the two.

Second, public theology involves *public discourse* with regard to *public issues, institutions, and interactions.* As discourse, it wrestles with how theology should go public. The Enlightenment heritage carved deep runes into the cosmological landscape of Western societies in the form of dichotomies, separating private from public, and sacred from secular. Western agents then transmitted their theology within the packaging of these dichotomies all around the world through the vehicles of colonialism, missions, and globalization. People continue to interpret the world around these dichotomies, even if in reality "religions are not only personal and private; they inevitably go public. They spill over the boundary of inner beliefs and individual convictions."[5] Public theologians do not merely want to break down these Enlightenment dichotomies but nurture healthy forms of going public. They further believe it is not enough to think theologically with regard to public issues, but discourse should lead to action. This bent toward praxis within the discipline of public theology leads them into political advocacy with regard to systems and institutions in society.

---

[4] E. Harold Breitenberg Jr, "What is Public Theology?" In Deirdre King Hainsworth and Scott R. Paeth (eds.) *Public Theology for a Global Society: Essays in Honor of Max L. Stackhouse* (Grand Rapids, MI: Eerdmans, 2010), 3–17: 5.

[5] Max Stackhouse, "Reflections on How and Why We Go Public," *International Journal of Public Theology* 1, no. 3 (2007): 421–430: 423.

Initially, public theologians were primarily concerned with secularism, pluralism, and globalization – as these were the pressing issues arising from within Western contexts. Over time, the discipline of public theology has received new energy from the issues raised within Asian, Latin American, and African contexts. This shift, which is still emerging through the tremendous contributions found within World Christianity, has foregrounded theological interaction with other religions, as well as taking up issues of the environment, liberation, power, health, marginalization and poverty. Majority World scholars have also reminded theologians that the *what* of theology is always carefully interconnected with the *who*. It is not just the elite intelligentsia who participate in public theology, but also people on the ground, in the streets, and those working in the fields. Public theology must take seriously the voices and needs of people who daily wrestle with poverty and marginalization. Social location is essential.

When public theologians wade into these complex issues, they usually do so through a range of Christian resources, such as biblical images like *shalom*, human flourishing, redemption, and/or the kingdom of God. Hence, Sebastian Kim defines public theology as "critical, reflective and reasoned engagement of theology in society to bring the kingdom of God, which is for the sake of the poor and marginalized, by engaging [the] academy, the church, and society."[6] Meanwhile Jürgen Moltmann says,

> It [public theology] gets involved in the public affairs of society. It thinks about what is of general concern in the light of hope in Christ for the kingdom of God. It becomes political in the name of the poor and marginalized in a given society. Remembrance of the crucified Christ makes it critical towards political religions and idolatries. It thinks critically about the religious and moral values of the society in which it exists, and presents its reflections as a reasoned position.[7]

---

[6] Sebastian Kim, "Mission's Public Engagement: The Conversation of Missiology and Public Theology," *Missiology* 45, no. 1 (2017): 7–24: 8.

[7] Jürgen Moltmann, *God for a Secular Society* (Minneapolis: Fortress Press, 1999), 1.

Both Kim and Moltmann highlight important linkages between the kingdom of God and the concerns of "the poor and marginalized." As such, the emergent voices of those around the world has allowed public theology to align more with the subject material of my course in international development, accentuating the lived experiences of people in global spaces.

Third, public theology relates with different publics in the world. The definition quoted above says it is *addressed to the church or other religious body as well as the larger public or publics*. Early on, David Tracy outlined three publics as: wider society, the academy, and church.[8] Scholars have subsequently included other publics, such as economics, politics, land, and other religions. The church itself functions as an important public in the world and intersects with the rest of public life. Elsewhere, I have described this through the imagery of weaving, showing how churches intersect with the publics around a local congregation in highly dynamic ways like the threads of an elaborate cloth.[9] Dirkie Smit argues something similar. He says,

> the church exists always as an integral part of human life in the world; it is interwoven always with public life in society and community; it should be aware of and interested in the resulting impact in both directions – the impact of public life on the church, its place, social form and self-understanding and also the impact of the church on public life and the many spheres that together constitute life in the world.[10]

While it is fashionable to castigate the church for the unhealthy role it has played in society (and any criticism is warranted), public theology accentuates the need for probing different intersections between church and society for the purpose of human flourishing.

Finally, according to the previous definition, public theology is *argued in ways that can be evaluated and judged by publicly available*

---

[8] David Tracy, *The Analogical Imagination: Christian Theology and the Culture of Pluralism* (New York: Crossroad, 1981), 3, 5.

[9] Gregg Okesson, *A Public Missiology: How Local Churches Witness to a Complex World* (Grand Rapids, MI: Baker, 2020), 5–6.

[10] Smit, "Notions of the Public," 441.

warrants and criteria. In other words, theology cannot just remain the privileged discipline of scholarly elites, nor rest comfortably behind the language spoken exclusively within the academy. Public theology must be accessible for the public realm. And for theology to be accessible to anything as complex as public life, it needs to translate the narrative, language, symbols, and embodied practices of the Christian faith into the narrative, language, symbols, and embodied practices of public life. This will invariably involve creativity and imagination. It also necessitates entire communities of witness.

How Does Public Theology Relate to Our Complex World?

Now that I have outlined some of public theology's primary contributions, let me connect this with the complexity of our contemporary world. One of the reasons I appreciate the resources found within public theology is that I believe it is well suited to enter into the complexity of public life. Other disciplines such as ethics, missiology, and sociology are likewise conducive to entering into complexity – and it should be noted we increasingly find interesting overlaps between these disciplines and the broader field of public theology.

We all live surrounded by complexity. That statement alone should be self-evident by anyone who daily swims in the currents of public life. This is as true for those living in my village in Tanzania as it is for the person residing in Singapore or New York City (though with notable differences in type, movement, and scope). Complexity is not a Western phenomenon, nor is it limited to what we find within large metropolises.

We purposely use the imagery of navigation in the title of this book as it communicates movement amidst complexity (or complexity amidst movement). Consider a busy urban thoroughfare, or the transmission of cultural elements within a diverse, cosmological town. However, even remote villages, such as where we lived in Tanzania, involve movement and complexity, though one needs different lenses in order to adequately comprehend the various flows. Complexity arises from movement, and globalization is a perfect example of that. Arjun Appadurai understands globalization through the imagery of -scapes, which he outlines as mediascapes, technoscapes, ethnoscapes, financescapes, and ideoscapes to capture the flows of media, technology, ethnicity and culture, economics, and ideas that permeate our world.[11]

We often think of globalization as a one-way street, where goods, ideas, and cultural artifacts move from the West to the rest of the world; however, globalization is more accurately a crisscrossing, multilane series of highways, where global agents "answer back" to what they receive, imparting new meanings into Western forms, while exporting their own cultural elements all around the world (and where these are subsequently altered by new audiences). Hence, we might say that globalization involves a multidisciplinary process of complexification within increased world compression. We don't often think of complexity (which implies diversity) and compression (suggestive of unification) occurring simultaneously, but that is precisely what we are experiencing within globalization.

For example, people associate media with Hollywood, and technology with Silicon Valley, but Hollywood and Silicon Valley are constantly influenced by what is happening around the world (for example, the technology behind sending money through cell phones first emerged in Kenya and is now being adopted in the West). Or, maybe a better example is food. We all know food is constantly reinterpreted by people all around the world. The U.S. borrows tacos from Mexico, and pizza from Italy, and invests both dishes with its own distinctive characters. American style tacos or pizza is then exported all around the world where it is given new tastes and meaning. In similar ways, the migration of people all around the world increasingly nurtures complex forms of human identity. People migrate for a variety of reasons and negotiate their identity through a multifaceted array of resources. An immigrant moving from Tripoli to Paris to Montreal, for example, combines different elements within his or her identity that are greater than the sum of the parts. Complexity is also seen within nationhood, where religion, ethnicity, and socio-economic status, as well as deeper mythic notions, such as "the remembered past," complexify what it means to be a citizen within a certain country.

---

[11] Arjun Appadurai, *Modernity at Large: Cultural Dimensions of Globalization* (Minneapolis: University of Minnesota Press, 1996).

Few scholars wade as deeply and intelligibly into contemporary forms of complexity as Max Stackhouse. One of his primary concerns lies with a theological engagement of globalization.

> Religion is always deeply embedded within the processes of globalization. Theology, at its best invigorates globalization with profound meanings of creation, life, fruitfulness, *shalom*, and guided by Christological visions of "reconciling everything on heaven and on earth" (Eph 1:10).

Stackhouse employs the biblical language of "powers" to describe the deeper spiritualities that undergird globalization. These spiritualities can be good and life-giving, as explained above, or they can be bad and destructive. In the case of the latter, he argues:

> If one of the spheres fails to simultaneously facilitate and channel the power that drives it, or begins to cannibalize other powers, destroying their integrity, or if it cannot be reformed by both the functional pressures of the other spheres and the recovery or reconstruction of a valid spiritual vision with viable ethic, the whole is likely to implode and the people suffer greatly.[12]

Public theology enters into the various movements of globalization in order nurture it from within. Stackhouse describes it as a "mandate for our time to invite all the peoples of the world to become participants in a global, civil society that is marked by the empowerment of the people."[13]

Organization of this Volume

Navigating Complexity in Our World, attempts to wade into contemporary public life through the resources of public theology. The chapters in this edited volume represent well what I have been discussing in this introduction. Each of the authors highlights a different aspect of our public realm. They don't always talk explicitly about the discipline of public theology, but we trust the reader will readily see how theology shapes their interactions. They draw upon such rich resources such as hospitality, love, creation, place, incarnation, and the church in order

---

[12] Max Stackhouse, *God and Globalization: Globalization and Grace, Volume Four* (New York/London: Continuum, 2007), 45.
[13] Ibid., 246.

to give new meanings to public realities such as privacy, food, land, and politics.

We have not divided the book into formal divisions; however, there is an underlying organization to the volume. The perceptive reader will see we structured the volume according to shared themes. In the first chapter, Jacob Tenney offers an interesting analysis to the changing shape of private-public in our contemporary world. The next two chapters deal with the theme of food. In Chapter Two, Sadie Sasser wades into predicament of food desserts in North America and draws insights from the theology of Christ's incarnation. In Chapter Three Graham Hoppstock-Mattson explores important linkages between food and place through a theology of hospitality. In Chapter four Kyeo Re Lee looks at what a public theology might look like for women within a Confucian society. The following two chapters deal with the environment and land, first in Chapter Five with Benjamin Foss's exploration of love as the impetus for environmental care in the context of global warming; and then in Chapter Six as Dwight Mutonono looks as theological meanings of land in Zimbabwe, especially with linkages between African Traditional Religions and the current political situation. Chapters Seven and Eight deal with health-related issues. First, Samuel Hood enters into the vaccine hesitancy debate within North American evangelical churches and seeks to unpack the varying meanings people give to vaccines. Michael Bennett then examines the high rate of suicides in Mongolia. He uses a theology of hospitality to guide a possible response by the local church. In the final chapter, Michael Schlatt interacts with sociologists and theologians alike to frame what a public ecclesiology might look like within Western Christianity. Amanda Allen then concludes the volume by reflecting back upon what we have learned.

It has been ten years since I created this course. My office in Kijabe, Kenya was not comfortable nor convenient. At the time, I was trying to integrate a theological view of health into a medical curriculum. Ever since that time I have been trying to nurture linkages between public theology and missiology, especially in regard to the urgent issues confronting international development.

I hope the reader will enjoy this rich, multifaceted, and diverse array of chapters dealing with the subject of public theology. None of the authors attempts to offer a one-size-fits-all answer to the problems they face. The issues of food, land, health, and the challenges confronting women resist any singular solutions. They do take us by the hand deeper into the complexity of global spaces and help us make important life-giving linkages between theology and public life.

Gregg A. Okesson

Chapter 1
A Public Theology for Privacy in the Technological Age

Jacob E. Tenney[1]

Abstract

There has been a struggle since the inception of the modern notion of the right to privacy to clearly identify what is private and what is public. This issue has become exaggerated in the technological age with no clear understanding of what and who should be protected from the authority and observation of the public. The Church has had an insignificant voice in the current debate on the individual's right to privacy, and this paper seeks to show why a public theology for privacy is vital in the current age, one which is defined by technology. An assessment of technological privacy issues currently occurring sheds light on the severity of the subject, and the use of historical, conceptual, and theological lenses aid in identifying the constant struggle between the public and private spheres. It has been determined that the public sphere, ruled and defined by power and authority, will seek to destroy and profit off of the safety found in the private sphere, and that a public theology for privacy should lovingly work towards the proper reconstruction of a private sphere that is others-focused and gives all individuals space for retreat, intimacy, and protection.

---

[1] Jacob E. Tenney is a student at Asbury Theological Seminary pursuing his Master of Theology degree. He is an ordained elder in the Free Methodist Church and is married with two daughters.

Introduction: A Crisis of Privacy

The world was presented with headline news when, on June 6, 2013, an investigative story titled, "US Orders Phone Firm to Hand Over Data on Millions of Calls: Top Secret Court Ruling Demands 'Ongoing, Daily' Data from Verizon," was published by *The Guardian*.[2] The story was the first of many revelations pertaining to how the United States government interacts with the private lives of people, and even foreign entities and governments around the globe without their knowledge or consent, through surveillance and access of internet and telecommunications records. At the center of this still ongoing saga between security and privacy stands the former U.S. Central Intelligence Agency (CIA) employee and subcontractor for the U.S. National Security Agency (NSA), Edward Snowden, the whistleblower who leaked an enormous amount of classified, top-secret documents to several newspapers. After being privy to classified government information for close to a decade, he decided he could no longer stand in silence to what he perceived was the United States government's destruction of "privacy, internet freedom and basic liberties for people around the world with this massive surveillance machine they're secretly building."[3]

Snowden describes his actions as civil disobedience; that is, an act of "deliberate disobedience of a law in order preserve one's moral integrity, protest, bring attention to an injustice, and/or catalyze the process of a change in a bad law or policy."[4] He confidently states that the reason he acted was to "inform the public as to that which is done in their name and that which is done against them," which he says in the eyes of the NSA includes "every conversation and every form of behaviour in the world known to them."[5] His passion and motivation throughout this entire ordeal lies in the simple creed he confessed at the very beginning of it all: "I don't want to live in a world where there's no privacy and therefore no room for intellectual exploration and creativity."[6]

---

[2] Glenn Greenwald, "Edward Snowden: The Whistleblower Behind the NSA Surveillance Revelations," *The Guardian*, June 11, 2013, https://www.theguardian.com/world/2013/jun/09/edward-snowden-nsa-whistleblower-surveillance).

[3] Ibid.

[4] Peter L. Jones, "Civil Disobedience," in *Dictionary of Scripture and Ethics*, ed. Joel B. Green (Grand Rapids: Baker Academic, 2011), 140.

[5] Greenwald, "Edward Snowden."

[6] Ibid.

At the heart of this entire issue rests the conundrum that Snowden wrestled with: "to keep some news (even if truthful) to [himself] so as to protect certain parties (such as loved ones); or to reveal information in the interest of public transparency or the common good."[7] As he wrestled with it initially, so now the entire world has been invited into the struggle, with a myriad of conclusions being reached. People have called Snowden "a whistleblower, a traitor, and a hero. He was honored with various awards for peace and integrity, but he was also indicted for theft of government property and communication of classified intelligence."[8] This issue of privacy in our ever-expanding technological society seems to have touched a sensitive nerve within the modern world.

Amidst the debate over what the right to privacy is and how it functions in today's world, several questions must be asked: how does the Christian, and the Church at large, respond to the rights attached to privacy and the issues that surround it? What does it mean to be a Christian that puts a value on privacy? Should a Christian fight for the right to privacy despite the notion that a healthy, evangelical faith requires a very public way of living? These questions (and many more) have gone unanswered by both the Church and Christian scholarship in a technological age; the number of theological conversations pertaining to the issue are few to none. There must be a concerted effort to work out a public theology, a Christian dialogue and engagement with the systems and movements embedded within the culture at large, for the issue of privacy.

In this paper I will focus on developing a public theology pertaining to the subject of privacy in the technological age. To accomplish this, I will provide an overview of current trends and issues pertaining to individual privacy; a brief history of privacy in the world; a conceptual primer in understanding the thought and debate between the public and private realms; along with a theological assessment of how to interact with healthy forms of privacy in our current culture. My hope is to offer a balanced understanding of how both the individual Christian and the communal Church can and should operate within the realms of privacy. Ignorance simply can no longer suffice in response to

---

[7] Cynthia Nolan, "The Edward Snowden Case and the Morality of Secrecy," *The Catholic Social Science Review* 22 (January 2017): 291-92.
[8] Ibid., 292.

an issue where the global population is desperately seeking clarity. To quote theologian Reinhold Niebuhr, "we are always part of the drama of life we behold; and the emotions of the drama therefore color our beholding."[9]

Current Privacy Trends and Issues

The Edward Snowden situation helps to shed some light on the perspective that many have concerning privacy in the today's day and age. In an interview on *CBS This Morning*, Snowden gave a moral defense of his civil disobedience: "what's the question that's more important here: was the law broken or was that the right thing to do?"[10] In his mind, privacy is a right, and its existence is necessary and essential to the common good. As powerful entities (governments, corporations, etc.) enter the lives of individuals in much more intimate ways, concern for the common good has increased and consequently privacy has become a highly contested topic.

In order to engage in a deeper conversation about privacy, it is important to first establish a cursory groundwork on the subject. Though the current privacy debate is often categorized as a technology and media issue, its scope goes far beyond that.

Supreme Court Justice Louis Brandeis, one of the early progenitors of the modern notion of privacy, wrote in 1891 that privacy is "the right to be let alone" for "the protection of the person."[11] One of his contemporaries, journalist E. L. Godkin, commented on this new category of rights by saying that "privacy is a distinctly modern product, one of the luxuries of civilization, which is not only unsought for but

---

[9] Reinhold Niebuhr, *Discerning the Signs of the Times: Sermons for Today and Tomorrow* (New York: Charles Scribner's Sons, 1946), 10, quoted in Martin E. Marty. "Reinhold Niebuhr: Public Theology and the American Experience," *The Journal of Religion* 54, no. 4 (1974): 332.

[10] *CBS This Morning*. "Edward Snowden wants to come home but says U.S. won't give him a fair trial". Filmed [September 2019]. YouTube video, 15:25. Posted [September 16, 2019]. https://www.youtube.com/watch?v=O4nFGOEeSP0

[11] Louis Brandeis and Samuel Warren, "The Right to Privacy," *Harvard Law Review* 4, no. 5 (December 15, 1890): 195.

unknown in primitive or barbarous societies."¹² Modern privacy, then, has a foundational aspect of separation and detachment, which are mostly foreign concepts in our always connected, consumption-driven, individualistic culture.

That said, the vast majority of privacy issues that are causing concern and sparking debate lie within the realm of technology and media. A helpful tool (one that will be revisited in this paper) for understanding our world's relationship to technology is provided by sociologist Jacques Ellul's assessment of modern society. Ellul argues that society is characterized by and dependent upon "technique," - which he defines as "the totality of methods rationally arrived at and having absolute efficiency (for a given stage of development) in every field of human activity."[13] Applying this explanation to the present culture, it can be contended that our current society functions in a way that prioritizes the most efficient ways to do anything, despite the ramifications that may occur as a result.

This dependence upon and prioritization of efficiency, both by individuals and powerful institutions, is made evident by a report published in 2019 by Amnesty International, a global human rights organization. The report identifies several concerns raised by the surveillance, data collection, and general lack of protection of personal data by companies such as Facebook and Google. It states that these two technology goliaths have "established dominance over the primary channels that most of the world... relies on to realize their rights online... [and] billions of people have no meaningful choice but to access this public space on terms dictated by Facebook and Google" if they wish to participate in the "new global public square."[14] The world's total dependence on the efficiency of technique through the personal use of technology and media, channels which are controlled by powerful corporations, has created a power struggle over the valuable commodity of the private spheres of individuals.

---

[12] E.L. Godkin, "The Right of the Citizen to his Reputation," *Scribner's Magazine* 8 (July-December 1890): 65.

[13] Jacques Ellul. *The Technological Society* (New York: Knopf, 1964), xxv.

[14] "Facebook and Google's Pervasive Surveillance Poses an Unprecedented Danger to Human Rights." Amnesty International, November 21, 2019. https://www.amnesty.org/en/latest/news/2019/11/google-facebook-surveillance-privacy/.

As has already been shown, national governments (beyond just the United States; including, China, Russia, and Syria) have also been accused of being major offenders of personal privacy. With the ability to craft and implement laws and policies that serve to enhance power and suppress dissension and opposition, many surveillance programs have been adopted (specifically by the US government) in order to "protect innocent Americans from the deadly plans of terrorists dedicated to destroying America and our way of life."[15] In the process of implementing such methods of protection, though, many have made the argument that the government has overstepped its bounds and has violated the personal privacy rights of those they claim that they are defending. Sascha Meinrath, the Palmer Chair of Telecommunications at Penn State University and an internationally renowned technology policy expert, provided some examples of ways that the US government may be infringing on individuals' personal lives:

> Everything from your financial records, to your phone calls, to your social media accounts, to your email – it's all being pulled into surveillance programs operating under different legal umbrellas. One is called "Section 215" – and is in danger of being re-authorized this fall – which enables information sharing between mega corporations like Google, AT&T and others, and the U.S. government. The other major legal umbrella is called "Section 702", which surveilles the flow of data over the Internet. Then there's executive order 12333, which gives government agencies far reaching cover to target people. And then likely, there are other surveillance regimes we don't even know about. In other words: The Snowden files were only the tip of the iceberg, and since the Snowden revelations in 2013, U.S. government surveillance has dramatically increased, not decreased.[16]

---

[15] United State Department of Justice, "The USA PATRIOT Act: Preserving Life and Liberty," accessed March 16, 2020, https://www.justice.gov/archive/ll/what_is_the_patriot_act.pdf.

[16] Sascha Meinrath, "The Erosion of Privacy, And Why We Need A New Social Contract," Forbes (*Forbes Magazine,* October 16, 2019), https://www.forbes.com/sites/ashoka/2019/10/15/the-erosion-of-privacy-and-why-we-need-a-new-social-contract/#27baecf37396)

The nation-state, much like an international corporation, has historically wielded incredible power over individuals and has been able to exert it in profound ways. The intrusiveness that characterizes a government that allegedly values and promotes its citizens' freedoms should be cause for reasonable alarm.

As the previous quote by Meinrath illustrates, multinational technology corporations (such as Facebook and Google) also have had major issues concerning the privacy of their customers and users. Facebook's Cambridge Analytica scandal left the information and data of an estimated 87 million people exposed for the purpose of "[building] a massive targeted marketing database based on each user's individual likes and interests."[17] Google has had numerous privacy scandals, including a 50 million euro fine levied by the French government "for not properly disclosing to users how data is collected across its services — including its search engine, Google Maps and YouTube — to present personalized advertisements."[18] Issues such as these, however, are commonplace in our technological society. These powerful corporations, using the most efficient means possible, aggregate the personal information of their users, information such as "sensitive details about their lifestyles, personal politics and even medical conditions," in order to sell the information to "data aggregators, data brokers, [and] data analysts."[19] These data-driven companies "are trading in our personal information… [collecting] thousands of data points on individuals from various companies we deal with, and [using] them to provide information about us to companies and political parties."[20] Technology giant Apple, recognizing the concerns people across the globe have related to privacy, went as far as placing privacy within their "core values" and announced their belief that it is "a

---

[17] Aja Romano, "The Facebook data breach wasn't a hack. It was a wake-up call.," *Vox*, March 20, 2018, https://www.vox.com/2018/3/20/17138756/facebook-data-breach-cambridge-analytica-explained.

[18] Adam Satariano, "Google Is Fined $57 Million Under Europe's Data Privacy Law," *The New York Times*, January 21, 2019, https://www.nytimes.com/2019/01/21/technology/google-europe-gdpr-fine.html.

[19] Katharine Kemp, "Here's How Tech Giants Profit from Invading Our Privacy, and How We Can Start Taking It Back," *The Conversation*, June 3, 2020, https://theconversation.com/heres-how-tech-giants-profit-from-invading-our-privacy-and-how-we-can-start-taking-it-back-120078.

[20] Ibid.

fundamental human right."[21] And though it may be viewed as the tech company that is most concerned with privacy, Apple still allows (and profits off of) apps and services on its ecosystem that collect and sell personal user data.[22]

Privacy has become an issue across the spectrum between individuals and authoritative entities, unearthing an age-old power struggle between the influential and the peripheral. Such a conflict between the two entities convinces individuals of the need for protection from outside dangers, instills a wariness toward the unknown and unfamiliar, and persuades them of the need for a guard from the intrusive and harmful attacks that may affect their ability to function and thrive in the present-day world. Identity theft protection services, a 10-billion-dollar market[23] including entities such as LifeLock, LegalSheild and IdentityForce, have recognized this fear and have profited off it by promising to provide the protection that consumers desire amidst the perils that await them in cybersphere. However, the peace of mind these companies offer is routinely supplied through monitoring services provided by credit bureaus Equifax, Experian, and TransUnion, services which collect and sell consumer credit information to marketers, banks, and credit issuers without the consumer's consent.[24] How, then, are individuals supposed to operate technology with any semblance of personal security when the perceived safety nets are actually elaborate snares and money-making endeavors?

All of these scenarios seem to paint a picture of the powerful (governments, corporations) exploiting and victimizing the weak (the

---

[21] "Privacy." Apple, n.d. https://www.apple.com/privacy/.

[22] Ian Bogost, "Apple's Empty Grandstanding About Privacy," *The Atlantic* (January 31, 2019), https://www.theatlantic.com/technology/archive/2019/01/apples-hypocritical-defense-data-privacy/581680/.

[23] Hayley Ringle, "Symantec completes acquisition of Tempe's LifeLock for $2.3B," *Phoenix Business Journal* (February 9, 2017), https://www.bizjournals.com/phoenix/news/2017/02/09/symantec-completes-acquisition-of-tempes-lifelock.html

[24] Michael Hiltzik, "Column: LifeLock offers to protect you from the Equifax breach — by selling you services provided by Equifax," *Los Angeles Times* (September 18, 2017) https://www.latimes.com/business/hiltzik/la-fi-hiltzik-lifelock-equifax-20170918-story.html.

common person).²⁵ Media theorist Neil Postman describes what it means to have power in the technological age:

> [Those who have power, the "winners"] tell [the powerless, the "losers"] that their lives will be conducted more efficiently. But discreetly they neglect to say from whose point of view the efficiency is warranted or what might be its costs. Should the losers grow skeptical, the winners dazzle them with the wondrous feats of computers, almost all of which have only marginal relevance to the quality of the losers' lives but which are nonetheless impressive… The result is that certain questions do not arise. For example, to whom will the technology give greater power and freedom? And whose power and freedom will be reduced by it?²⁶

As I continue to work toward establishing a public theology of privacy in the technological age, it is imperative to ask the right questions: Who holds technological power? Who is suppressed and downtrodden because of technology? Who are the beneficiaries of the ease and efficiencies provided by technology? By briefly surveying history through the lens of privacy, it becomes clear that if these questions are not being asked, the powerful will consistently and increasingly invade the privacy of the powerless for their own benefit.

History of Privacy

In painting a portrait of the history of privacy (or the private life), it is important to remember the previously quoted words by Godkin: privacy as we know it is a "distinctly modern product." That said, it would be a catastrophic mistake to portray the pre-modern world as one that was void of privacy, for "all societies of any complexity distinguish between public and private… it is primarily cultural discourse that

---

[25] Other areas that technological invasion of personal privacy frequently occurs in (that I am unable to include in this paper's scope) are the banking industry and the healthcare industry, both of which house intimate details of countless people.

[26] Neil Postman, *Technopoly: The Surrender of Culture to Technology* (New York: Vintage, 1993), 11.

determines what is private and what is not."[27] The private life, a sphere of concealment, has been a necessary construct throughout human history, for it is this non-public realm that has acted as "a zone of immunity to which we may fall back or retreat, a place where we may set aside arms and armor needed in the public place... This is the place where family thrives, the realm of domesticity... The private realm contains our most precious possessions, which belong only to ourselves, which concern nobody else."[28] Beginning with the establishment of the Christian Church in the ancient Roman context and working toward the present day, this next section will provide a very brief survey of the history of privacy in Western civilization to show the drastic shifts that have taken place between the public and private spheres of personal life and the part that technology has played in these developments.

The rise of Christianity in the midst of the paganism of the Roman Empire is the most helpful place to locate the starting points for the modern notion of privacy, simply because of the massive influence both Greco-Roman culture and the rise of Christianity have had on the history of the (predominantly Western) world. The *res privata* (the private affairs of an individual) in the Greco-Roman world was viewed as a necessary subordinate to the *res publica* (the affairs held in common by the people). Law professor and privacy expert Raymond Wacks describes the Greco-Roman distinction between public and private as a necessity for the sustainment of the public: "The Greeks regarded a life spent in the privacy of 'one's own' (*idion*) as, by definition, 'idiotic'. Similarly, the Romans perceived privacy as merely a temporary refuge from the life of the *res publica*... Only in the late Roman Empire can one discern the initial stages of the recognition of privacy as a zone of intimacy."[29]

---

[27] Evelyne Patlagean, "Byzantium in the Tenth and Eleventh Centuries." In *A History of Private Life*, Vol. 1, *From Pagan Rome to Byzantium*, edited by Phillipe Ariès and Georges Duby, translated by Arthur Goldhammer, (Cambridge, MA: The Belknap Press of Harvard University Press, 1987), 641.

[28] Georges Duby. Forward to *A History of Private Life*, Vol. 1, *From Pagan Rome to Byzantium*, edited by Phillipe Ariès and Georges Duby, translated by Arthur Goldhammer, vii-ix (Cambridge, MA: The Belknap Press of Harvard University Press, 1987), viii.

[29] Raymond Wacks, *Privacy: A Very Short Introduction*. (Oxford, UK: Oxford University Press, 2010), 32.

It is in this context that the newly founded Christian sect of the first and second centuries developed its private community for the purpose, argues historian Peter Brown, of strengthening its followers to operate in the turmoil and opposition that they would face in the public realm: "If singleness of heart was to survive in the Christian churches and be seen to survive before a suspicious pagan world on the relentlessly public stage of everyday life in the city, it could survive only if caught in the fixative of a group life consciously structured according to habitual and resilient norms."[30] The private life, as seen in the early church, was formed out of necessity, in order to nurture a strength for the sake of survival. "[The Christians] created a new group, whose exceptional emphasis on solidarity in the face of its own inner tensions ensure that its members would practice what pagan and Jewish moralists had already begun to preach… [They] differed from those of their pagan and Jewish neighbors only in the urgency with which such attitudes were adopted and put into practice."[31] Privacy, emphasized by the early Christians of the Roman Empire, was a necessity that demanded absolute commitment in order to develop the ability to exist; in the midst of a perilous public realm, the private life had taken on a new role of increased importance.

Several centuries following the explosion of Christianity within the structure of the Roman Empire, the Medieval Age ushered in a new way to view privacy. After the barbarian Odoacer took control of Rome and unequivocally ended the reign of the Roman Empire in 476 CE, Christianity (through the influence of the institutional Church) gained significant influence over the pagan people and regions associated with the Germanic and Celtic tribes of Europe. With the romantic view of the bustling metropolis of Rome now far removed from both the common and bourgeois mindset, the ideal shifted away from the chaos of the city to the tranquility of rural areas, centered around communal farming, and, as historian Michel Rouche contends, grounded in an idyllic sense of privacy:

---

[30] Peter Brown, "Late Antiquity." In *A History of Private Life*, Vol. 1, *From Pagan Rome to Byzantium*, edited by Phillipe Ariès and Georges Duby, translated by Arthur Goldhammer (Cambridge, MA: The Belknap Press of Harvard University Press, 1987), 235-311: 260. Much of the following section draws from several essays featured in several different volumes of the celebrated *History of Private Life* five-volume opus.

[31] Ibid., 260.

Private life assumed much greater importance in the Middle Ages than it had in Roman antiquity. The eclipse of the city by the countryside is the most striking proof of this. The joy of living, once cultivated in urban streets and buildings, now took refuge in rude houses, even huts. The empire had held a public place as an ideal, promoted by its laws, its troops and its aediles. But in the age of the Germanic kingdoms, the cult of urbanity collapsed and private life took its place.[32]

This drastic change meant that the private sphere no longer existed simply as a state of mind, but instead it had moved to actual physical locations and spheres: specifically, the family and personal households. The Church, now a dominant force in the world, no longer needed privacy for the sake of its public survival; instead, the ecclesial body, along with the authority of the local rulers, began to assert their power within the private lives of the people they were charged to lead.

The Medieval Age transitioned into the Renaissance which then led into the Enlightenment, which eventually brought the Western world into the state of modernity. This centuries-long evolution is lumped together here because within the realm of privacy, one major development took place: the rise of autonomous individualism. Through the humanistic endeavors characterized by Renaissance art and writing, to the triumph of reason in the Enlightenment, the private individual began replacing the empire, the Church, and the local rulers as the public decision-maker. In 1850 the French diplomat Alexis de Tocqueville heralded the advantages of individualism, proclaiming that it is "a feeling of comfort, which allows each citizen to withdraw from the mass of his fellow men in order to keep company with his family and friends, in such a way that, having created a small society that suits him, he willingly leaves the larger society to its own devices."[33] Slowly,

---

[32] Michel Rouche, "The Early Middle Ages in the West." In *A History of Private Life*, Vol. 1, *From Pagan Rome to Byzantium*, edited by Phillipe Ariès and Georges Duby, translated by Arthur Goldhammer (Cambridge, MA: The Belknap Press of Harvard University Press, 1987), 415-549: 415.

[33] Michelle Perrot, "Conclusion." In *A History of Private Life*, Vol. 4, *From the Fires of Revolution to the Great War*, edited by Phillipe Ariès and Georges Duby, translated by Arthur Goldhammer(Cambridge, MA: The Belknap Press of Harvard University Press, 1990), 669-672: 669.

through a centuries-long process of escalating importance given to the autonomous individual, society had finally come to celebrate and exalt the uncompelled withdrawal of the individual from the public sphere. Consequentially, the influence of the private sphere expanded exponentially and allowed increased space for individuals to find opportunities for rest and intimacy.

It is important to pause here and recognize that the expansion of the private realm in the "ages of individualism" is told through a very specific lens – that is, the lens of privilege. The ever-expanding privileges of privacy that were being introduced during this era were, in reality, something only select elites enjoyed. Those lucky enough to be wealthy, born into a respected family, had the appropriate skin color, or, at the very minimum, born a male, experienced a private life that others did not, and in some cases, could not. For women throughout most of human history, a claim can be made that "a significant cause of women's subjugation is their relegation to the private realm of home and family."[34] Additionally, "the shroud of privacy may conceal domestic oppression, especially of women by men."[35] While the private life was at times a haven of harm and oppression for women, this intended sphere of intimacy was similarly violated or used as an instrument of repression for racial minorities (and other unprivileged people groups). In American history, having dark colored skin was the ticket into this disreputable category. Professor Henry Giroux, a renown cultural critic, commenting on the voluntary loss of privacy by many in today's culture, says that:

> People of colour, especially poor dissenting blacks, for whom privacy has never been an assumed right… [their] right to privacy was violated in the historical reality of slavery, the state terrorism enacted under deep surveillance programs such as COINTELPRO, and in the current wave of mass incarcerations. What has changed, particularly since 9/11, is that the loss of privacy now extends to more and more groups.[36]

---

[34] Wacks, *Privacy: A Very Short Introduction*, 32.
[35] Ibid., 32.
[36] Henry A. Giroux "Selfie Culture in the Age of Corporate and State Surveillance." *Third Text* 29, no. 3 (May 2015): 157.

It is imperative to remember these societal distinctions that exist within the structure of the public and private spheres; for when we observe the historical precedent that has been established for the privacy rights of the vulnerable and subjugated populations, it is clear that absolute power has overwhelmed those who are least equipped to defend themselves.

As we move into the twentieth century of this brief historical survey, the perceived divisions between the public sphere and private spheres were shattered by the two great world wars. In order to feed the war machine and pledge allegiance to one's nation, citizens were required (via military conscription, supply rationing, ethnic internment, etc.) to give up their individual privacy in order to assist in the public struggle toward victory. In the midst of war (and especially after its conclusion), aspects of the private life were restored, and some new opportunities were created. However, "people had to dissimulate and hide these new private activities, especially if they did not contribute directly to the war effort."[37] As a result of the world wars, the public sphere in the United States swelled with power while the private sphere was attacked and put under scrutiny, best exemplified by The Sedition Act of 1918,[38] President Truman's Executive "Loyalty Order" of 1947,[39] and the McCarthyism campaign that started in the late 1940s and lasted through the 1950s.[40] Ever since the post-war period, we in the West have experienced an age defined by the continual power struggle between the public and private sphere, between the autonomy of the individual and the authority of institutions. As the current Western society meanders through the

---

[37] Ibid., 671.

[38] The Sedition Act of 1918 enabled the United States government to fine and imprison any individual who said or printed "disloyal, profane, scurrilous, or abusive language about the form of government of the United States, or the Constitution of the United States, or the military or naval forces of the United States, or the flag of the United States, or the uniform' of the Army or Navy of the United States."

[39] Truman's Executive Order 9835, often referred to as the "Loyalty Order," allowed for the government to investigate all government employees by collecting information on their personal lives and beliefs in order to determine whether or not they were loyal enough to the United States government; if they were deemed "disloyal," they were dismissed from their employment.

[40] Also known as the Second Red Scare, McCarthyism defines a period of anti-communist propaganda produced by the U.S. government that led to the creation of the House Committee on Un-American Activities, a committee which utilized its power to investigate private citizens and, if they were found guilty of disloyalty or subversion, effectively blacklist them from the American public sphere.

ill-defined age of late-modernity and postmodernity, the individual's place in both public and private spheres has become a constant struggle between the individual's right to privacy and the desire of powerful establishments to commodify and exploit those rights.

A history of privacy is complicated, mostly because of how dependent it is upon the context it is situated within. For Christianity within the Roman Empire, privacy was a means of survival. For the Medieval Age, privacy was an escape into the countryside from the chaos of the public city, with the caveat of submitting one's private life to the feudal ruler. During "ages of individualism," the all-encompassing influence of the public sphere shrunk as the expansion of the autonomous individual and his or her private sphere retreated to a make the space of intimacy more accessible. In today's technological age, privacy is heralded as an individual right, yet it is routinely treated as a commodified medium. Ellul argues that the conflict over the commodification of individual privacy finds its root in society's succumbing to the rational allure of a "technique" that powerful entities control: "Drawn by self-interest (the ideal of comfort, for instance), the masses went over to the side of technique; society was converted... groups of the most conflicting interests united to hymn its praises. Literally everyone agreed on its excellence."[41] Contemporary privacy exists in a precarious position: individuals desire a curated private life, but they abhor the intrusion of the public in order to do so; privacy is valued, but its true nature and function is terribly misunderstood and misapplied.

A Conceptual Primer on Privacy

At the heart of understanding the basic, fundamental values and reasons relating to the concept of *privacy*, it is imperative to be able to see it as a contrasting sphere situated alongside public. That said, it is important to define *public* alongside *private*. Philosopher Hannah Arendt, seeking a new way to view human life amidst the horrors of the world wars, defined the public sphere as "everything that appears in public [that] can be seen and heard by everybody and has the widest possible publicity.... The world itself, in so far as it is common to all of us and distinguished

---

[41] Ellul, *The Technological Society*, 55.

from our privately owned place in it."[42] The private, she contends, should simply be defined as "a sphere of intimacy" which functions to "shelter the intimate."[43] Similarly, philosopher Charles Taylor, seeking to clarify the moral order present in the amalgam that is modernity, defined the public sphere as "a common space in which the members of society are deemed to meet through a variety of media: print, electronic, and also face-to-face encounters; to discuss matters of common interest; and thus to be able to form a common mind about these."[44] Privacy, he contends, is a sphere that focuses on the individual's concept of the "good life," a sphere that protects "ordinariness" and includes the domain of intimacy, which is concerned with access and is "shielded from the outside world and even from other members of a large household."[45] Both Arendt and Taylor argue that the public sphere is defined by commonality, a space where individuals reside, communicate and interact with one another, whereas both authors assert that the private sphere is characterized by a restriction of access to the most ordinary and intimate aspects of life, an area that controls what is being seen and heard by others. Privacy, they argue, lies in the occlusion of certain entities and individuals from a person's innermost being.

In order to better comprehend the abstract underpinnings of *privacy*, it may help to bring actual application into this conversation. Let us, then, briefly turn our attention toward the process that privacy undertook in becoming recognized as a human right. In 1890, the aforementioned Louis Brandeis, along with his law partner, Samuel Warren, acted as some of the first advocates for the development of privacy rights in the United States legal system by publishing their celebrated article "The Right to Privacy" in the *Harvard Law Review*. Their advocacy was in response to perceived personal invasions brought about by Eastman Kodak's new "snap camera," an inexpensive and portable technological wonder that quickly produced cheap photographs

---

[42] Hannah Arendt, *The Human Condition* (Chicago: The University of Chicago Press, 1958), 50, 52.

[43] Ibid., 38.

[44] Charles Taylor, *Modern Social Imaginaries* (Durham, NC: Duke University Press, 2004), 83. Taylor draws from Jürgen Habermas' work *The Structural Transformation of the Public Square* as the basis of his discussion.

[45] Ibid., 105.

for the benefit of so-called "yellow journalism."[46] Because of an increasing amount of technologies entering into the public sphere that had the capability to encroach on the individual's privacy (telephone, faster printing press, cinematography, etc.), the barrier surrounding the private life became more important to protect.

The importance of privacy continued to bubble underneath the surface, without any resolution, until 1964, over seventy years after Warren and Brandeis's article was published, when the Supreme Court established a precedent for the right to privacy via a "challenge to Connecticut's statute proscribing the use of contraceptives,"[47] in the case *Griswold v. Connecticut*. This ruling established that "the right of privacy is taken to protect personal autonomy," and was then strengthened by the 1977 case *Roe v. Wade*. On the global scale, the newly formed United Nations, in its inaugural general session, established the *Universal Document of Human Rights* in response to the atrocities of World War II. It included an article on the right to privacy, which stated that, "No one shall be subjected to arbitrary interference with his [sic] privacy, family, home or correspondence, nor to attacks upon his honour and reputation. Everyone has the right to the protection of the law against such interference or attacks."[48] Whether it be protection against unnecessary intrusion or violence, or protection of abstract spaces or physical bodies, privacy as a right has been established to protect the autonomous human in his or her sphere of private space and intimacy.

An important thing to note in these laws is a point that Arendt makes pertaining to human interaction in a world of competing public and private spheres: "No human life, not even the life of the hermit

---

[46] Wacks, *Privacy: A Very Short Introduction*, 53. See W. Joseph Campell, *Yellow Journalism: Puncturing the Myths, Defining the Legacies* (Westport, CT: Praeger Publishers, 2001), 25-41, in which Campell argues that "Yellow Journalism" was a term coined in the late 19th century by New York journalist Ervin Wardman to describe the lack of dignity and virtue exemplified by the sensationalist newspapers owned by William Randolph Hearst and Joseph Pulitzer. The use of the term "yellow" is debated, but Campell contends that it either draws from a yellow-dressed cartoon character used by both newspapers (the "Yellow Kid") or as a reference to "decadence, given the color yellow was sometimes associated with depraved literature in the 1890's" (32).

[47] Thomas Huff, "Thinking Clearly About Privacy." *Washington Law Review* 55, no. 4 (1980), 785.

[48] "Universal Declaration of Human Rights." *United Nations*, United Nations, https://www.un.org/en/universal-declaration-human-rights/.

in nature's wilderness, is possible without a world which directly or indirectly testifies to the presence of other human beings."[49] The right to privacy does not protect you from existing in the society; instead, it protects you from being violated while participating in society. In fact, legal philosopher Charles Fried claims that privacy is "necessarily related to ends and relations of the most fundamental sort: respect, love, friendship, and trust. Privacy is not merely a good technique for furthering these fundamental relations; rather without privacy [respect, love, friendship, and trust] are simply inconceivable. The qualities require a context of privacy or the possibility of privacy for their existence."[50] The public sphere and the private sphere depend upon each other, existing in an uncomfortable symbiotic relationship: humanity needs both spheres in order to survive, yet the private sphere, often the locus of personal safety and intimacy, is prone to be trampled and violated without safeguards to protect it.

Philosopher Stanley I. Benn, in his book, *A Theory of Freedom*, argues that the theoretical foundation of freedom lies in a personal commitment to the belief that the individual choice of others deserves protection. Thus, with the respect for persons as the subject of free action, humanity will be driven to treat others in a manner conformed to principles of justice, deference, and truth, "simply by virtue of that subject's being a person, and quite irrespective of the outcome of our conforming to or departing from these principles."[51] This person-centered notion, in Benn's view, is the best way to argue for an individual's right to immunity from observation. If not others-focused, the modern public sphere may convince the masses that freedom lies in a generic understanding of unrestricted choice and actualized desires, removing the focus from an others-centered view and instead placing it on a values-centered view. Values-centered views exist under the umbrella of "shared values," a concept which inevitably will lead individuals and groups toward universal interpretations and applications onto specific situations. Such a shift would seek to unite free people in support of general applications that remove the emphasized right to individual autonomy, which would consequently limit the ability for others to experience an uninterrupted

---

[49] Arendt, *The Human Condition*, 22.
[50] Fried, C. 1968. "Privacy: A Moral Analysis." *Yale Law Journal* 77, no.1: 477.
[51] Stanley I. Benn, *A Theory of Freedom* (Cambridge: Cambridge University Press, 1988), 8.

and free expression of personal privacy. In the debate between values-centered and others-centered notions of freedom, these questions must be answered: "Do all people deserve the same amount of privacy? Or, are there some individuals who require more privacy than others?"

Philosopher Albert Borgmann, who specializes in the philosophy of technology, adds to the argument by claiming that the notion of prosperity that was offered to the individual in the ages of industrialization has carried through to the present age in the form of a weakened public sphere "that has been taken over by instrumentality (i.e., production and administration)."[52] Similarly, because of the opportunity of such prosperity, he argues that the "realm of privacy is in each case occupied by one consumer" who affirms their consumption "as an exercise of freedom that would be encumbered by judgmental intrusion."[53] Thus, between the constant labor of a public realm that is defined by production, and the individualistic focus of a private realm defined by personal comfort and consumption, there is truly no space left for intimate coexistence; privacy has been commodified and transformed into an individualistic, therapeutic zone of imagined freedom.

Through this brief primer on the conceptual concerns related to privacy, it is easy to see that a true understanding of the private sphere cannot be reached without a concept of what the public is as well. With a proper balance between the two established, it is imperative to remember that privacy is most sincerely perceived through the lens of respect for others' intimacies, a view that helps to buoy the established, worldwide awareness of privacy as an essential human right. This others-focused approach stands in stark contrast to the production-focused public sphere and the consumeristic private sphere of the present age. Consequently, both spheres have become so malformed that neither is working correctly and are therefore disappearing into each other, leaving one amorphous realm void of any distinction.

---

[52] Albert Borgmann, *Power Failure: Christianity in the Culture of Technology* (Grand Rapids: Brazos Press, 2003), 40.
[53] Ibid., 41.

Theological Reflection on Privacy

It is important to establish a vital truth before diving too deep into this theological discussion: nothing is kept private from the omnipresent, omniscient God. Hebrew 4:13 states, "And no creature is hidden from his sight, but all are naked and exposed to the eyes of him to whom we must give account." And Isaiah 40:28 declares, "Have you not known? Have you not heard? The Lord is the everlasting God, the Creator of the ends of the earth. He does not faint or grow weary; his understanding is unsearchable." That said, there are things that God has kept private from his creation, as evidenced by Deuteronomy 29:29, which announces that, "The secret things belong to the Lord our God." Nothing lies hidden from the all-knowing God who is mysterious beyond comprehension.

At the very same time, however, we must speak of God as Father, Son, and Holy Spirit, the economic and immanent Trinity. Second Corinthians 13:14 speaks to this dynamic relationship: "The grace of the Lord Jesus Christ and the love of God and the fellowship of the Holy Spirit be with you all." The Trinitarian God, three distinct persons yet all of one substance, is constantly at work while intimately indwelling with each other. Jesus says in John 15:26, "But when the Counselor comes, whom I shall send to you from the Father, even the Spirit of truth, who proceeds from the Father, he will bear witness to me." The Trinity is bound in loving intimacy, yet that intimacy is not confined to the private sphere. Eastern Orthodox theologian Nicu Dumitrașcu summarizes this public expression of the Trinity's intimacy by saying that, "the intra-divine love of the Father towards the Son is extended also over the people through the intermediation of the Holy Spirit. For nothing is done separately within the Holy Trinity, but is done within a trinitarian soteriological 'economical' framework."[54]

It can be seen, then, that the Trinitarian God does not adequately fit within the framework of the very human concepts of public, private, or privacy. Therefore, it is more helpful instead to theologically assess the subject of privacy through the lens of ecclesiology. The body of Christ, enlivened by the Spirit, is the instrument of God's continued redemption of all creation. This body, the Church, is an active participant in God's

---

[54] Nicu Dumitrașcu, "A New Trinitarian Vision: Orthodox Ecclesiology--Embodied within a Secularized Society." *Theology Today* 70, no. 4 (January 2014): 446.

creation; the Church is where the coming kingdom is being proclaimed, but also where it has already been established. As Dumitrașcu declares, "within the light of the Holy Trinity the mysterious depths of the being of the Church are discovered as well as the true meaning of every communion and unity in Christ."[55]

Because the Church has such a prophetic position within the world, it, in theory, should often encounter those who are outside of the body of Christ. The book of 1 Peter speaks at lengths about how the people of God, identified as "aliens and exiles" (2:11) in a culture that rejects their identity, should interact with the world it exists within, and offers up the statement that before Christ's gift of divine grace, the Church was "not a people, but now you are the people of God; once you had not received mercy, but now you have received mercy" (2:10). Jesus Christ gives the Church its identity, inner substance, and being. It would not be a stretch, then, to state that these core dispositions should be displayed in a way that almost eschews privacy and protection. The reasoning behind such a notion is that if these dispositions find their source in Jesus Christ the Son of God then they should emulate the radical self-giving that Jesus modeled through His incarnation, passion, and resurrection. The author of 1 Peter concludes the exhortation by stating that the Church is to "live such good lives among the pagans that, though they accuse you of doing wrong, they may see your good deeds and glorify God on the day he visits us" (2:12). Only a publicly transparent life, one that does not give privacy utmost primacy, would be able to draw such attention in order to warrant such a response.

Even though the body of Christ is called to radically transparent ways of life and speech, that does not mean that it is barred from healthy expressions of privacy. Each person of the Trinity, whom the Church is to be intimately connected with, gives Biblical witness to privacy: praying to the Father "who is in secret" and "who sees in secret" (Matthew 6:6); the frequent retreats by Jesus to places of solitude for times of prayer or grief (Luke 5:16, Matthew 14:13); and the characteristic mysteriousness and covertness of the Holy Spirit, who is compared to the invisible wind (John 3:8) and is said to individually reside within the people of God (1 Corinthians 6:19). Following the Trinitarian example, as was laid out in the earlier discussion on the history of the private life, early Christians

---

[55] Ibid., 445-46.

depended on privacy as a source of strength for the purpose of survival. Likewise, in 1 Corinthians 12:23, Paul provides a category of the body of Christ that is different from the others: "On the contrary, those parts of the body that … are unpresentable are treated with special modesty." Though Christ has called these "unpresentable" parts into new life and has mercifully included them into His fold, there are still aspects and characteristics that require the use of "special modesty." These are the "private" parts of the body of Christ, and they necessitate careful protection and appropriate use and deployment.

These concealed parts of the body of Christ are an important distinction to comprehend in a theological discussion of privacy. The Greek word ἀσχήμων is translated as "unpresentable" in 1 Corinthians 12:23, but it carries more weight than a single-word definition. The scope of ἀσχήμων, instead, includes things not openly done "in reserved society because it is considered 'shameful, unpresentable, indecent', or 'unmentionable'… [it] is applied especially to sexual matters… those that elicit special modesty, genitalia."[56] Drawing on a theology of the body, it is well known that God made humankind in his own image and likeness, and after forming the parts into a whole he proclaimed that the entirety of the male and the female body were "very good."[57] So, these unpresentable, private parts (genitalia), are not evil, or wrong, because they must be concealed; instead, Paul says that they are to "receive even greater presentability," (or modesty) because of their private status.

Biblical scholar Richard Hays, in commenting on this passage, asserts the power struggle that drives this entire section: "The comparison between the body and human societies was a rhetorical commonplace (*tapas*) in the ancient world… [Paul] employs the analogy not to keep subordinates in their places but to urge more privileged members of the community to respect and value the contributions of those members who appear to be their inferiors, both in social status and in spiritual potency."[58] Power, then, is the motivation behind the special

---

[56] Walter Bauer, *A Greek-English Lexicon of the New Testament and Other Early Christian Literature*, rev. and ed. Frederick W. Danker, 3rd ed. (Chicago: University of Chicago Press, 2000), 147.

[57] Genesis 1:26-30; 2:7.

[58] Richard Hays, *First Corinthians: Interpretation: A Bible Commentary for Teaching and Preaching* (Louisville, Ky: Westminster John Knox Press, 2011), 213.

consideration given to the private parts. Hays continues by painting the picture offered by Paul's ecclesial ordering in the body of Christ:

> The social class dimension of this tension between strong and weak is suggested by Paul's further elaboration of the body metaphor in verses 24-25: those members that are considered "dishonorable" or even "shameful" (in the metaphor, the sexual organs) must be treated with all the greater respect... The high-status Corinthians may look down their noses at their uncouth lower-class brothers and sisters in the faith, regarding them as something of an embarrassment, but Paul insists that they must be "clothed" with dignity and honor. This echoes his earlier insistence that the strong must accommodate their behavior to the needs of the weak (8:7-13; 10:28-29a), as Paul himself has done (9:19-23; 10:31-11:1).[59]

Within this pastoral message concerning ecclesial cohesion we discover an important precedent concerning personal privacy: a biblical mandate for privacy must start and end with the dignity, honor, and well-being of the weak, and an attitude of concern and loving-kindness must be held by those who hold power and status.

Holding these two opposites in tension (transparency for the sake of God's glory vs. privacy required of unpresentable parts) is the difficult task of trying to construct a systematic theology of privacy. Additionally, the biblical text is "a poor resource for the modern concept of privacy,"[60] and is quite silent regarding direct commands and instructions on how privacy should be handled. To be fair, though, the contemporary notion of privacy was unheard of in the time and context of the biblical authors. Be that as it may, when ideas related to privacy do appear in the biblical text, Scripture passages "reflect a respect for human dignity in which the parties communicate freely in mutual trust."[61] That is why modesty, as commanded in 1 Corinthians 12:23, is so important in regards to the private sphere. Theologian Cara Anthony, grounding her work in Thomistic virtue theory, states that Christian modesty, "regulates human

---

[59] Ibid., 215-16.
[60] Lawrence M. Stratton, "Privacy," in *Dictionary of Scripture and Ethics*, ed. Joel B. Green (Grand Rapids: Baker Academic, 2011), 628.
[61] Ibid., 628.

assertiveness (mental and physical) in order to make space for other persons to freely exercise their own appropriate power. That is, modesty keeps in check any form of self-assertion that comes at the expense of another person's dignity or freedom."[62]

This, then, is where the lens of ecclesiology helps to bolster the theological implications of privacy. Drawing off of earlier points made, communicating freely in mutual trust is akin to the transparency that is commanded of the body of Christ in 1 Peter for the sake of God's glory. At the same time, reflecting a respect for human dignity can be found in the notion of privacy required for the "unpresentable" parts of the body of Christ that is mentioned in 1 Corinthians. Through it all, however, the Spirit directs, enables, and empowers the body of Christ to be as self-giving or withholding as necessary in order to participate in the kingdom of God and its continued redemption of creation. Within a theological framework of privacy, the freedom to live transparently must constantly find balance with the necessity for the protection of human dignity from the oppressive misappropriation of authoritative power.

A Public Theology of Privacy

The domain of public theology is a helpful context in which to bring the issues of privacy. Though it may seem strange to look for clarification regarding the private sphere through a discipline that is focused on the public sphere, my argument throughout this paper emphasizes the fact that the public and private spheres depend upon each other. That is why public theology, or as theologian Mary Doak explains it, "a theology that is not simply concerned about the public but intends to contribute to the reconstruction of public discourse," is necessary for a holistic dialogue pertaining to this topic.[63] In attempting to translate the meaning of the revelation of Jesus Christ and His gospel message of good news to the specific problem of technological privacy within a pluralistic world, a Christian public theology can offer a fresh, loving perspective to view this significant issue.

---

[62] Cara Anthony, "Modesty in the Service of Justice: Retrieving Tradition and Reversing the Gaze." *Horizons* 36, no. 2 (Fall 2009): 277.

[63] Mary Doak, *Reclaiming Narrative for Public Theology*. SUNY Series, Religion and American Public Life (Albany: SUNY Press, 2004), 11.

That being said, as I have worked toward a conclusion, it is clear that a reassessment and reconstruction of our preconceived notions about privacy are needed. In our modern-day "Ellulian" society of technique that does not place privacy on a balance between freedom and protection, but instead strives toward maximum efficiency by encouraging maximum consumption, the public and private realms have been distorted. Because of the erosion of these realms, our modern-day society has stripped away the human rights associated with privacy and instead subjected them to the category of human luxury, awarding them to those who have the means and ability to secure it. This has left the vulnerable groups of society (the poor, the elderly, the uneducated, and minorities to name a few) stuck in a perpetual state of fear regarding misappropriations of influence and power over their spheres of personal information, intimacy, and retreat.

The Lawyers' Committee for Civil Rights Under Law, a nonpartisan, nonprofit organization seeking to "secure equal justice for all through the rule of law,"[64] wrote a letter to Congress in 2019, signed by dozens of civil rights, civil liberties, and consumer protection groups, imploring a "comprehensive privacy reform" that would "empower consumers, protect against discrimination, and promote equal opportunity for all in the modern public square and marketplace."[65] Written for the leaders of today's technological age, the letter appealed to:

> the importance addressing data-driven discrimination and equal opportunity in comprehensive consumer privacy legislation. Fundamentally, the right to privacy exists to, among other things, protect against unfair and inappropriate uses of personal information. Any legislation addressing data practices must recognize and address how the exploitation of personal information can disproportionately harm marginalized communities, including by enabling discrimination—intentionally or unintentionally—against

---

[64] "Letter to Congress on Civil Rights and Privacy," Lawyers' Committee for Civil Rights Under Law, April 19, 2019. https://live-lawyers-committee-2020.pantheonsite.io/wp-content/uploads/2019/04/Letter-to-Congress-on-Civil-Rights-and-Privacy-4-19-19.pdf.

[65] Ibid.

People of color, women, religious minorities, members of the LGBTQ+ community, persons with disabilities, persons living on low income, and immigrants.[66]

The specific harms they went on to name included: voter suppression, digital redlining, discriminatory policing, retail discrimination, exacerbation of digital inequity, amplification of white supremacy, identity theft, and endangering personal safety.[67] Unjust practices that manipulate the weak through the immoral use of power have become the norm in today's technological society.

The body of Christ should be the perfect witness and response to systems of oppression and exploitation. With Christ is its head, and through the manifestation and action of the Kingdom of God, the Church should confidently and prophetically take a stand in the midst of these discussions on privacy and proclaim: "There is no fear in love, but perfect love casts out fear" (1 John 4:18). The unjust and immoral use of power that many governments and multinational institutions have exhibited through the predatory actions of data accumulation, surveillance, and invasion of privacy has created a wellspring of fear among countless individuals; the actions of these institutions are reckless and completely void of perfect love. It must be the Church's job, then, as the acting agent and eschatological vision of the Kingdom of God, to join in and support campaigns and advocacy groups that are seeking the common good of the global population by standing in opposition to powerful and exploitative technological practices and demand that changes be made.[68]

Nevertheless, perfect love does not always require perfect transparency. Theologian Lewis Smedes wrote that, "we will not discover and we will not demonstrate the common life in the body of Christ unless we honor private life in the body of Christ."[69] It is here that it must be asserted that the world is populated by individuals and groups who

---

[66] Ibid.

[67] Ibid.

[68] See https://privacyinternational.org/ and https://www.aclu.org/issues/privacy-technology for examples of organizations seeking to restore privacy in the technological world.

[69] Lewis B. Smedes, "In Praise of Privacy," in *The Reformed Journal* 16, no. 8 (October 1966): 6.

desire to injure, harm, and destroy; these people and institutions are intent on abusing others for their own selfish gain. As the body of Christ seeks to join God's preeminent public mission in redeeming all creation, it should also be empowered to seek privacy as a means of protection from evil and its harmful effects.

The Church's response to the issue of privacy must be bold. Ellul, the constant critic of the efficiency of technique, wrote strong words to the Church on how to change the broken and unjust structures which dominate our age and lead toward death:

> Christians can never consider themselves as on the right side, looking contentedly upon the perdition of everything else; to do so is to fail the charity of Christ and cease in this way even to be Christians. Being joined with others (through economic, sociological, and other such laws, and also by God's will), they cannot agree to watch them trapped in their distress and dissolution, handed over to tyranny, unceasing labor, and unfounded hope. They need to immerse themselves in social and political problems so that they can act in the world, not in the hope of making it a paradise, but only of rendering it tolerable. Not of attenuating the opposition between this world and the kingdom of God, but only the opposition between this world's disorder and the order of preservation that God wants for it. Not of making the kingdom of God come, but so that the gospel may be proclaimed, that all people may hear truly the good news of salvation and resurrection.[70]

Rooted in a love toward others, the Church must strive to reorder the brokenness that defines the world around us, and this reordering can only come from the Church, who alone can offer the good news of salvation and resurrection through Jesus Christ. How, then, does the good news of the gospel help to reorder the broken structure of individual privacy in the technological age? Borgmann suggests that "we can begin to reform the personal and private sphere of our lives if we center it

---

[70] Jacques Ellul, *Presence in the Modern World* (Eugene, OR: Cascade Books, 2016), 29.

on focal things and practices."[71] The Eucharist, for instance, a means of grace that Christ established for the life of the Church, "transform(s) the partakers into a body with a social dimension"[72] and brings the Church together in celebration of the ongoing public and private salvation of all of creation. And that is where the reconstruction of a public theology of privacy must happen: the endgame of privacy should not be fear-quelling. Instead, privacy should be recalibrated and properly presented so that individuals (and groups) are enabled to operate in solitude, rest, retreat, intimacy, and perfect love within the public Kingdom of God. Privacy must stand hand-in-hand with freedom, a freedom rooted in a respect for persons, or else the end result is shallow and individualistic; such a privacy would be void of any empowerment, intimacy, and true rest. So, may the Church, empowered by the Holy Spirit, recapture a vision of privacy that demands human dignity, respect, and justice. May it publicly model transparency for the sake of God's glory while also exhibiting a deference toward the privatization of individual rights that is grounded in trust and love.

---

[71] Borgmann, *Power Failure*, 61.

[72] William Cavanaugh, "Is Public Theology Really Public?: Some Problems with Civil Society." *The Annual of the Society of Christian Ethics* 21 (2001): 119.

Works Cited

Anthony, Cara. "Modesty in the Service of Justice: Retrieving Tradition and Reversing the Gaze." *Horizons* 36, no. 2 (Fall 2009): 265-284.

Apple. "Privacy." n.d. https://www.apple.com/privacy/.

Arendt, Hannah. *The Human Condition*. Chicago: The University of Chicago Press, 1958.

Bauer, Walter. *A Greek-English Lexicon of the New Testament and Other Early Christian Literature*, rev. and ed. Frederick W. Danker, 3rd ed. Chicago: University of Chicago Press, 2000.

Benn, Stanley I. *A Theory of Freedom*, Cambridge: Cambridge University Press, 1988.

Brandeis, Louis, and Samuel Warren. "The Right to Privacy." *Harvard Law Review* 4, no. 5 (December 15, 1890): 193–220.

Bogost, Ian. "Apple's Empty Grandstanding About Privacy," *The Atlantic*, January 31, 2019, https://www.theatlantic.com/technology/archive/2019/01/apples-hypocritical-defense-data-privacy/581680/.

Borgmann, Albert. *Power Failure: Christianity in the Culture of Technology*. Grand Rapids: Brazos Press, 2003.

Brown, Peter. "Late Antiquity." In *A History of Private Life*, Vol. 1, From Pagan Rome to Byzantium, edited by Phillipe Ariès and Georges Duby, translated by Arthur Goldhammer, 235-311. Cambridge, MA: The Belknap Press of Harvard University Press, 1987.

Campell, W. Joseph. *Yellow Journalism: Puncturing the Myths, Defining the Legacies*. Westport, CT: Praeger Publishers, 2001.

Cavanaugh, William. "Is Public Theology Really Public?: Some Problems with Civil Society." *The Annual of the Society of Christian Ethics* 21 (2001): 105-123.

CBS *This Morning*. "Edward Snowden wants to come home but says U.S. won't give him a fair trial". Filmed [September 2019]. YouTube video, 15:25. Posted [September 16, 2019]. https://www.youtube.com/watch?v=O4nFGOEeSP0

Doak, Mary. *Reclaiming Narrative for Public Theology*. SUNY Series, Religion and American Public Life. Albany: SUNY Press, 2004.

Duby, Georges. Forward to *A History of Private Life*, Vol. 1, *From Pagan Rome to Byzantium*, edited by Phillipe Ariès and Georges Duby, translated by Arthur Goldhammer, vii-ix. Cambridge, MA: The Belknap Press of Harvard University Press, 1987.

Dumitraşcu, Nicu. "A New Trinitarian Vision: Orthodox Ecclesiology--Embodied within a Secularized Society." *Theology Today* 70, no. 4 (January 2014): 445-454.

Ellul, Jacques. *The Technological Society*. New York: Vintage Books, 1964.

Ellul, Jacques. *Presence in the Modern World*. Eugene, OR: Cascade Books, 2016.

Fried, Charles. "Privacy: A Moral Analysis." *Yale Law Journal* 77, no. 1 (1968), 475-493.

Giroux, Henry A. "Selfie Culture in the Age of Corporate and State Surveillance." *Third Text* 29, no. 3 (May 2015), 155-164.

Godkin, E.L. "The Right of the Citizen to his Reputation," *Scribner's Magazine* 8 (July-December 1890): 58-67.

Greenwald, Glenn. "Edward Snowden: the Whistleblower behind the NSA Surveillance Revelations." *The Guardian*, June 11, 2003. https://www.theguardian.com/world/2013/jun/09/edward-snowden-nsa-whistleblower-surveillance.

Hays, Richard. *First Corinthians: Interpretation: A Bible Commentary for Teaching and Preaching*. Louisville, Ky: Westminster John Knox Press, 2011.

Hiltzik, Michael. "Column: LifeLock offers to protect you from the Equifax breach — by selling you services provided by Equifax," *Los Angeles Times*, September 18, 2017, https://www.latimes.com/business/hiltzik/la-fi-hiltzik-lifelock-equifax-20170918-story.html.

Huff, Thomas. "Thinking Clearly About Privacy." *Washington Law Review* 55, no. 4 (1980), 777-794.

International, Amnesty. "Facebook Twitter Facebook and Google's Pervasive Surveillance Poses an Unprecedented Danger to Human Rights." November 21, 2019. https://www.amnesty.org/en/latest/news/2019/11/google-facebook-surveillance-privacy/.

Jones, Peter L. "Civil Disobedience," in *Dictionary of Scripture and Ethics*, ed. Joel B. Green. Grand Rapids: Baker Academic, 2011: 140-41.

Lawyers' Committee for Civil Rights Under Law. "Letter to Congress on Civil Rights and Privacy." April 19, 2019. https://live-lawyers-committee-2020.pantheonsite.io/wp-content/uploads/2019/04/Letter-to-Congress-on-Civil-Rights-and-Privacy-4-19-19.pdf

Meinrath, Sascha. "The Erosion of Privacy, And Why We Need A New Social Contract," *Forbes Magazine*, October 16, 2019. https://www.forbes.com/sites/ashoka/2019/10/15/the-erosion-of-privacy-and-why-we-need-a-new-social-contract/#27baecf37396.

Nations, United. "Universal Declaration of Human Rights." *United Nations*. https://www.un.org/en/universal-declaration-human-rights/.

Niebuhr, Reinhold. *Discerning the Signs of the Times: Sermons for Today and Tomorrow*. New York: Charles Scribner's Sons, 1946, 10, quoted in Martin E. Marty. "Reinhold Niebuhr: Public Theology and the American Experience," *The Journal of Religion* 54, no. 4 (Oct., 1974): 332-359.

Nolan, Cynthia. "The Edward Snowden Case and the Morality of Secrecy." *The Catholic Social Science Review* 22 (January 2017): 291–310.

Patlagean, Evelyne. "Byzantium in the Tenth and Eleventh Centuries." In *A History of Private Life*, Vol. 1, *From Pagan Rome to Byzantium*, edited by Phillipe Ariès and Georges Duby, translated by Arthur Goldhammer. Cambridge, MA: The Belknap Press of Harvard University Press, 1987, 551-641.

Perrot, Michelle. "Conclusion." In *A History of Private Life*, Vol. 4, *From the Fires of Revolution to the Great War*, edited by Phillipe Ariès and Georges Duby, translated by Arthur Goldhammer, 669-672. Cambridge, MA: The Belknap Press of Harvard University Press, 1990.

Postman, Neil. *Technopoly: The Surrender of Culture to Technology*. New York: Vintage, 1993.

Ringle, Hayley. "Symantec completes acquisition of Tempe's LifeLock for $2.3B," *Phoenix Business Journal*, February 9, 2017, https://www.bizjournals.com/phoenix/news/2017/02/09/symantec-completes-acquisition-of-tempes-lifelock.html.

Romano, Aja. "The Facebook data breach wasn't a hack. It was a wake-up call.," *Vox*, March 20, 2018, https://www.vox.com/2018/3/20/17138756/facebook-data-breach-cambridge-analytica-explained.

Satariano, Adam. "Google Is Fined $57 Million Under Europe's Data Privacy Law." *The New York Times*, January 21, 2019. https://www.nytimes.com/2019/01/21/technology/google-europe-gdpr-fine.html.

Smedes, Lewis B. "In Praise of Privacy," in *The Reformed Journal* 16, no. 8 (October 1966): 6-7.

Stewart, Emily. "What You Need to Know about Facebook's New Privacy Settings." *Vox*, April 18, 2018. https://www.vox.com/technology/2018/4/18/17251480/facebook-privacy-scandal-changes-europe-gdpr.

Stratton, Lawrence M. "Privacy," in *Dictionary of Scripture and Ethics*, ed. Joel B. Green. Grand Rapids: Baker Academic, 2011, 628.

Taylor, Charles. *Modern Social Imaginaries.* Durham, NC: Duke University Press, 2004.

United State Department of Justice, "The USA PATRIOT Act: Preserving Life and Liberty," accessed March 16, 2020, https://www.justice.gov/archive/ll/what_is_the_patriot_act.pdf.

Wacks, Raymond. *Privacy: A Very Short Introduction.* Oxford, UK: Oxford University Press, 2010.

Chapter 2
From Heaven to the Food Desert: How the Incarnation Speaks to Issues of Poverty and Obesity in the United States

Sadie V. Sasser[1]

Abstract

This essay identifies the public issue of poverty-related obesity in the United States and broadly explains possible contributing factors. Upon conveying the limits of current economic and government-related responses, it turns to the Church for insight on this issue and suggests that Christians should form a more robust, theological answer to poverty-related obesity based in the doctrine of the Incarnation. By drawing heavily on the self-sacrificing love of Jesus portrayed in Philippians 2, the essay urges Christians to recognize the body as good and thus to care for its individual bodies as well as the bodies of others. Finally, this paper presents stewardship and advocacy as categories in which individuals and churches may act to alleviate the prevalence of poverty-related obesity, and it ends with examples of current responses in a local church atmosphere.

---

[1] Sadie V. Sasser is a graduate student at Asbury Theological Seminary and currently working on her Master of Divinity, which she plans to complete in May 2021. She is seeking ordination to the diaconate in the Anglican Church of North America. Sadie acquired her Bachelor of Arts from Ouachita Baptist University and is originally from South Arkansas.

Introduction

In recent years, obesity has become a public health crisis in the United States.[2] A study published in 2017 by the Center for Disease Control shows that 38.9 percent of US citizens are obese, and over the past twenty years, this number has risen by almost 10 percent.[3] The effects of this widespread obesity include an increased frequency of disease related to obesity (e.g. Type II Diabetes, heart disease, some types of cancer, etc.) and, as a result, an increase in the cost of medical care across the board; costs have risen over 8 percent in the last 8 years.[4] Obesity and its results function like a domino effect: obesity leads to more disease, disease leads to increased medical costs, and these increased costs affect not only those who are obese, but also the entire nation.

If obesity is the first domino to fall, what exactly pushes it over? There are multiple factors and causes that contribute to obesity. The CDC recognizes a lack of physical movement, the community environment (e.g. infrastructure, lack of walking paths, etc.), genetics, and disease as major contributing factors.[5] These causes are widely known by the public; however, the National Institute of Health conducted a separate study in 2011 that brings an interesting trend to the forefront. This study showed that "people who live in the most poverty-dense counties are those most prone to obesity."[6] After surveying rates of poverty and obesity in 3,139 counties in the United States, scientists concluded that "Counties with poverty rates of >35% have obesity rates 145% greater than wealthy counties."[7] This study shows that, along with factors specified above, socioeconomic status and poverty heavily affects obesity.

---

[2] Michael Pollan, *The Omnivore's Dilemma: A Natural History of Four Meals*, (New York: Penguin Books, 2006), 101-102.

[3] Craig M. Hales, Margaret D. Carroll, Cheryl D. Fryer, and Cynthia L. Ogden, "Prevalence of Obesity Among Adults and Youth: United States, 2015-2016," *NCHS Data Brief 288* (October 2017): https://www.cdc.gov/nchs/data/databriefs/db288.pdf

[4] Adam Biener, John Cawley, and Chad Meyerhoefer, "The High and Rising Costs of Obesity to the US Health Care System," *J Gen Intern Med* 32 (April 2017): https://www.ncbi.nlm.nih.gov/pmc/articles/PMC5359159/.

[5] Centers for Disease Control and Prevention, "Adult Obesity Causes & Consequences," *Centers for Disease Control and Prevention* (November 2019) https://www.cdc.gov/obesity/adult/causes.html

[6] James A. Levine, "Poverty and Obesity in the U.S.," *Diabetes* 60 no. 11 (November 2011): https://www.ncbi.nlm.nih.gov/pmc/articles/PMC3198075/

[7] Ibid.

How can this be the case? Although the study does not overtly claim that poverty is the cause of obesity, there is a correlation between poverty and obesity. This correlation is not known and accepted among the broad public, especially among those who occupy higher socioeconomic tiers. Considering the data and contributing factors that connect poverty and obesity, we can logically conclude that poverty is not just one among many factors, but instead accounts for one of the biggest influences on obesity in the United States. The fact that the wider public is relatively unaware and has offered no response to this correlation indicates that education and action are needed. Indeed, it is the responsibility of both the "secular" world *and* the Church to speak into this issue.

The purpose of this essay is to discuss how Christian theology should have a say in the poverty/obesity epidemic. My main concern, therefore, is not a detailed overview of all factors at play and I will not discuss them at length nor demand a full understanding of the issue. Rather, my main goal is to provide an introduction to the correlation between poverty and obesity as a public issue that can be influenced by theology, specifically by the doctrine of the Incarnation. I will offer a brief overview of the factors that relate poverty and obesity and will give a summary of the current theological response to these issues. The bulk of the essay will address how the doctrine of the Incarnation necessarily leads to Christian engagement with topics of poverty and obesity, specifically through advocacy. I will conclude with some examples of churches that have engaged these issues with a call for the Church to remember its place in the world and to be intentional about bringing about human flourishing.

Correlation Between Poverty and Obesity

Imagine you are in the middle of a poverty-dense urban area. You have five dollars to spend on a meal, you can only use public transport to arrive at your destination, and the nearest grocery store is twenty minutes away. Where would you buy food? The nearest fast food restaurant with a good dollar menu is probably your best option, or perhaps the nearest gas station can offer a few snacks that would appease your hunger. You probably would not go out of your way to go to the grocery store because of the time and effort necessary to get there, not to mention that five dollars will not buy very much fresh food at a grocery store. Now, to make this even more difficult, add the fact that you have two small children at home with you as the primary caregiver. Would this affect your choices for food?

This is the type of situation in which millions of Americans find themselves daily. People experiencing poverty face multiple factors that affect their decisions around food, including availability of utilities and appliances, time to prepare food for a family, transportation, money, etc. The example above generalizes the notion of what poverty may look like, but the multiplicity of aspects that are related to poverty-related obesity make it more complicated. There is a complex web of issues at play that are important to poverty-related obesity, and it is not possible to discuss them all. Three specific factors, however, are necessary to discuss: government welfare, economics, and the USDA and Big Agriculture.

The American government does, in fact, attempt to provide relief to those experiencing poverty and food insecurity in the form of SNAP benefits (formerly known as Food Stamps). This is a key virtue in our society, but we must ask what kind of effect SNAP benefits have on poverty-related obesity, if any. A 2011 study done by Charles L. Baum, a professor of economics, surveys the effect that Food Stamps has on recipients and how it relates to obesity. His findings revealed that although receiving government assistance has a small effect on the national trend of obesity overall, those who receive these benefits long-term are indeed more likely to become obese. An interesting caveat in the study shows that this mostly impacts women.[8] However, the nature of government food assistance has changed drastically in the last twelve years. With the passing of the 2008 Farm Bill, the program changed its name to SNAP (Supplemental Nutrition Assistance Program) and initiated the SNAP-ed program that seeks to provide more nutritional education.[9]

While the 2008 Farm Bill and its extension in 2018 have surely raised the quality of government food assistance,[10] the question remains:

---

[8] Charles L. Baum, "The Effects of Food Stamps on Obesity," *Southern Economic Journal* 77 no. 3 (January 2011): 645-646.

[9] The United States Department of Agriculture, "A Short History of SNAP." USDA, 11 Sept. 2018, www.fns.usda.gov/snap/short-history-snap.

[10] The United States Department of Agriculture, "Agriculture Improvement Act of 2018: Highlights and Implications." *USDA ERS*, 1 (Oct. 2019), www.ers.usda.gov/agriculture-improvement-act-of-2018-highlights-and-implications/.

do SNAP benefits contribute to obesity? While government welfare is not the main antagonist in the story of poverty-related obesity (provided funds can be used on whole foods and fresh produce, and nutritional education programs exist), the mere availability of government assistance does not solve the more pressing issue. The problem is not the availability of government welfare, but the availability of healthy food. The most accessible foods to people in impoverished areas are highly processed and sanctioned by the USDA. The reason for this points mostly to the economic system of the United States.

Economic factors play a huge part in the complexity of poverty-related obesity. The United States operates in a free market economy, allowing free trade and private business ownership. While the free market can be a virtue for a society, it also leads to setbacks and blind spots surrounding food insecurity. A study published in the *American Journal of Agricultural Economics* states that higher fruit and vegetable prices are linked to higher rates of obesity in poor women and women with children.[11] The same study asserts that the availability of supermarkets in low-income areas of the United States are much lower than middle- to high-income neighborhoods.[12] Both of these factors are directly related to economic impact; the free market has encouraged the industrialization of food manufacturing while also allowing business owners to pull out of poverty-dense areas, thus creating what is known as a food desert, both in urban and rural areas of the United States.

Food deserts makes the availability of processed and calorie-dense foods very high while the availability of whole foods and fresh produce increasingly low. Thus, families and individuals who are food insecure in the United States are more likely to purchase cheap and heavily processed foods because of availability and cost. Such foods are plenteous, available in gas stations as well as grocery stores and supermarkets. On the opposite side of the spectrum, families and individuals who have the means can shop at Whole Foods, where people buy carefully grown organic products. Additionally, Whole Foods stores exist few and far between and require reliable transportation and

---

[11] Lisa M. Powell and Euna Han, "Adult Obesity and the Price and Availability of Food in the United States," *American Journal of Agricultural Economics* 93 no. 2 (January 2011): 378-384.

[12] Ibid.

extra money for fuel to shop there. This difference in the availability of processed food versus whole, fresh food is a direct result of economic structures, and people experiencing poverty draw the short end of the stick that capitalism offers.

The United States Department of Agriculture, along with Big Food corporations, are entangled with economics in this complex web of poverty-related obesity. The USDA is the arm of the government that provides SNAP benefits and nutritional education while simultaneously regulating food production and sales.[13] When the free market reigns, efficiency is king because it begets cheap prices. Unfortunately, this efficient and cheap method of production results in unhealthy food. Whole foods that are healthier are far more expensive than calorie-dense and high-sugar foods because, while whole and organic foods are less predictable and are slaves to the whims of nature and time, industrialized food manufacturing can be mostly controlled, measured, and counted on for profit. *Sojourners Magazine* featured an article several years ago that discussed this issue. "With commodities so cheap, food fortunes belong to those who sweeten and supersize a handful of kernels into a box of Corn Pops... The winners in this game are the Big Food corporations, whose profiteering (financed by taxpayers) not only endangers public health at home but also undermines agriculture markets abroad."[14] The USDA manages agriculture and food production, but as the article put forth, self-serving business practices pervade the system.

For a closer look, we can explore the corn industry to illustrate the mechanisms of how food became a business that focuses on maximizing profit. Michael Pollan discovered that in the 1970s, agricultural yields of corn were pushed to a maximum not yet achieved, causing overproduction to be a huge issue. This extra corn was processed into multiple different additives for manufactured foods, the most prominent of which is high fructose corn syrup. High fructose corn syrup is used as a sweetener, but notably this addition of sweetener did not statistically reduce *regular* sugar consumption in the American diet; thus, the amount of overall sugars consumed by the average American increased exponentially

---

[13] https://www.usda.gov/.

[14] Bethany Spicher, "Toward Food Justice: The wealthy feast, the poor go hungry. Surprise," *Sojourners Magazine* 33 no. 7 (July 2004): 8.

with the inclusion of high fructose corn syrup.¹⁵ In what foods is one more likely to find high fructose corn syrup? In highly processed foods that are calorie-dense, cheap, and have a long shelf life. The USDA is efficient, wealth-producing, and capitalistic. However, this system, while economically profitable, does not promote human flourishing, and the poor suffer as a result.

The government does reach out a hand to its citizens who need help acquiring food, but the government also allows people to buy food that is not healthy and will not result in a healthy citizenship. If the government allows it, the USDA encourages it. And because the free market operates on its own whims without much accountability, the businesses that provide the best, most whole and ethically grown food are nowhere to be found in poverty-dense areas both rural and urban. These subtleties are precursors to the poverty-related obesity epidemic. Clearly the correlation between poverty and obesity is more than a question of scientific or economic data; it is an issue of justice. Why would the same government that provides relief for the poor and carries the weight of increasing medical costs also continues to allow Big Food corporations to produce food that increases the rate of obesity? Although fault cannot be given to any one factor, the overall system at work here is one of oppression. The poor in the US are, in the end, not helped by the government at all because the systems supported by the government result in declining health, lack of availability of healthy foods, obesity, and cyclical poverty in family systems.

If a founding ideal of the American experiment is equality for all, we must continue to pursue that end as best as we can, thus reforming dysfunctional systems that bring oppression instead of freedom. This is itself an irony: at what length can a secular society bring true equality and functionality when it is constantly pursuing its own ends? Furthermore, does America pursue some ends for itself that sometimes compete with the good of its citizens (e.g., subsidized foods for global market competition results in excess corn production that is then made into heavily processed foods for American consumption)? The moral goals of secular society will always fail when divorced from the gospel of Jesus Christ, and it is at this point that the Church must step in. Following this

---

¹⁵ Pollan, *Omnivore's Dilemma*, 103-104.

track, the question must be asked: how has the Church responded to both issues of poverty and of obesity?

Current Theological Response

Why should the Church care about poverty-related obesity, or any so-called public issue for that matter? Miroslav Volf argues that human flourishing is at the center of the major faiths including Christianity.[16] It is an aspect of Christianity that our devotion to God necessarily extends itself to just treatment of others. Israelite laws protected foreigners (Leviticus 19:34), Jeremiah urges the exiles to "seek the peace of the city" (Jeremiah 29:7), and Jesus himself declares himself to be a savior to the oppressed (Luke 4:18-19). Volf defines human flourishing as "love of God and neighbor, universal beneficence, [and] experiential satisfaction."[17] If the pursuit of human flourishing is a central concern of Christianity, then social systems and structures that effect a portion of any population negatively should cause concern and merit a response.

Both poverty and obesity are affected by these systems and structures, and the response to these issues are just as complicated inside the Church as out. Current cultural narratives surrounding both poverty and obesity in the present-day United States have completely changed from Bible times, when abundance was a signifier of God's blessing (Deuteronomy 30:9-10). Poverty and obesity are now both labeled as immoral, and the person who finds him or herself in poverty or obesity is culpable. One Christian response specific to obesity has been put forth by Peter Browning, who asserts that a moral category has been attributed to people who are overweight or obese. By using such words as "gluttony" or "sloth," those who are obese are seen as bad or sinful. Inherent in this accusation is the assumption that those who are obese have made conscious choices to overeat or to be sedentary.[18] It should be noted that the discipline-centric style of monasticism might have contributed to this assumption of obesity being immoral. Spiritual fathers like Saint

---

[16] Miroslav Volf, *A Public Faith: How Followers of Christ Should Serve the Common Good* (Grand Rapids: Brazos Press, 2011).

[17] Ibid., 60.

[18] Peter Browning, "The Global Obesity Epidemic: Shifting the Focus from Individuals to the Food Industry," *Journal for the Society of Christian Ethics*, 37 no. 1 (Spring-Summer 2017): 161.

Benedict created very strict rules for their followers to only consume as much food as one needs,[19] but importantly most monastic movements were born out of a desire to live differently than the prevailing culture; thus, monastics chose temperance towards food to show difference in comparison to rulers who might have taken advantage of their wealth.[20]

This assumption is completely incorrect in the modern-day United States, proven by data signifying a trend between poverty and obesity. Not only is obesity affected by socio-economic status but is also a product of genetics. I highly doubt that any Christian today who was asked about obesity would flat out call it a sin. However, the underlying belief that obesity should be assigned to a moral category seems very prevalent. As stated in an article from *Christianity Today* by Virginia Stem Owens, "Fat, if not sinful, is at best unfortunate, at worst obscene. In this culture, we pity the anorexic, but we avoid the obese."[21] Not only does injustice exist in the systems at work in our economics related to food and poverty-related obesity, but the moral categories in which we operate regarding this topic are dysfunctional.

From my own personal experience growing up in a rural town in the South, those whose socioeconomic status was high enough to control their weight with healthy eating if they wished seemed to ostracize those who were obese, thereby reducing a person's moral value to their body size. Peter Browning does a good job of bringing these moral judgments to the forefront, reminding the Church that the marginalized and oppressed should be offered compassion and acceptance by the Church.[22] Alas, in all the searches to find a healthy theological approach to dealing with obesity, it seems that all the Church has to offer is imitation or judgment. This is in no way a robust response to the injustice at hand.

At the same time as the Church has no current helpful response to obesity, there is likewise no helpful response to poverty. Julie A. Mavity Maddalena wrote an important article in 2013 speaking to

---

[19] St. Benedict, *The Order of Saint Benedict*, ed. Timothy Fry, O.S.B. (Collegeville: The Order of St. Benedict, Inc., 1981).

[20] Justo L. Gonzalez, *The Story of Christianity, Vol 1: The Early Church to the Dawn of the Reformation* (New York: HarperOne, 2010).

[21] Virginia Stem Owens, "The Fatted Faithful: Why the Church may be harmful to your waistline," *Christianity Today* 43 no. 1 (January 1999): 72.

[22] Browning, "The Global Obesity Epidemic," 174.

the treatment of women and children in poverty. She identifies the prevalent ideal of self-sufficiency in American culture and traces this theme through history. Maddalena comes out with a strong case that "the predominant current in America moves to hold all people morally and practically responsible for self-sufficiency, regardless of whether the currents actually move against them."[23] In other words, Americans tend to ascribe moral categories to individuals and behavior (a person is obese because they didn't make good decisions) rather than the systemic forces at play in everyday life (a person is obese because of cyclical poverty, lack of helpful education, etc.). Especially as it relates to people in poverty, a widely held belief is that self-sufficiency is a moral virtue and those who cannot care for themselves are in some way morally deficient. Again, I saw this kind of thinking constantly growing up in the rural South in a politically conservative environment. The issue with the poor was always about the fact that they wanted to live off the government's money and never do any work for themselves – this was the argument I was indoctrinated with. The American idol of self-sufficiency becomes all too clear here.

As Maddalena continues her argument, she begins to call on the resources of Christian theology to answer for the problem of self-sufficiency. Her main framework is the image of the Body of Christ being an interdependent organism. It is this idea of interdependency that Maddalena uses to combat the rhetoric of self-sufficiency that so pervades American culture and undervalues the plight of the poor.[24] Maddalena's thesis is beautifully done, but while her article addresses public issues with thoughtful theological dialogue and therefore sets a precedent to expand and replicate this methodology, she does not go far enough. Maddalena's assumptions and suggestions for new policies and economic changes are all correct and agreeable, but they remain highly theoretical. It is the job of the Church to take her work and create new ways of responding in the world.

It is obvious that the Church desperately needs a response to issues of obesity and poverty. Poverty and obesity are mentioned

---

[23] Julie A. Mavity Maddalena, "Floodwaters and the Ticking Clock: The Systematic Oppression and Stigmatization of Poor, Single Mothers in America and Christian Theological Responses," *Cross Currents* 63 no. 2 (June 2013): 158.

[24] Ibid., 167-9.

separately here because it has been shown that the Church gives a very meager, if any, response to these issues individually; if there is no present individual response, we can be sure that there is no response to the interplay and correlation of these two issues in current culture. Given the gap in both robust theological ideas about and practical Christian responses to obesity and poverty, it is the purpose of this essay to offer an introduction.

Incarnation as a Christian Response

The Christian doctrine of the Incarnation speaks to the God of the universe appearing in human flesh in Jesus Christ. Rather than discussing orthodox understandings of the Incarnation, the purpose here is to outline three ways the Incarnation applies to the Church today, which I link specifically with the correlated issue of poverty and obesity.

The Body is Good

The Incarnation reminds us that our physical bodies are good. The first section of scripture we come to that speaks boldly to the Incarnation is John 1:14. "The Word became flesh and made his dwelling among us. We have seen his glory, the glory of the one and only Son, who came from the Father, full of grace and truth."[25] This is one of the most well-known verses about the Incarnation. The word "dwelling" is rendered "tabernacled" in *The Living Bible*. This is probably an allusion to Exodus 40, in which the tabernacle is finally built, and God's glory comes down in the cloud so that it completely fills the tabernacle. In Exodus 40, Moses is not able to enter the tabernacle because of the incredible glory of God. By contrast, the author of John also talks about God's glory, but makes an incredible claim: we *have* seen his glory. The Incarnation is, of course, the doctrine that God came to earth in human form to reconcile and redeem humanity.[26] However, divorced from passages of scripture like this it seems sterile and distant. In light of the biblical context of John, the Incarnation signifies a paradigm shift – the glory of God has been inaccessible and even absent from Israel for some time, but it has arrived

---

[25] *The Holy Bible, New International Version*, (Grand Rapids: Zondervan, 2011).

[26] Thomas C. Oden, *Classic Christianity: A Systematic Theology* (New York: HarperCollins, 1992).

again in Jesus and is able to be seen, touched, and heard. The glory of God is in bodily form, and we are able to experience it.

The presence of God with humanity is not the only point that I wish to highlight here. The fact that God is present in a *human* body is equally important to understanding the lesson that human bodies are inherently good. The Church throughout history has struggled with the implications of this, but now an integral truth comes to the forefront: because God came in human form, God affirms that the body is inherently good. If this fact were truly and fully accepted, I believe the Church would act much differently today. Dualistic ideas about the separation of the body and the spirit that originated with Plato have subtly persisted through history and still impact our current moment.[27] The Church at large still struggles to accept that human beings are not tripartite but integrated – the aspects that have so often been separated into different categories are in fact inseparable. This distinction means that the body, soul, and spirit are not distinct categories but all work together to create being and existence. An integrated existence is what God called "good" when he created humanity.

Although this may seem easy to accept, we have already seen how an integrated existence is not an aspect of theology that most Christians currently live in to. To take the Incarnation seriously means that the understanding of the body and thus that of food is drastically different. Part of this is eating what is good. In what ways can food bring us closer to God? Stephanie Paulsell writes about Christian practices of honoring the body and introduces the idea of Christian kosher – a practice of eating that puts parameters around which foods one should consume. "A way of eating that draws deeply on Christian faith would be shaped by such choices, choices that honor the body – our bodies and the bodies of others."[28] Surely a more ordered way of eating, based in ideas about the goodness of the body, brings us closer to God and more in tune with the created order. If this is the case, we should be concerned not only about what we eat but also what is provided for the poor – "the bodies

---

[27] Margaret R. Miles, *Beyond the Centaur: Imagining the Intelligent Body* (Eugene: Cascade Books, 2014).

[28] Stephanie Paulsell, *Honoring the Body: Meditations on a Christian Practice* (New York: Jossey-Bass, 2002), 95.

of others." It is necessary to think about right action and right ways of eating and then extend those practices to those who are vulnerable.

Norman Wirzba has spent a considerable amount of time thinking and writing about the theology of food. He approaches a theology of eating from a heavily philosophical point of view, but uses it to tackle current issues in the world related to food production and the divorce of food from Christian community. Wirzba acknowledges the effects of food production, not only on the body, resulting in obesity, but specifically on bodies that experience poverty. His statement summarizes the thrust behind this essay: "The economic divide between the rich and the poor is not confined to bank statements. It is being worked out in their bodies in the forms of good versus poor nutrition."[29] Later in the book, Wirzba writes an entire chapter focused around food and how the Eucharist speaks to a theology of food. When one considers the sacrament of the Eucharist and the weight it carries for the community of believers, it becomes obvious that the act of eating is a spiritual thing. Christians ingest the bread and wine, and the body of those believers becomes the body and blood of Christ for the world. It is not enough for Christians independent from the entire body of Christ to care for their bodies, but not care for the bodies of others.

This idea that the body of Christ has an obligation to care for other people leads us to a deeper question: what is the role of the Church in the world? My answer to this question is rooted in a biblical theme found in both the Old and New Testaments, that of a "kingdom of priests" (Exodus 19:6; Revelation 5:10). God did not choose Israel to be his own people so that he would have mere companions. Scripture makes it clear that God chose a people for himself so they could be a witness to his character for the rest of the world. The "kingdom of priests" idea asserts that the purpose of the Church is to be a witness for Christ to the world, and this is done merely by the way we live. If the Incarnation says to Christians that the individual body matters, it follows that the bodies of those who are not part of the Church matter as well. Christians should be the foremost proponents of healthy bodies, not only for our individual health but for the health, of all people for the sake of human flourishing and to the glory of God!

---

[29] Norman Wirzba, *Food and Faith: A Theology of Eating* (Cambridge: Cambridge University Press, 2019), 151.

Therefore, the Incarnation causes a shift in the Church's current conceptions of not only the body and of food, but also what is meant by "health." Concern for the health of the Church should expand to concern for health in public spheres. We should take the health of the public very seriously, and this is why the intersection of poverty and obesity should matter immensely to the Church. We as Christians have the resources to address this issue in the public sphere.

Disposition towards poverty

A second incredibly important portion of Scripture that speaks to the truth of the Incarnation is Philippians 2. Personally, Philippians 2 has had a vast impact on my life and the way I view my own existence within the body of believers. When one surveys Philippians 2, a few points come to mind. First, Paul urges the believers at Philippi to practice self-giving love by putting others before themselves. There is a deep well for us in this section, which I will return to later. The second major thing communicated by Philippians 2, and the theology of interest here, is how Christ's actions change our disposition toward poverty.

Philippians 2:6-8 portrays a beautiful picture of the God of the Incarnation. God exists in glory, maker and sustainer of everything on earth, yet he lays it aside to become nothing. This passage tells us that God willingly entered into poverty. This in fact is exactly what happened in Bethlehem the night of his birth – a baby born into shame in a barn with no bed but a feeding trough. It would be interesting to apply Jesus' conditions to a present-day rhetoric surrounding those in poverty. Perhaps one might use the trusted burden of self-sufficiency, discussed by Maddalena above, to give Jesus some hope for his future outside poverty: if he works hard enough, he'll rise above it. It is extremely ironic, though, that in the context of Philippians 2, self-sufficiency is completely destroyed. Jesus, who was God, was sufficient on his own; one could say he was *sufficiency*. Yet, Jesus makes a conscious decision to rely not on his sufficiency, but rather on his humility. This trajectory continued to get worse for him from the human vantage point, where this laying aside of divine rights and entering into humanity escalated into a death on a cross, yet Jesus knew this was what he needed to do to be victorious for the sake of the world and the humans he loves. This should sober the mind of the Church. Poverty, in the view of scripture, is not a vice but a virtue. Philippians 2 is meant to show the virtue of Jesus, proven by the fact that he laid aside heavenly wealth to enter into earthly poverty. At the very least, this unveiling of the heart of God toward poverty should cause the Church to rethink its disposition toward poverty.

Ideals of caring for the poor were present in the Old Testament even before the Christ event. God's kingdom of priests was supposed to care for the poor through gleanings, the year of Jubilee, etc. However, there is no evidence that those guidelines were ever carried out.[30] The Old Testament prophets made it one of their main messages to remind the people of Israel that they had fallen into sin. Injustice abounded in Israel's society, where care for the widow, orphan, and foreigner, while commanded by God, had not been taken seriously.[31] This aspect of injustice was one of the factors leading to the exile of Israel and Judah.[32] The Incarnation of Jesus steps into the trajectory of God's narrative of caring for his creation in need, even to such an extent that God himself would become human. To highlight this care, that human, Jesus, even says that the poor are more fit for the kingdom (Matthew 5:3). In the present day, it is the Church's job to continue this trajectory and bring the love and care of the creator into the public sphere. We must reframe our ideas of what poverty means and help it fit within the biblical narrative, and this results in holding people experiencing poverty in high esteem and using our resources to help them.

Stewardship and Advocacy

Philippians 2 has already shown us that Jesus Christ, God enfleshed, humbles himself in such a way that he becomes poor, which changes our view of poverty. Philippians 2 offers other insights, especially when it comes to action towards each other. In 2:1-4, Paul urges the church at Philippi to practice humility with one another to the point that the other becomes more important than oneself. Paul goes on to use 2:5-8 as a starting point for that behavior, exhorting the reader to

---

[30] Christopher J. H. Wright, *Old Testament Ethics for the People of God* (Downers Grove: IVP Academic, 2004).

[31] J. Daniel Hays, *The Message of the Prophets: A Survey of the Prophetic and Apocalyptic Books of the Old Testament*, ed. Tremper Longmann III (Grand Rapids: Zondervan, 2010).

[32] Ibid.

imitate Christ in this way of humility: "In your relationships with one another, have the same mindset as Christ Jesus" (v. 5). In what particular way is the Church supposed to do this? For Christians to imitate Christ, it must look something like when Jesus "did not consider equality with God something to be used to his own advantage; rather, he made himself nothing" (vv. 6-7). Of course, humans are the creation, not the creator; we are not equal with God and cannot choose to give up our divine rights for the sake of creation like Jesus did. It does seem to follow, though, that although we as humans can never fully imitate the actions of Christ, we do have things at our disposal that can be used for the good of others. The resources God has blessed us with can be laid aside or given away for the sake of another – this is the doctrine of stewardship.

John Wesley took stewardship very seriously. Across many of his sermons, stewardship is a recurring theme that encompasses all areas of life. Gary L. Ball-Kilbourne wrote an article in 1984 overviewing this theme in Wesley's theology, and the extent to which Wesley takes this idea of stewardship is very challenging. Ball-Kilbourne states "Wesley believed the human being to be accountable to the Creator in every corner of human life. In financial matters, personal habits, public policy, and political affairs, God has given the human being resources for the working of the good in the world and for the edification of the individual and society."[33] In his sermon titled "The Most Excellent Way," Wesley himself states:

> You may consider yourself as one in whose hands the Proprietor of heaven and earth, and all things therein, has lodged a part of his goods, to be disposed of according to his direction. And his direction is, that you should look upon yourself as one of a certain number of indigent persons, who are to be provided for out of that portion of his goods wherewith you are entrusted. You have two advantages over the rest: the one, that 'it is more blessed to give than to receive;' the other, that you are to serve yourself first, and others afterwards.[34]

---

[33] Gary L. Ball-Kilbourne, "The Christian as Steward in John Wesley's Theological Ethics," *Quarterly Review* 4 no. 1 (Spring 1984): 53.

[34] John Wesley, "The Most Excellent Way," *The Sermons of John Wesley: A Collection for the Christian Journey*, ed. Kenneth J. Collins and Jason E. Vickers (Nashville: Abingdon Press, 2013).

This is Wesley's challenging call for believers to reframe our belongings and all our resources not as our own but as God's. Wesley does not do away with providing for ourselves, but reminds us that closely behind the importance of caring for ourselves is the importance of caring for others. Ball-Kilbourne comments on this, saying "This remarkable image… suggests the essential solidarity the Christian experiences with the rest of humankind."[35] It is clear that Wesley himself took Philippians 2 seriously, and not only in a theoretical sense. He desired for Christians to not only have the right belief about stewardship, but also to take initiative in the world for the sake of others.

If there was a social issue in his day about which Wesley was most concerned, it was the issue of poverty. Not only was humanitarian aid an integral part of the Methodist societies he founded, Wesley was also highly engaged with public policy and offered critiques of how that policy served the rich and oppressed the poor. Ball-Kilbourne states that one of Wesley's small writings, *Thoughts on the Present Scarcity of Provisions*, if written today would come under the discipline of public policy.[36] He comments that "Wesley went beyond suggestions of humanitarian relief to recommend legislative remedies, many of which were rather harsh, if not impractical."[37] Since Wesley firmly believed in the Christian as steward, it was not a question merely of money and how much money a Christian should give to the poor; Wesley desired to give of every resource God had given him. It is clear from his engagement with public policy that this included his mental energy, his time, and surely more personal resources not relegated to money.

It is important here to recognize that one theologian encouraging these things of Christians is not the only reason to act on them. Moving past mere exhortation, Wesley lived a life worth imitation and is a helpful figure through which to see the posture of Jesus working itself out in a political context. It is precisely this political context which I believe Christians are called to, especially in response to the oppression of the poor resulting in health issues like obesity.

---

[35] Ball-Kilbourne, "The Christian as Steward," 45.
[36] Ibid., 49.
[37] Ibid., 50.

It is one thing to give money to those in need. It is surely a good use of the five-dollar bill in your wallet to give it to someone who needs food or some type of material help. I would argue, though, that to be truly self-giving in the imitation of Jesus, our response to the poor in our society should claim more resources than just money. I have heard it said that time is a person's most precious resource; it cannot be saved, so it should be spent wisely. I would agree that time and energy rather than money is a human being's greatest resource. The good thing is that almost everyone has at least a little time and energy to give.

A helpful concept in this vein that has come to the forefront in more modern times, one that Wesley did not have at his disposal, is that of advocacy. A recent definition of advocacy from an Evangelical Christian lens is as follows:

> Evangelical transformational advocacy [is] intentional acts of witness by the body of Christ that hold people and institutions accountable for creating, implementing, and sustaining just and good policies and practices geared toward the flourishing of society. Transformational advocacy challenges injustice and obstacles to human flourishing at whatever level it is practiced by humbly engaging with people who can address the wrong, trusting God's Spirit to change all those involved as well as the institutions themselves.[38]

Thus, the Church can and should engage public issues through advocacy, using our voices to help those who are not heard, because by advocating for justice in society, we are being the hands and feet of Jesus and attempting to promote flourishing for all people.

This idea of advocacy obviously involves the use of time, energy, and other resources one may have available. Advocacy is a big task, but I believe if the Church truly takes the Incarnation seriously – the self-giving love of God appearing in a human body and in poverty to redeem his creation – this ministry of advocacy is a very necessary calling. How can Christians go about advocacy in the face of the poverty-related

---

[38] Stephen Offutt, David Bronkema, Krisanne Vaillancourt Murphy, Robb Davis, and Gregg A. Okesson, *Advocating For Justice: An Evangelical Vision for Transforming Systems and Structures* (Grand Rapids: Baker Academic, 2016), 11-12.

obesity epidemic? Should we advocate in an attempt to reform the USDA and Big Food corporations? Should Christian businessmen and -women take a risk and open a grocery store in the midst of a food desert? Can Christian men and women ask for better SNAP-ed programs, or even fill the gap that exists now? There are many different opportunities for advocacy that speak to the issue at hand. Drawing on Maddalena's theme of interdependency, I would assert that the best way to approach advocacy is through the local church, working together to bring about change and community. This will take creativity and awareness of the surrounding community needs that are present where a certain church is situated, but it is very possible. Here, we turn to some examples of how this is being done.

Applications

There are modern-day examples of John Wesley's public stewardship and advocacy at work today. *Sojourners Magazine* ran an article in 2012 telling the story of two separate initiatives in obese- and poverty-dense areas of the US. In Mississippi, an African-American pastor, Rev. Michael O. Minor started initiatives inside his church to specifically address the issue of obesity. In fact, he is known as "the Baptist preacher who banned fried chicken."[39] Minor used a grassroots style of education and began discussing health in small groups in his church which then led to discussions in larger contexts. Minor's initiative started with small communities but the success of it has extended to the denomination as a whole. Learning from this enterprise, the basic sociological principles were transferred to the context of white, rural Appalachia where churches began to teach on health and the theological implications of having a body (in a way the congregants could understand). Danny Collum states "people are seeing that to change individual behavior [related to obesity] also means resisting economic and cultural forces, a challenge best met in the context of community."[40] These churches are taking the incarnational view of health seriously.

---

[39] Danny Duncan Collum, "Diet, Exercise, and Temples of the Holy Ghost: from Mississippi to Kentucky coal-mining country, Churches are taking on the public health crisis of obesity," *Soujourners Magazine* 41 no. 5 (May 2012): 16.

[40] Ibid.

Similarly, a religious study was done in 2016 to survey how two different Baptist churches were engaging this issue of poverty in their contexts. Saddleback Church in California operates on the belief that the Church should be the main arbiter of justice in society; "Saddleback pastors [had] confidence in the local church as the primary vehicle for social change."[41] Saddleback situates the reality of the world and of poverty inside an eschatological vision and urges the Church to be the factor of transformation in the world "with or without government or 'secular' business." They take this seriously by engaging in humanitarian efforts, especially overseas, with the help of a huge part of their congregation. A different example is Ebenezer Baptist Church in Atlanta, Georgia. Ebenezer is the "historic church home of Martin Luther King Jr." and therefore finds roots in the Civil Rights movement.[42] Ebenezer emphasizes "collaboration" with groups who advocate for human rights and houses a complex of multiple nonprofits who work alongside the church to help alleviate poverty in the area.[43] Both of these examples bring up the important point that engagement with social issues by the church can be approached in different ways. We have seen examples of grassroots movements in education about obesity, the reframing of a response to poverty into an eschatological vision where the church is the main actor, and political advocacy and partnerships with government entities who fight against systemic poverty. These are churches that are functioning as a kingdom of priests in the world.

Conclusion

It is my theological perspective that the truth of the Incarnation urges us toward intentional action and self-giving love. Thus, I believe the Church needs to respond to issues of poverty and obesity with continued advocacy and calls for policy makers to change the systems that oppress those who are poor. However, ultimately, the Church needs to respond in whatever way they are equipped to do. The fact that Churches are intentionally facing issues of poverty and obesity at all is incredibly encouraging, and the rest of us should learn from them.

---

[41] Kristopher Norris and Samuel Hand Speers, "The Hope of the Poor: Ecclesial Practices of Politics, Hope, and Transformation," *Perspectives in Religious Studies* 43 no. 1 (Spring 2016): 107.
[42] Ibid., 108.
[43] Ibid., 109, 111-112.

If the Church is to be a kingdom of priests, it is absolutely necessary for us to seek human flourishing. Miroslav Volf is again worth quoting when he says that seeking human flourishing is very simple: "love God and neighbor rightly so that we may both avoid malfunctions of faith and relate God positively to human flourishing."[44] The injustice of the nature of poverty and its effects on obesity and overall health are an issue of human flourishing, and Christians need to respond. God incarnate came to earth to redeem his people from their sin and suffering. This image of God urges us to not only care about our own health but also the health of others, and we can do so by being intentional stewards and by advocating for others. When we are generous with the resources we have been given by God, we imitate the Incarnation of Christ.

---

[44] Volf, *A Public Faith*, 73.

Works Cited

Ball-Kilbourne, Gary L. "The Christian as Steward in John Wesley's Theological Ethics." *Quarterly Review* 4 no. 1 (Spring 1984): 43-54.

Baum, Charles L. "The Effects of Food Stamps on Obesity." *Southern Economic Journal* 77 no. 3 (January 2011).

Biener, Adam, John Cawley, and Chad Meyerhoefer. "The High and Rising Costs of Obesity to the US Health Care System." *J Gen Intern Med* 32 (April 2017): https://www.ncbi.nlm.nih.gov/pmc/articles/PMC5359159/.

Browning, Peter. "The Global Obesity Epidemic: Shifting the Focus from Individuals to the Food Industry." *Journal for the Society of Christian Ethics* 37 no. 1 (Spring-Summer 2017): 161.

Centers for Disease Control and Prevention. "Adult Obesity Causes & Consequences." *Centers for Disease Control and Prevention* (November 2019): https://www.cdc.gov/obesity/adult/causes.html.

Collum, Danny Duncan. "Diet, Exercise, and Temples of the Holy Ghost: from Mississippi to Kentucky coal-mining country, churches are taking on the public health crisis of obesity." *Soujourners Magazine* 41 no. 5 (May 2012): 14-17.

Justo L. Gonzalez. *The Story of Christianity, Vol 1: The Early Church to the Dawn of the Reformation*. New York: HarperOne. 2010.

Hales, Craig M., Margaret D. Carroll, Cheryl D. Fryer, and Cynthia L. Ogden. "Prevalence of Obesity Among Adults and Youth: United States, 2015-2016." *NCHS Data Brief 288* (October 2017): https://www.cdc.gov/nchs/data/databriefs/db288.pdf.

Hays, J. Daniel. *The Message of the Prophets: A Survey of the Prophetic and Apocalyptic Books of the Old Testament*. Ed. Tremper Longman III. Grand Rapids: Zondervan. 2010.

Levine, James A. "Poverty and Obesity in the U.S." *Diabetes* 60 no. 11 (November 2011): https://www.ncbi.nlm.nih.gov/pmc/articles/PMC3198075/.

Maddalena, Julie A. Mavity. "Floodwaters and the Ticking Clock: The Systematic Oppression and Stigmatization of Poor, Single Mothers in America and Christian Theological Responses." *CrossCurrents* 63 no. 2 (June 2013): 158.

Miles, Margaret R. *Beyond the Centaur: Imagining the Intelligent Body*. Eugene: Cascade Books. 2014.

Norris, Kristopher and Samuel Hand Speers. "The Hope of the Poor: Ecclesial Practices of Politics, Hope, and Transformation." *Perspectives in Religious Studies* 43 no. 1 (Spring 2016): 103-114.

Oden, Thomas C. *Classic Christianity: A Systematic Theology*. New York: HarperCollins. 1992.

Offutt, Stephen, David Bronkema, Krisanne Vaillancourt Murphy, Robb Davis, and Gregg A. Okesson. *Advocating For Justice: An Evangelical Vision for Transforming Systems and Structures*. Grand Rapids: Baker Academic, 2016.

Owens, Virginia Stem. "The Fatted Faithful: Why the Church may be harmful to your waistline." *Christianity Today* 43 no. 1 (January 1999): 70-73.

Paulsell, Stephanie. *Honoring the Body: Meditations on a Christian Practice*. New York: Jossey-Bass, 2002.

Pollan, Michael. *The Omnivore's Dilemma: A Natural History of Four Meals*. New York: Penguin Books, 2006.

Powell, Lisa M. and Euna Han. "Adult Obesity and the Price and Availability of Food in the United States." *American Journal of Agricultural Economics* 93 no. 2 (January 2011): 378-384.

St. Benedict, *The Order of Saint Benedict*, ed. Timothy Fry, O.S.B. Collegeville: The Order of St. Benedict, Inc.

Spicher, Bethany. "Toward Food Justice: The wealthy feast, the poor go hungry. Surprise." *Sojourners Magazine* 33 no. 7 (July 2004): 8.

The Holy Bible, New International Version. Grand Rapids: Zondervan. 2011.

The United States Department of Agriculture. https://www.usda.gov/.

The United States Department of Agriculture. "A Short History of SNAP." *USDA.* 11 Sept. 2018, www.fns.usda.gov/snap/short-history-snap.

The United States Department of Agriculture. "Agriculture Improvement Act of 2018: Highlights and Implications." *USDA ERS.* 1 Oct. 2019. www.ers.usda.gov/agriculture-improvement-act-of-2018-highlights-and-implications/.

Volf, Miroslav. *A Public Faith: How Followers of Christ Should Serve the Common Good.* Grand Rapids: Brazos Press, 2011.

Wesley, John. "The Most Excellent Way." *The Sermons of John Wesley: A Collection for the Christian Journey.* ed. Kenneth J. Collins and Jason E. Vickers. Nashville: Abingdon Press, 2013.

Wirzba, Norman. *Food and Faith: A Theology of Eating.* Cambridge: Cambridge University Press, 2019.

Wright, Christopher J. H. *Old Testament Ethics for the People of God.* Downers Grove: IVP Academic. 2004.

Chapter 3
Food as Other:
The Manifestation of Hospitality in Food and Place During the Global Age

Graham Hoppstock-Mattson[1]

Abstract

Globalization has revealed itself to have a perilous relationship to existence, notably our existence in place and with food. The problems with globalization, as shown in this study, were mostly seen in their full existential and metaphysical capacities in the works of Nietzsche and Heidegger. Both projects, however, fail to overcome the violence of globalization in their reliance on total rupture. In this chapter, I will argue that Christianity has the only complete answer to the phenomenon of globalization. I will show this through revealing existence as something grounded in the Trinity, which itself becomes manifested in hospitality. As such, both food and place will be shown as the crucial ethical epicenters for the transfiguration of globalization into a moral phenomenon through a properly Trinitarian mode of existence from Christian life. This study will, further, reveal the shortcomings of philosophical attempts to answer to this phenomenon and Christianity's overcoming of such shortcomings.

---

[1] Graham Hoppstock-Mattson is a Masters of Divinity Student at Asbury Theological Seminary, where he will be graduating in the summer of 2020. Upon graduation Graham and his wife Brooke will be moving to Vancouver where she will be starting her PhD. Graham is currently a certified candidate in the United Methodist Church, Kentucky Annual Conference.

Introduction

Globalization, place, and culture have a tepid history together, with some anthropologists—like Marc Augé—claiming that bastions of globalization[2] like the airport have potentially even killed place and by extension culture. Amidst the languishing of place of culture we have seen the rise of a perilously convoluted reality. We have, on the one hand, seen the desolation of place and culture at the sake of ideals—what I will call materialistic nihilism— as well as the challenge towards place and culture that comes through transnational migration. In this chapter I will attempt to problematize globalization and, perhaps through this, also present its redemption through looking at food as other. When looking at food as other we are radically placed back within a more biodynamic and phenomenological understanding of community and what it means to exist, e.g. we see place as something fundamental to our being and the other as someone who is fundamental to our existence. In this sense food becomes not merely a mechanistic and simply metaphysical act of nutritional intake, but rather a profound statement of what it means to be—which is in community. Further, it will be shown that food itself is a vital tool for public theology as its permeability allows both a sociological and theological lens through which to view the complexities of a given culture. To show this, I will transition the dialogue into a more global conversation about what it means to exist globally and how food offers a way to value both place and global migrations, and even further show how when it is viewed theologically it provides the necessary antidote to the violence and malaises of globalization. To do so, it will also bear to show the relevance of public theology as a theological mode that extends theology into being itself for the world.

---

[2] Here I am using the term globalization to speak of the complex phenomena rising out of the technological advances of modernity and into late modernity that have given rise to an international economic system, unparalleled access to international travel, a new broadened awareness of geopolitics, and a heightened awareness of the permeability and the ease of transgression upon culture. It should also be argued in this chapter that globalization has ushered in a new ecological age which needs to be understood and argued lest its more nefarious interactions be left unfettered.

The Problem of Globalization

Globalization seems a rather amoral phenomenon; in that it is most predominantly descriptive of an age in which global migration and markets are made more accessible to all and can be done with remarkable expediency. In this sense, we should not evaluate the morality or the ethics of globalization as a flat phenomena— that is in the sense that globalization could be a catch all term for its broadest presencing.[3] More precisely, it will proffer us to view globalization from its source. As such, the problem of globalization, and global migration more minutely, need to be analyzed from its source and therein will we find its ideological commitments. Principally, then, the systems by which globalization has constructed itself within the modern age have trended towards a system of ideals which we will call materialistic nihilism. This materialistic nihilism has had a corrosive effect on food, what it means to eat, and by extension food's irreducible relationship with place.[4] To understand the construction of materialistic nihilism we will need to consult with its most keen preceptors in Friedrich Nietzsche and Martin Heidegger.

Will-To-Power and the Technological Mindset

Friedrich Nietzsche, as such, is most well-known for his statement, "God is dead."[5] Nietzsche, however, does not flatly proclaim the death of God. He also proclaims our complicity in his death, showcasing that we all are his murders. Understanding Nietzsche's proclamation, "God is dead" is pivotal for understanding his concept of the will-to-power that he employs and thus for our understanding of materialistic nihilism's effects on food and place—as experienced through globalization. We

---

[3] Note, I will use the term 'presencing' under a phenomenological guise. Taking my cue then from Heidegger's use of the term in which it signifies a mode of revealing— the coming to presence of Being.

[4] Borrowing my understanding of anthropological place from, Augé, Marc. *Non-Places: An Introduction to Supermodernity*. Second Edition. trans. John Howe. (New York: Verso, 2008). Augé defines anthropological place as a space within which people necessarily reside. Meaning that place is a meaning for all who reside within that space, 42.

[5] The quote appears in "The Madman" in his, *The Gay Science*. There Nietzsche proclaims, "God is dead. God remains dead. And we have killed him.", 181. Here, Nietzsche is proclaiming our role within the death of God, which gives way to the revaluing of all values as he desires to do.

cannot hear these words flatly, we must exegete Nietzsche carefully and think well about his statements. In other words, we cannot hear "God is Dead" as simple antagonism to the Christian god or the will-to-power as something merely about a desire towards rule.

Martin Heidegger's essay "The Word of Nietzsche: 'God is Dead,'" in this regard, warns us against taking Nietzsche this way.[6] Heidegger warns against an understanding of "God is dead" as merely a statement from Nietzsche about his anger towards, or desire, against god, (and particularly the Christian god). Instead, as Heidegger guides us, we only understand Nietzsche's word once we have understood the will-to-power and his view of Nihilism which follows. Nietzsche's proclamation means that the suprasensory world is without effective power—we no longer abstract from the body.[7] Put another way, the spiritual world is dead and this allows for Nietzsche to say, "That the highest values are devaluing themselves."[8] In this sense, while high values are being devalued, new values are being posited and valued *differently*, (it should all bear that is is a constant process in flux).

The re-valuation of all values is then the key to understanding the true essence of the will-to-power and of how this modern age embodies it in its Nietzschean mold. The will-to-power is established through the value-orientation of this age and its *points-of-view*, which Nietzsche defines as "preservation-enhancement conditions."[9] These preservation-enhancement conditions makes values proper to the subject and it is in this sense that the will-to-power is noted by Nietzsche to be "super-abundant life."[10] The will-to-power is, then, the *see-er* in which value is posited—that which brings to life— that establishes "becoming", and

---

[6] Heidegger, Martin. "The Word of Nietzsche: 'God is Dead'" in *The Question Concerning Technology: And Other Essays*. trans. William Lovitt. Harper Perennial Modern Thought (New York: Harper Perennial Modern Classics, 2013). Heidegger says, "So long as we confine ourselves to looking at this unbelief turned aside from Christianity, and at the forms in which it appears, our gaze remains fixed merely on the external and paltry façades of nihilism... So long as we understand... "God is dead" only as a formula of unbelief, we are thinking of it theologically in the manner of apologetics..." 63.

[7] *Ibid.*, 61.

[8] This is aph. 2 in Nietzsche's *Will to Power* as is cited in Heidegger, *Ibid.*, 66. Even more, Nietzsche says that this devaluing is the essence of nihilism.

[9] *Ibid.*, 72.

[10] Aph. 14 in Nietzsche's *Will to Power* as is cited in Heidegger, *Ibid.*, 70.

further it establishes the willingness of the willer to will towards mastery. Thus, the revaluation of all values that gives way to the will-to-power is, in and of itself, a desire to master all things before the subject. Mastery, in that sense, is not simply command over others but the bringing together of ones self for any given task. This is the true task of Nietzsche's *der Übermensch* (the Overman), that is the man who is from out of the will-to-power and destined for that reality in which to master it. It is in this way that Nietzsche is able to claim that God is dead, and the will-to-power is that which has killed him. In god's space here is not another god, but *der Übermensch*, who is meant to adapt to the transient wills of the willer's will-to-power which rise from the values that are given dominion over earth through each epoch. Yet, crucially, these values are as the willer (*der Übermensch*) decides they need to be in order for the preservation and enhancement of life.

Heidegger notes that in this essence Nietzsche's metaphysics is truly that of nihilism. The will-to-power, which is the crux of Nietzsche's system, is not trying to gather all things up in a fear of a lack of life, but rather a certainty and secureness of superabundant life—of material life.[11] Thus, for Heidegger, Nietzsche is the realized nihilism of centuries of metaphysical causality which found itself realized and situated in the thought of Descartes.[12] Metaphysics through Descartes found itself only secure and true within the thinking self, and then most palpably in the value-positing of the will-to-power in Nietzsche. Certainly truth, and even being itself, is now under the will-towards-mastery of the thinking subject of which to speak value onto any object. Even the being of humanity is not secure in this sense, unless it is ordained into being through the will-to-power. This is the essence of Nietzsche's nihilism, but Heidegger notes how this metaphysical idolatry is taken even a step further into the technological thinking of this age by which Nietzsche's thought is given full nutrition to grow in society.[13]

---

[11] *Ibid.*, 81.

[12] David Bentley Hart adopts the term "realized nihilism" in "A Philosopher in the Twilight" *First Things* (February 2011): 46. Hart also notes the metaphysical inheritance Heidegger was arguing against well.

[13] Focusing on the metaphysical nature of this is key to understanding both Heidegger's critique and Nietzsche's thought. There must be a strict understanding of causality and therein the mastery of the thinker is given towards the power of ordering.

Heidegger's clearest vision of this comes in his landmark essay, "The Question Concerning Technology." Here Heidegger asserts the danger of technology to Being is in nothing technological itself, rather technology is dangerous in becoming a way of seeing/perceiving and therein destines all being towards a fixed end. Heidegger says, here, that technology is not merely a means to an end but a way of revealing, a bringing-forth.[14] All *techne* is, then, bringing something forth into being from which did not exist before. Heidegger then says that modern technology is ruled by the principle of *Ge-stell* (Enframing),[15] which is something that reveals the real itself as a standing-reserve. This Enframing principle, as such, is the ordering upon something—namely in nature. Heidegger does not see this as a categorical negative, but simply as the true essence of technology—of which can certainly become a moral negative. Heidegger utilizes the example of a hydro-electric power plant which is set up in the Rhine River by which to utilize the river for energy as a way of revealing the essence of technology. Heidegger says that in this manner the Rhine appears as something under our control and by which we have ordered and mastered, and in this sense the Rhine now becomes not a river, but instead a water power supplier for the technology which destines something into a way of being.[16]

Heidegger sees this hydroelectric dam as part of the modern realization of technology—something of which our picture of *der*

---

[14] Heidegger, *The Question Concerning Technology*, 12-13.

[15] When we hear *Gestell* we should be reminded of Heidegger's understanding of Being as Da-Sein or more interpreted, "openness-to-being". Enframing then denies this openness in that it closes Being into a fixed destination, as something determined. It is in this sense that Nietzsche is the metaphysical error *par excellence*, because he finds in the will-to-power the consummation of Enframing. Being is given a fixed and technological destination. See the introduction to Heidegger's *The Question Concerning Technology* by William Lovitt.

[16] *Ibid.*, 15-16. Interestingly so too we find echoes of this in Berry, Wendell. *The Unsettling of America: Culture & Agriculture*. (San Francisco: Sierra Club, 1996.) Notably Berry says this shifts allows us to see nothing beyond the quantifiable and thus how it applies mechanistically. He says, "It is typical of the mentality of our age that we cannot conceive of infinity except as an enormous quantity. We cannot conceive of it as an orderly process, as pattern or cycle, as shapeliness. We conceive of it as inconceivable quantity," 84. Heidegger also echoes this in his criticism of Descartes and his explication on nihilism, asserting that "The claim move towards secureness that consists of this, that everything to be represented and representing itself are driven together into the clarity and lucidity of the mathematical *idea* and there assembled," in *The Question Concerning Technology*, 89.

Übermensch epitomizes. Heidegger does not decry the windmill because it does not order itself onto nature and as such destine its being into one mode of revealing—which Heidegger shows that *Ge-Stell*, as Enframing, must do[17] — instead it is dependent upon nature for its energy thus allowing the wind into a more poetic revelation.[18] It is in this way that Heidegger says that modern technology banishes Being into ordering, into a purely object-oriented metaphysic. Regulating and securing a standing-reserve become the mark of all revealing.[19] In this way, modern technology is an expression of the will-to-power that Nietzsche describes, and it is why we can make the claim that we live in an age of materialistic nihilism. Modern technology and its creation of instrumental reason, as such, has challenged-forth all that is into securing a superabundant life based on our universally accessible ordering of things into that which has value. The essence of globalization then falls within this materialistic nihilism—metaphysical certainties given towards the ordering of being— and it has been corrosive onto many things, but has been particularly destructive towards food.[20] With this framework of materialistic nihilism established we can begin to see how through globalization it has had destructive effects on place and food.

The Death of Place

For all it is worth, the airport could be considered a shimmering symbol of the successes of globalization and modernity. Within its terminals and through its commodity, we can move across the globe with stunning efficacy. In this sense, through globalization we now have a world that is without frontiers, and hopefully without exclusion— meaning that it is necessarily available to all. Of course we should now know that this universality of accessibility is predicated on an Enframing upon which all is ordered up into the useable. All things are accessible,

---

[17] Heidegger talks about this in *The Question Concerning Technology* most notably from p. 25-29.

[18] *Ibid.*, 14. Also finding the notion of poetic revealing in p. 34-35.

[19] *Ibid.*, 27.

[20] Hart, "A Philosopher in the Twilight", 48. A point can be made about the nihilistic machinations of globalization in Kleber, Marco. "The Metaphysics of Globalization in Heidegger" in *Philosophy of Globalization*. Concha Roldán, Daniel Brauer, Johannes Rohbeck eds. (Berlin: De Gruyter, 2018): 369-378.

then, through our ability to access them through a robust certainty of what it is that they are— the metaphysics of modernity through technology. Yet, what has this universal accessibility, which necessarily predicates itself on materialistic nihilism, to do with place?

Place, specifically through architecture though not limited towards it, should restore the meaning of time in rooting us towards a past and towards helping us imagine a future.[21] This is the imagination of the modernist poet Baudelaire who imagined the chatter of the workplace amidst the chimneys and the spires of the Church, signifying a world in which the modern has transplanted itself into the traditions of the polis.[22] The anthropologist Marc Augé, however, believes we have superseded even this imagination of modernity into what he denotes as supermodernity. Supermodernity, as Augé posits, does not produce spaces—places where the modern workplace is in balance with the ancient cathedral—which inhabit rooted places, but instead non-places which do not integrate themselves into anything. Instead we receive a world in which space becomes a "place of memory", they are no longer anthropological places, and instead worlds in which people are born and die in hospitals, complete transactions wordlessly through abstract computations of commerce, and are shuttled into dense networks of transport which contains transit points and temporary abodes by which to service itself. In this world, Augé posits, we see ourselves surrendered to solitary individuality, communicating most often with only mere images of humanity— or place.[23]

For Augé, then, where place is always defined against as relational, historical, and out of which identity is given and found— which necessarily contrasts itself with space— non-places give nothing relational, historical, or disposed towards identity.[24] Instead of being relational, non-places promote a contractual metaphysic onto those who

---

[21] Augé, *Non-Places*, xvii.
[22] From Baudelaire's *Tableaux parisiens* as cited in Augé, *Ibid.*, 62.
[23] *Ibid.*, 63-64.
[24] *Ibid.*, 63.

inhabit them.[25] No longer are we simply born into place,[26] but instead we are validated in place through contractual moments only to again recede to anonymity.[27] Here we see most poignantly that non-places erode the relational nature of place— here then we should see the concealment of being under the principle of Enframing (*Gestell*). Even further, symbols of non-place like the highway erode the historicity of place by making place merely a landscape-text addressed to the driver impersonally amongst a sea of a million others.[28] This transformation of place into mere text should make it easy to see, then, how identities of both of place and of the individual within that place begin to erode. To *be* at all, then, is to be challenged-forth into being, into giving being a value by which to enhance the conditions of existence, to use our framework from above. Non-places throw us into and come from out of an ordering of the world, a narcissistic relationship towards space and others simply because the value-ordering of the world by which we live under challenges us to do as other do simply to be ourselves.[29]

With the pervasiveness of non-place and the materialistic nihilism described above it should stand that places in general are given over to the will of the subject who is given to the creation of their own subjectivity as a means of enhancing their existence. Even beyond the creation of non-places in which humanity becomes a standing-reserve to the will-to-power, natural places have become standing-reserves given over to enhancement of "life." Energy, as something that is in reserve to be used towards the enchantment of life—typically through technology—necessarily becomes the confines towards which place can exist. Energy, understood this way, is that which at once gives life and takes away life.[30] Unfortunately under the materialistic nihilism we have

---

[25] It is then worthy of note that in his essay, "Of Other Spaces", Michel Foucault notes, "…the anxiety of our era has to do fundamentally with space…", 331 in *Rethinking Architecture: A Reader in Cultural Theory*. Ed. Neil Leach (New York: Routledge, 1997).

[26] Augé, *Non-Places*, 43. We can see similarly in Edward S. Casey's work on place, most notably in his *Getting Back into Place: Toward a Renewed Understanding of the Place-World*, where he says, "To be is to be in place," 14.

[27] Ibid., 82.

[28] Ibid., 83.

[29] Augé, *Non-Places*, 85. Cf. also Heidegger's "The Age of the World Picture" in *The Question Concerning Technology*, where he pronounces, "[In modern space] every place is equal to every other", 119.

[30] Berry, *The Unsettling of America*, 81.

previously described, the place in which we must necessarily have to be, is ordered up and destined into being a vessel of energy under the all ordaining principles of a materialistic metaphysics.[31] This understanding of the world, as a world that is to be ordered and utilized to the necessities of our need to feel alive, is necessarily corrosive to place.

From Feast to Meal: Food and Commodity

As we have seen, the metaphysical ordering of materialistic nihilism has led necessarily to the destruction of place—something which has become necessary to globalization. One of the principle reasons for the destruction of place we have identified is a disposition towards ordering of the world. From out of this framework we can observe what this has done in relation to food. There are, as such, two presenting illnesses in relation to food. The first presents itself in the commodification of agriculture and consequently food within the economy. The second comes in that food itself becomes a standing-reserve that stores up energy that can be given to us, or critically not given.[32]

First, it follows, we must examine the commodification of food and, by its nature, agriculture. As Wendell Berry notes, "The only escape from this destiny of victimization has been to 'succeed'— that is to 'make it' into the class of exploiters…"[33] Within this statement we see the principle of the standing-reserve that comes from the materialistic nihilism we are speaking of. Berry makes explicit what it means to become the *der Übermensch* of our materialistic nihilism. As it is a basic principle for us that all must eat in order to survive, it would follow that in order to have mastery over that source we must create a standing-reserve of that

---

[31] I would argue, here, that this is how we should best understand Heidegger's critique of ontotheology, his rage against the theology of a supreme being. The metaphysics of much of modernity is indeed a materialistic metaphysic wherein the realm of first causes is inhabited primarily by the all powerful and the gift of all being and all life is understood primarily as a power itself and not that which it is, a gift.

[32] Though it is not a central aspect of this essay, it could be argued that the metaphysics of the will-to-power, as necessarily located in the self-thinking self, as it relates to food does principally lead to a quantifiable mastery of eating that has presented itself in our modern eating illnesses.

[33] Berry, *The Unsettling of America*, 5.

source by which life is preserved and enhanced—that it is made into an object under our control. This, especially when it comes to agriculture and as such food, is known then as a commodity. In this sense we should see that commodities are not something trivial as we may expect, but rather something riddled with metaphysical subtleties.[34] The commodity presents itself as a universality—something basic to globalization—which gives agriculture over to a world market of standing-reserves. Essentially this means that food is no longer something that comes from a place and represents that place and its people, but is instead simply an image of food; it is consumed as a food product as opposed to food itself, (a great example of this would be the fast food menu wherein a stunning visual logic is placed onto our relationship with food. Here we order explicitly based on images and typically our phenomenal understanding of what we are eating is based on its marketing imagery and the mood it represented to us upon ordering).[35] This image-oriented society becomes a society of spectacle in which mere appearance is taken as something becoming of goodness.[36]

Beyond this, something that represents a densely packed cultural exchange of social and ecological relations and is deeply rooted in place like food, becomes merely a commodity or stated otherwise, a product.[37] It is in this sense that food becomes mere image and, even further, non-

---

[34] Cf. Debord, Guy. *The Society of the Spectacle* (Detroit: Black & Row, 1977). Debord states, "…we recognize our old enemy, *the commodity*, who knows so well how to seem at first glance something trivial and obvious, while on the contrary it is so complex and so full of metaphysical subtleties," (Aph. 35).

[35] Hence Debord's aphorism, "The spectacle is not a collection of images, but a social relation among people, mediated by images," (aph. 4). Further, note that most packaged food consumed is sold to us via images of itself and comes as a "product" of something and under the visual categorization in a market.

[36] Again Debord, "The spectacle presents itself as something enormously positive, indisputable and inaccessible. It says nothing more than, 'that which is good, is that which appears.' The attitude which it demands in principle is passive acceptance which in fact it already obtained by its manner of appearing without reply, by its monopoly of appearance," (Aph. 12).

[37] Wirzba, Norman. *Food and Faith: A Theology of Eating*. Second Edition (Cambridge: Cambridge University Press, 2019), 58-60, here Wirzba argues for the de-culturalization of food. In this way it becomes a certain type of the non-food imagery which I am arguing for. See also Paul Roberts' important *The End of Food* (Boston: Mariner Books, 2009) where he makes a similar argument about modern agribusiness and globalization's success in the food market being predicated on its being like any other consumer product.

food—to play on Augé's flourish—in that food becomes de-placed and de-culturalized through its commodification, as such food becomes unified through misery and alienation.[38] That is, food no longer represents a region and its culinary ability as we can still see in Mexican taco culture, but rather corn can be farmed anywhere for whatever shadowy purpose it is deemed to by those who think of it—it is merely a standing reserve to be given over as a source of energy. As a result for this total control, ecological systems and rhythms no longer are allowed to have their own transience, their own meaning in and of themselves, but rather they are ordered and manipulated by the logic of supply and demand.[39]

In reality, then, these illnesses are one and the same. This is nearly true, though crucially they show one difference. They both predicate a notion that Being must be given value, and that it must be secured. This, then, denotes that beyond agricultural practices themselves, we have corroded what it means to truly eat. We have forgotten how to eat and as such we have destroyed its expression in place through agriculture. This metaphysical existentialism denotes an isolated individual[40] who paradoxically has universal access to all of the globe through their rational ordering of objects and values towards a value-being—the culmination of the metaphysical eating and materialistic nihilism.

The logic of materialistic nihilism established, then, it should make sense that nationalism and populisms are on the rise in response to the desolation of food, the isolation of the individual, and the destruction of place.[41] Yet these attempts—nationalism/populism—at overcoming this materialistic nihilism are misguided on all accounts. While nationalism gives the guise of re-establishing a place because it is not personal, it

---

[38] How fitting it is, then, that most of us eat our meals alone or in small specialized groups. Rarely do we pause to appreciate the locality of food, the places in which we eat it, or the people who produce our food or share it with us.

[39] Wirzba, Norman. *From Nature to Creation: A Christian Vision for Understanding and Loving Our World*. The Church and Postmodern Culture. Ed. James K.A. Smith. (Grand Rapids: Baker Academic, 2015), 12.

[40] It is notable that the notion of an isolated individual is argued by Debord (aph. 20), Augé (82-83), and Heidegger (102-104) in their respective works. Thus the principle of modernity, in which globalization is its triumph through its universal accessibility, is an isolated and self-thinking individual.

[41] Augé, *Non-Places*, makes this argument as well stating, "…the 'resurgence' of nationalisms, which is giving it [place] new relevance, could pass as a 'return' to the localization from which Empire… might seem to have represented a withdrawal," 91.

is still non-historical or relational. It orders up and controls all being and places through a similar metaphysical idolatry, instead this time with more ideological fervor—an ideological fervor that contains a very narrow vision of what it is to be a person and a people. Both reflect a profound sense of idolatry, and idolatry is never something banal, but reflects the scope and gaze of the person who is doing the looking.[42] Here, then, we find ourselves in a tenuous place. Globalization and it would seem its alternative, nationalism through naïve localization, despite their popularity and dominance are failing to bring much more than violence and malaise outside of their momentary glimmers. Much against this prognosis, it should be argued that Christian theology, and particularly the sub-discipline of public theology, is the most productive and indeed the only total option for recovering existence, and e.g. *being*, from the materialistic nihilism we have described.

Theological Existence

In order to rescue food and place from materialistic nihilism we first need to develop a sense of what it means for us to exist theologically— and indeed at all. Through a recovery of theological existence, and only then, can we again be able to appreciate the existential importance of food and place. Further, through a robust understanding of what it means to exist theologically we can come into a true relationship with eating, and by default food. Finally, if all of these things hold true, hospitality should be the natural manifestation of a properly theological existence. Through hospitality the problem of globalization can be done away with while global migration can be integrated. Further, the status of public theology will be fundamentally established as a vital discourse and one that realizes the task of a truly dogmatic theology to extend the Church beyond its walls. More clearly, public theology will be shown to be an indispensable mode of theological reflection and crucial to the Church's task of being indisputably for the world.

---

[42] Jean-Luc Marion is his work *God Without Being* (Chicago: University of Chicago Press, 1995) says of idolatry, "The idol thus acts as a mirror, not as a portrait: a mirror that reflects the gaze's image, or more exactly, the image of its aim and the scope of its aim," 12.

Ontology and God

With Descartes "*Cogito ergo Sum*," ("I think therefore, I am"), Being—and as we have seen, all existence—was found within the mathematical certainty of the self-thinking self.[43] This rationality, as such, has become the predominant validation of what it means to exist in the Modern era, particularly as the technological mindset has come to prevalence.[44] Yet, if what we have previously stated is true, any such ontology is a inherently nihilistic one predicated on the will-to-power that Nietzsche's metaphysics lay bare. In this regard, we will need a new idea of what it means to exist, and we should do this theologically.

For many the Doctrine of Creation has very little existential capacity beyond being a starting point, a necessary causality.[45] This thinking can be echoed by Kirillov in Dostoyevsky's *The Demons* where he says, "No one asked me if I wanted to be born"[46]; we have been thrown, or created, into existence in which that existence is a mere causal necessity.[47] In this sense, the human is never truly or freely a person. It is bound by the necessity of its existence, which would then prompt Kirillov to proclaim that, "Whoever dares to commit suicide becomes God."[48] For this reason philosophy, on its own, is unable to understand

---

[43] Heidegger, *The Question Concerning Technology*, 88-89.

[44] Charles Taylor affirms this as he speaks of the isolation of the individual through material reason in *The Ethics of Authenticity* (Cambridge: Harvard University Press, 1991); esp. 1-12.

[45] Starting here is of extra significance if we are to heed to works of Aquinas, "Any error about creation also leads to an error about God." *Summa Contra Gentiles*, II. 3.

[46] Fyodor, Dostoyevsky, *Demons: A Novel in Three Parts*. Trans. Richard Peaver & Larissa Volokhonsky. Vintage Classics (New York: Vintage Books, 1995), 394. Similarly helpful in this regard is Ocean Vuong's statement in his *On Earth We're Briefly Gorgeous* (New York: Penguin Press, 2019) in which he states, "To be or not to be. That is the question. A question, yes, but not a choice," 63.

[47] Dreyfus, Hubert. *Being-in-the-World: A Commentary on Heidegger's Being and Time*, Division I. (Cambridge: MIT Press, 1991), 240-244. Heidegger's concept of *Geworfenheit* (throwness) then expertly articulates the necessity of being and our recognition that we are true creation, not God.

[48] Again, Dostoyevsky, *Demons*, 105. This, then, really becomes the literary focus of Albert Camus in his work *The Myth of Sisyphus* in which he states, "The reasoning is classic in its clarity. If God does not exist, Kirilov is god. If God does not exist, Kirilov must kill himself. Kirilov must therefore kill himself to become god. That logic is absurd, but it is what is needed."

this existence. The implications of *creatio ex nihilio* therefore have profound ontological and moral meaning for the human.

To understand the existential importance of creation we must look at the words of Genesis 1:26. While God creates, he does so under the maxim, "Let it be", but in making human-beings God says, "Let us *make* humankind…,"[49] (Gen. 1:26). The implication of this is that humankind is an ongoing creation, something that has not yet ceased to be, or to be made. It is in this mode that we can begin to understand what Karl Barth means when he suggests that the Covenant—as Incarnation and Redemption— is the ground of creation.[50] Further, it is not just the ground of creation, but it is the entire pageant of creation, that creation itself is not just the story of humanity's genesis, but that it is the setting of Revelation and redemption, and what comes through Jesus Christ.[51] Attending to this, we should note that the prelude to John's Gospel pronounces "In the beginning…" (Jn. 1:1) echoing again the story of Creation, and when Jesus dies on the cross he states, "It is finished" (Jn. 19:30).

This denotes something entire about the pageant of Creation, that at the beginning of humanity God says, "Let us make…" and upon Christ's death it is pronounced, "It is finished." It suggests that a new creation has been made; or, more pointedly, that creation is only actually now finished and interpretable as such. This creation, then, is not bound to the necessity of existence, and can therefore truly become alive— this does give "Let the dead bury their own dead" (Mt. 8:22, Lk. 9:60) a whole new connotation.[52] In this sense, to become human and to truly exist is to be in communion with the Divine— to come from out of biological

---

[49] All quotations of Scripture will come from the NRSV.

[50] Hans Urs von Balthasar, *The Theology of Karl Barth* (New York: Holt, Rinehart & Winston, 1971), 108.

[51] *Ibid.*, 110.

[52] This is the central argument of John Behr's magisterial *The Mystery of Christ: Life in Death* (Crestwood: St. Vladimir's Seminary Press, 2006) and is further explored in his *Becoming Human: Meditations on Christian Anthropology in Word and Image* (Crestwood: St. Vladimir's Seminary Press, 2013). In the latter he shares the story of Ignatius of Antioch writing to Roman Christian's as he is on his way to be martyred in which he asks them not to interfere in his death, because through his death he will become truly human.

existence constrained by death, and into the eternality of God.[53] Thus, to truly exist means to take on a Divine ontology, something revealed through the incarnation.[54] To take on the divine ontology, then, cannot be individual. It must take on a hypostatic character, defined by love, in order to become the very *reality* of a person.[55] This means that personhood is something necessarily given from the hypostatic Trinity, which is by nature personal and relational—meaning that God exists in perfect relation to an *Other*, which is necessary for his own existence.[56] It is given assurance through the Incarnation of Jesus Christ in his death and resurrection. Jesus is, then, the savior because he is the very reality of the person in that he hypostatizes personhood to humanity.[57] Thus in order to exist, to become alive, we must ourselves "let it be" as we enter into communion with the Divine *being*, God himself as revealed to us through His Trinitarian persons, who transforms and perfects our being into a new creation unconstrained by the finitude of biological existence. No longer do we suffer like Kirillov, protesting at the necessity of our existence, but we chose to become alive through Christ.

Theological Existence and Hospitality

It should follow, then, that if we become truly alive in our participation in the Triune ontology, we must become truly alive by assuming the nature of God which is personal.[58] By extension, we cannot exist as merely individuals—though the particularity of subjectivity can never be entirely done away with. When we come into true existence, when we "take on the cloak of Christ", we are de-individualized, (or

---

[53] A particularly poetic example of this is Charles Wesley's hymn "Idumea (Am I Born to Die?)" found in *The Sacred Harp*. 1991 Edition (Carlton, GA: Sacred Harp Publishing, 1991), 47. In which death is questioned and life is found in participation with Christ's glory.

[54] This can be witnessed most fully in Athanasius' understanding of the Doctrine of the Incarnation in his, *On the Incarnation*. Trans. John Behr. Popular Patristics Series, vol. 44a. Ed. John Behr (Crestwood: St. Vladimir's Seminary Press, 2011); esp. 115-119.

[55] John D. Zizioulas, *Being as Communion: Studies in Personhood and the Church*. Contemporary Greek Thought. Christos Yannaros, Bishop Kallistos, Costa Carras eds. (Crestwood, NY: St. Vladimir's Seminary Press, 1985), 53-55.

[56] *Ibid.*, 41-46.

[57] *Ibid.*, 54.

[58] *Ibid.*, 41. Pulling also, then, on the Byzantine ascetical traditional.

perhaps, de-egoized), and we come into a personal mode of being.⁵⁹ We, as such, come into being through becoming part of the ecclesial body of Christ, through our birth into the Virgin Mother of the Church.⁶⁰ Yet again, and most basically, true humanity, true existence, is predicated upon otherness. That is, we do not first come into existence then relate, it is through our relations that we come to be.⁶¹ It is in this sense that we have otherness for the sake of oneness. This is the *ousia* and the *hypostasis* of Trinity and its necessary implications through which we see the particularly of the self necessarily bound in relation—self-hood for the sake of love.⁶² To become a person, as understood theologically, is done through participation in God's being, which is love.⁶³ This participation in the love that comes from and is God establishes for us that in order to exist properly we must be in a loving relation, ergo hospitality (as the nonviolent reception of the other as other) is the manifestation of what it means to truly be alive.⁶⁴ Hospitality is the way of being that is revealed in the Trinity itself as it is the self-offering love that gives life to the Other—*kenosis*.⁶⁵

Otherness, which predicates our hospitable and loving being, responds rather negatively towards an anthropology of the self-thinking individual because this anthropology is revealed as violent. The Other, in this way, evades our attempts to bring them into the certainty of the will-to-power, and in this the Other paralyzes our desire to master it.⁶⁶ The Other calls us into ethics by showing that it is not an object, but a distance revealed—something to be related to rightly.⁶⁷ The Other

---

⁵⁹ *Ibid.*, 110-114.

⁶⁰ *Ibid.*, 113.

⁶¹ *Ibid.*, 105-107.

⁶² This borrowing from the typology of Barth's theology as expressed by von Balthasar on what it means to become God's partner (*Theology of Karl Barth*, 113) in synthesis with Zizioulas' hypostatic Trinitarian personhood.

⁶³ Zizioulas, *Being as Communion*, 46. Also this is the central thesis of Marion's *God Without Being*.

⁶⁴ To this point Zizioulas says, "Love is not a feeling towards the Other but a gift coming from them." *Communion and Otherness: Further Studies in Personhood and the Church*. Ed. Paul McPartlan (London: T&T Clark, 2007), 55.

⁶⁵ This point is developed in Wirzba, *Food and Faith*, 217-224.

⁶⁶ Emmanuel Levinas, *Totality and Infinity: An Essay on Exteriority*. Trans. Alphonso Lingus (Pittsburgh: Duquesne University Press, 1969), 217.

⁶⁷ Norman Wirzba, "From Maieutics to Metanoia: Levinas' Understanding of the Philosophical Task", in *Emmanuel Levinas: Critical Assessments of Leading Philosophers*,

cannot be owned or controlled; the Other cannot be mastered. The Trinity as the primordial ontological concept, through which we become truly human—through Christ's death and resurrection and our birth into the Church as our new mode of existence—is manifested through hospitality.

Hospitality and Food: Food as Other

It should then follow that food is no longer a metaphysical substance that enhances life or acts as an energy source, but instead it is fully representative of the Other.[68] Food is then the culmination of our relationship with the Other—animal and otherwise. Thus, it should stand that food is symbolic of how we respond to the call towards ethics of the Other— towards doing and being the good. The way we eat is, as such, a statement about how we exist in place and what we think of the Other, and most importantly whether or not we care to exist ourselves at all. Most pointedly, how we eat—whether is it hospitable or not— becomes the modicum of manifestation for our new Trinitarian being. In this way, we can see why the theologian Jürgen Moltmann would proclaim that to witness towards Creation would be the most profound Christian statement at the end of modernity.[69] What Moltmann sees is that we must manifest the Christian life for the sake of the other and in the modern era, the other in need is creation itself.

Hospitality is then here the paramount manifestation of Christian being. The Christian faith is not a moving towards an eschatology in which one's creaturely status is abandoned but it is instead about become a true person; it is about the transformation of all earthly life.[70] We cannot eat well, then, if we abandon the health and the infinite otherness

---

Vol 1: Levinas, Phenomenology and his Critics. Ed. Claire Elise Katz and Laura Trout. (Abingdon: Routledge, 2005), 395-396.

[68] Pannenberg in his essay, "God and Nature", in *Toward a Theology of Nature: Essays on Science and Faith*. Ed. Ted Peters (Louisville, KY: Westminster John Knox Press, 1993): 50-71, argues similarly as I am intending here that any theology of nature must come from out of the Trinity. Only a theology of the Trinity in view of the history of salvation will be adequate to explain the presence of God with his creatures through space and time, e.g. the necessary Otherness of Food.

[69] Jürgen Moltmann, *The Way of Jesus Christ: Christology in Messianic Dimensions*. trans. Margaret Kohl (Minneapolis, MN: Fortress Press, 1990), 307.

[70] Wirzba, *Food and Faith*, 197.

of pristine ecological and biological cycles for quantity and commodity. Eating when received as something Other, that is as something *given*, becomes something in which we absorb—through consumption—the very relationship with the Other whose self-offering brings to us life.[71] In this most radical way food is a profound statement upon culture, and Christian being—manifested in hospitality—finds itself bound into an intricate membership with food and the complex ecological memberships which connote the Christian's very alive-ness. It is in this sense that John Zizioulas says, "Man's responsibility is to make a eucharistic reality out of nature, i.e., to make nature, too, capable of communion."[72]

Food and Place

Seeing food as an other helps us to regain a vision of agriculture as something truly *cultural*. No longer is food just a metaphysical object of nutritional consumption, but it is something densely symbolic of what it means to live. There is, even further, a deep sacramentality to food in which religious meaning is not merely added but *unveiled* as part of the divine liveliness and loveliness already inherited.[73] What we then must remember is that food and also, necessarily, ourselves always come from somewhere— to be at all is to be in a place.[74] In this way, to truly become human is to recognize ourselves within these thick memberships within place that is culminated in food, and to make ourselves capable of response and love. The only possible ethic here, then, is a virtue ethic,[75] and one cultivated upon a sacramental and ascetic understanding of life.

Food is now no longer something utilitarian, but something greatly more than mere eating and drinking. It is now given a

---

[71] Wirzba, *Food and Faith*, 207. Wirzba also compares eating, in this sense, to the most profound sexual intimacy, it is an erotic encounter with an Other.

[72] Zizioulas, *Being as Communion*, 119. Zizioulas continues on, "If man does this, then truth takes up its meaning for the whole cosmos, Christ becomes a cosmic Christ, and the world as a whole dwells in truth, which is none other than communion with its Creator."

[73] Wirzba, *Food and Faith*, 260.

[74] Edward S. Casey, *The Fate of Place: A Philosophical History* (Berkley: University of California Press, 2013), ix.

[75] This very argument has been recently made and sustained in Bouma-Prediger, Steven. *Earthkeeping and Character: Exploring a Christian Ecological Virtue Ethic* (Grand Rapids: Baker Academic, 2019).

fundamental reverence, it is recognized as *given*.[76] To eat we must see God's givenness within creation and our response-ability towards land and place as necessary to our eating. Fr. Schmemann, then, notes that it is no accident that the Fall is predicated on a wrongful relationship with food in which man's desire is to come into communion with himself and not with God.[77] In this way, we must begin to understand God not in his essence, but from the grandeur and givenness of his creation and his care for it.[78] This denotes a necessary sacramentality to our eating, but also a necessary asceticism in which we participate in the validation of eating as given by God towards his creatures and then in which we must recognize and bring into communion by protesting against its death.[79] Hence fasting, and also feasting, take on a necessary role in the practice of Christian faith towards eating. It establishes the necessary practical grounds upon which hospitality becomes the link to the Other—in this case place and food in their necessary symbiotic relation. In fasting we can abstain from our desire to master as well as to protest against the death of place and the abuse of food. In feasting we come to recognize and celebrate givenness and by extension otherness—in which rumination on our personhood and necessarily communality can be digested in that givenness.[80] To put it another way, to eat well is to manifest our hospitality to the Other and in which to turn a mere meal into a manifestation of Trinitarian particularity and oneness. Our meal becomes a feast, then, it becomes as Icon of God in His persons.

It is in this sense that Christian existence is realized in the way we eat. Christian existence invites us to see our being as constituted by our relation to the other. In this case, it causes us to reflect on how we have existed in membership towards creation as *given* by God to us. This necessarily asks us whether we are bringing all things into communion

---

[76] Alexander Schmemann, *For the Life of the World: Sacraments and Orthodoxy* (Crestwood: St. Vladimir's Seminary Press, 1973), 16.

[77] Schmemann, *For the Life of the World*, 16.

[78] St. Maximus the Confessor. *On Love I*, 96, trans. G.E.H. Palmer, Phillip Sherrard, and Kallistos Ware. In *The Philokalia*, vol. 2 (London: Faber & Faber, 1981), 64.

[79] Moltmann argues for the Christian movement against death in economic and environmental practices in *Experiences in Theology: Ways and Forms of Christian Theology*. trans. Margaret Kohl (Minneapolis: Fortress Press, 2000), 26-27.

[80] Wirzba, *Food and Faith*, 219-222.

with Him who gives life in all.[81] The essence, then, of our Eucharistic ontology—a movement from New Creation in baptism to communion with God— is an appreciation of the Other, which then evokes our gratitude[82]— this should also necessarily bring us into an appreciation of the glory of the lord and e.g. beauty.[83] To eat well is to regain a pristine sense of God's intentions of Creation from which he saves upon and not out from, it is to enter into rhythms of life which see Creation as a true sacrament— in this regard the Sabbath has great existential as well as theological implications.[84] In this we hear afresh the groaning of Creation as it waits for the revealing of God's Church, (Rom 8:19-23), as Creation too seeks its sabbath and its communion.[85] From this vantage, having now understood what it means to exist for Christian theology and for what this means towards its relationship towards food and place, we can offer the phenomenon of globalization a new home.

Food, Hospitality, & the Global Age: A Discourse on Eucharist

We have previously sketched out a theological existence in which to exist is to come alive as an ecclesial being; a being who is saved from individuality and brought into communion with the Triune God. Out of our communion with the Trinity we come to seen ourselves as constituted by the our relation to the Other, formed by a givenness and brought into life through love. We have then see that this fundamentally changes the way we eat and in our relationship to place—we necessarily come to see the sacramentality of both. With these things now in mind,

---

[81] Again Schmemann, *For the Life of the World*, 16-17.

[82] Zizioulas, *Communion and Otherness*, 90.

[83] Though the aesthetic aspect of this argument won't be followed here, we should heed the warning of von Balthasar in volume I of his theological aesthetics where he pronounces, "In a world without beauty— even if people cannot dispense with the word and constantly have it on the tip of their tongues in order to abuse it— in a world which is perhaps not wholly without beauty, but which can no longer see it or reckon with it: in such a world the good also loses its attractiveness, the self-evidence of why it must be carried out. Man stands before the good and asks himself why it must be done and not rather its alternative, evil," 19.

[84] See von Balthasar's treatment of Barth on creation and sabbath in *The Theology of Karl Barth*, 110-113.

[85] It is in this sentiment we should hear Barth commenting on Romans 8:19-21 saying, "The creation waiteth together with us—no, for us." In *The Epistle to the Romans*. Sixth Edition. trans. Edwyn C. Hoskyns (Oxfrod: Oxford University Press, 1933), 308.

we can see how Christian existence manifested in hospitality renders the materialistic nihilism of the current global phenomena banal. No longer are things universally accessible to the rational mind, but all things are now an Other to be related to rightly and seen as given towards that givenness of all things—the imago Dei is a strong retort against globalization. In this sense the manifestation of Christian existence through hospitality, most poignantly through food and place, offer its strongest critique of globalization and nationalisms respectively, and reveals itself as the only truth about existence. Yet, Christianity in its truthfulness does not entirely destroy the global phenomenon, but rather presents its transfiguration.

To see this we must begin to see that Christian existence and its inherently public witness, brings a moral capacity to what was otherwise an amoral aspect of globalization, that is in its global migrations. Where globalization says that all places are equal to every other place—as a universality, as something destined for the preservation-enhancement of life—Christian existence reveals the dignity of the particular and the frontiers. (Indeed, as we're coming to see, the world must have frontiers, it must have particularity).[86] The nature of the Trinity does give us an ample example of particularity and otherness as constitutive towards good existence, yet it does not offer strict particularities or hierarchies, but instead grounds our Otherness on oneness and vice-versa. It suggests to us the necessity of particularity, even the necessity of frontiers and localizations, but it does not allow them to be rigidly controlled. It asserts that any frontier must itself be permeable, be capable of opening.[87] In this way, global migrations are now validated with a capacity for the Good itself.

Food, as it has been argued, roots us into a healthy appreciation of place as it represents the culmination of our relation to place and its members. From our choice in meats, spices, even to where we eat our food, we are representing a deep cultural—even sacramental—impulse

---

[86] Augé, *Non-Places*, ix-xii.

[87] Certainly this dialogues crucially with understandings of migrations and national immigration. It would seem to me, then, that migration should be championed in as much as it does not destroy place. The frontiers of place are always adaptable inasmuch as they are relational, historical, and given towards identity. Any rigid totalitarian understanding of place is again given towards the will-to-power over place in which place becomes a space and an image of reality.

which has a *place* to be. Ergo in the regionality of cuisine, from the dried meats of Northern Italy, to the BBQ of the south, food represents a culture, a people with an identity based on how they relate towards the land and the places they are—it reveals hospitality or the lack thereof. We see this as an intricate and beautifully mysterious relationship with food, people, and their given place.[88] We also see, however, the permeability of place within the Otherness of migrations. We see French technique guiding cuisine in Patagonia, Argentina, or the styling of barbecue in Scandinavian food.[89] Most notably where this is best done, place is also well cultivated—there is an inherent appreciation for the beauty of space and its relation towards our being, e.g. it becomes a place.

To recognize the Eucharistic ethos, and therein its predilection towards food, roots us into a responsible relationship with place and the Other—it guides us back to our hospitable existence. We see the ability of food to migrate and, in this sense, we see the dense culture and otherness inherit within food and people. Hospitality is indeed inherent within this mode of being, as to eat is necessarily to welcome the Other into a consummate relationship with ourselves. To welcome the Other well, similar to erotic phenomena, we must do this virtuously— e.g. our ethics must become immersed in virtue.[90] Meaning, boundaries must be constructed in which particularity remains still for the sake of oneness, and where love can be properly expressed. Put differently, boundaries where the Other calls us into ethics and we respond with hospitality. As it dialogues with globalization, then, global migrations are encouraged and revealed as something predisposed towards goodness. So too, place is given a rightful seat at the table as the question is always being raised as to whether we are in right relationship with our environs—whether or

---

[88] For a poignant example of this the Netflix Docu-Series *Chef's Table* should be consulted. Particularly the episodes revolving around Dan Barber, Magnus Nilsson, and Francis Mallmann. All, in one way or another, showcase a deep relationship to place whilst utilizing more international techniques and ways of spicing food.

[89] On the interconnectedness of technique see Netflix's other Docu-Series *Ugly Delicious* in which the permeability to technique and even style are given within various places.

[90] To pull from Steven DeLay's presentation of Jean-Luc Marion's thought, "To abandon oneself in this way is to enter into a domain of experience where everything appears against the background of charity. I no longer live concerned with how others view me, but instead a life first preoccupied with how God sees me." In *Phenomenology in France: A Philosophical and Theological Introduction* (London: Routledge, 2019), 93.

not we have accepted our membership in a dense ecological community.[91] This permeability is made possible because of the very givenness of all things as juxtaposed on the very certain mastery of individuality in materialistic nihilism. It is made possible through a recognition, then, of thanks—to God and neighbor—and humility.[92] Food itself, then, as an icon of the trinity manifested through hospitality, which is a radical retort to the metaphysical certainty of Modernity and its prize of globalization.

Another, perhaps smaller though still important, point can be distilled. It is through food that we can witness to the stunning vitality of public theology. Public theology, with food as a lens, does not content itself to remain in an arid doctrinaire status, but rather returns theology to the things themselves—to borrow Husserl's famous idiom. With food as a properly theological lens, public theology is able to give itself things in which to experience the phenomena of Christian existence and to evaluate where the being of the Church for the world is best expressed. In the case of this study, then, the Trinity is no longer merely an economic relation towards an other-worldly salvation—though it remains within Pro-Nicene logic—but reveals itself to permeate and have transformative implications for the entire food process from farm to table. Food, here, further reveals itself to be a useful tool insofar as it reveals a multivalence of meanings; showing itself to have ecological, ontological, cultural, and geopolitical significance. Thus, both public theology and the theological reflection upon food should constitute an ongoing significance for theology as both an academic field and as the vital tool of reflection for the Church as it necessarily makes the Church a gift for the world.

Conclusion

Our sketch of theological existence and its implications towards food and place in recognition of their otherness and givenness should

---

[91] Heidegger in his essay "Building Dwelling Thinking" then says, "The old word *bauen*, which says that man is insofar as he *dwells*, this word *bauen*, however, also means at the same time to cherish and protect, to preserve and care for, specifically to till the soil, to cultivate the vine. Such building only takes care— it tends the growth that ripens into fruit of its own accord." In *Basic Writings*. Revised Edition. trans. David Farrell Krell. Harper Perennial Modern Thought (San Francisco: Harper Perennial Modern Classics, 2008), 349.

[92] Borrowing then from, Norman Wirzba, "The Touch of Humility: An Invitation to Creatureliness". *Modern Theology* 24, no. 2 (April 2008): 225-244.

lead us into a new understanding of grace. Karl Barth speaks of the turn we have attempted here in saying, "We would rather not live by grace. Something within us energetically rebels against it. We do not wish to receive grace; at best we prefer to give ourselves grace."[93] We should see the problems inherit in globalization as it is eloquently totaled in the prophetic metaphysical evaluations of Nietzsche and Heidegger. Our sketch of theological existence, however, one in which we become alive in self-offering and through the givenness of the Other, then has far more radical implications. It questions the certainty of the self-thinking self to order all things based on their usefulness. It invites us to stop shouting at the shallow end of a pool and take our practices of being-in-the-world into the deep end where we must be more silent and more humble.[94]

For our purposes, the strongest retorts to globalization come through food because of its natural ascetic disposition— in that to be in proper relation to it we must have a sacramental understanding of eating which invites us into a mode of feasting and fasting. Food roots us into a place and questions us as to how we treat our membership within that place; it demands of us hospitality which manifests our Trinitarian being. It is, further, a dense cultural product in which Otherness is offered towards consummation; food is radically intimate. Food invites us into a celebration of the givenness of the Other, something we recognize only through its being given. For the Christian to exist and then to eat well is to manifest the Trinity through hospitality. Food invites us as an extension into speaking grace, towards celebrating God's gifts towards us, towards recognizing the infinite within the Other.[95] In summation, it should be argued that to combat the illness of globalization, and all of its metaphysical certainties, is to eat well. Recovering, then, what it means to exist theologically helps us to receive the gift of creation and as Zizioulas notes, "make it worthy of communion."[96] This will take a necessary dying

---

[93] Karl Barth, *Dogmatics in Outline*. Trans. G.T. Thomson (New York: Harper & Row, 1959), 20.

[94] Borrowing then from Sarah Coakley, "Deepening Practices: Perspectives from Ascetical and Mystical Theology". In *Practicing Theology: Beliefs and Practices in Christian Life*. Miroslav Volf & Dorothy C. Bass eds. (Grands Rapids, MI: Eerdmans, 2002): 78-93. Coakley argues that these "deep" practices encourage us into contemplation and question the order in which we've given ourselves. This corrects our attempts to control our own purgation into holiness.

[95] Wirzba, *Food and Faith*, 239-245.

[96] Zizioulas, *Being as Communion*, 119.

unto self and becoming alive through Christ, a step towards becoming the ecclesial being which is itself a protest against death and destruction. Eucharistic eating provides us a necessary way out of the violence of globalization and into a more beatific vision here and now.

Works Cited

Augé, Marc. *Non-Places: An Introduction to Supermodernity*. Second Edition. Trans. John Howe. New York: Verso, 2008.

Aquinas, St. Thomas. *Summa Contra Gentiles: Book Two, Creation*. South Bend: University of Notre Dame Press, 1976.

Athanasius, St. *On the Incarnation*. Trans. John Behr. Popular Patristics Series, Vol. 44a. Ed. John Behr. Crestwood: St. Vladimir's Seminary Press, 2010.

Barth, Karl. *Dogmatics in Outline*. Trans. G.T. Thomson. New York: Harper & Row, 1959.

———. *The Epistle to the Romans*. Sixth Edition. Trans. Edwyn C. Hoskyns. Oxford: Oxford University Press, 1933.

Behr, John. *Becoming Human: Meditations on Christian Anthropology in Word and Image*. Crestwood: St. Vladimir's Seminary Press, 2013.

———. *The Mystery of Christ: Life in Death*. Crestwood: St. Vladimir's Seminary Press, 2006.

Berry, Wendell. *The Unsettling of America: Culture & Agriculture*. Third Edition. San Francisco: Sierra Club, 1996.

Bouma-Prediger, Steven. *Earthkeeping and Character: Exploring a Christian Ecological Virtue Ethic*. Grand Rapids: Baker Academic, 2019.

Camus, Albert. *The Myth of Sisyphus*. Second Edition. Vintage International. New York: Vintage Books, 2018.

Casey, Edward S. *Getting Back Into Place: Toward a Renewed Understanding of the Place-World*. Second Edition. Bloomington: University of Indiana Press, 2009.

———. *The Fate of Place: A Philosophical History*. Berkley: University of California Press, 2013.

Coakley, Sarah. "Deepening Practices: Perspectives from Ascetical and Mystical Theology." In *Practicing Theology: Beliefs and Practices in Christian Life*. Miroslav Volf & Dorothy C. Bass eds. Grands Rapids: Eerdmans, 2002: 78-93.

Debord, Guy. *The Society of the Spectacle*. Revised Edition. Detroit: Black & Row, 1977.

DeLay, Steven. *Phenomenology in France: A Philosophical and Theological Introduction*. London: Routledge, 2019.

Dostoyevsky, Fyodor. *Demons: A Novel in Three Parts*. trans. Richard Peaver & Larissa Volokhonsky. Vintage Classics. New York: Vintage Books, 1995.

Dreyfus, Hubert L. *Being-in-the-World: A Commentary on Heidegger's Being and Time*, Division I. Cambridge: MIT Press, 1991.

Foucault, Michel. "Of Other Spaces: Utopias and Heterotopias." In *Rethinking Architecture: A Reader in Cultural Theory*. Ed. Neil Leach. New York: Routledge, 1997: 330-336.

Hart, David Bentley. "A Philosopher in the Twilight." *First Things* (February 2011): 44-51.

Heidegger, Martin. "Building Dwelling Thinking". In *Basic Writings*. Revised Edition. trans. David Farrell Krell. Harper Perennial Modern Thought. San Francisco: Harper Perennial Modern Classics, 2008: 343-364.

———. *The Question Concerning Technology: And Other Essays*. Trans. William Lovitt. Harper Perennial Modern Thought. New York: Harper Perennial Modern Classics, 2013.

Kleber, Marco. "The Metaphysics of Globalization in Heidegger." In *Philosophy of Globalization*. Concha Roldán, Daniel Brauer, Johannes Rohbeck eds. Berlin: De Gruyter, 2018: 369-378.

Levinas, Emmanuel. *Totality and Infinity: An Essay on Exteriority*. Trans. Alphonso Lingus. Pittsburgh: Duquesne University Press, 1969.

Marion, Jean-Luc. *God Without Being: Hors-Texte*. First Edition. Trans. Thomas A. Carlson. Religion and Postmodernism. Ed. Mark C. Taylor. Chicago: University of Chicago Press, 1995.

Maximus the Confessor, St. *On Love I*, 96, Trans. G.E.H. Palmer, Phillip Sherrard, and Kallistos Ware. In *The Philokalia*, vol. 2. London: Faber & Faber, 1981.

Moltmann, Jürgen. *Experiences in Theology: Ways and Forms of Christian Theology.* trans. Margaret Kohl. Minneapolis: Fortress Press, 2000.

———. *The Way of Jesus Christ: Christology in Messianic Dimensions.* Trans. Margaret Kohl. Minneapolis: Fortress Press, 1990.

Nietzsche, Friedrich. *The Gay Science: With a Prelude in Rhymes and an Appendix of Songs*. Trans. Walter Kaufmann. New York: Vintage Books, 1974.

———. *The Will to Power*. Trans. Walter Kaufmann & R.J. Hollingdale. Ed. Walter Kaufmann. New York: Vintage Books, 1968.

Pannenberg, Wolfhart. "God and Nature." In *Toward a Theology of Nature: Essays on Science and Faith*. Ed. Ted Peters. Louisville: Westminster John Knox Press, 1993.

Roberts, Paul. *The End of Food*. Boston: Mariner Books, 2009.

Schmemann, Alexander. *For the Life of the World: Sacraments & Orthodoxy*. Crestwood: St. Vladimir's Seminary Press, 1973.

Taylor, Charles. *The Ethics of Authenticity*. Reprint Edition. Cambridge: Harvard University Press, 2018.

von Balthasar, Hans Urs. *The Glory of the Lord: A Theological Aesthetics, I: Seeing the Form*. Trans. Erasmo Leiva-Merikakis. San Francisco: Ignatius Press, 1982.

———. *The Theology of Karl Barth*. New York: Holt, Rinehart & Winston, 1971.

Vuong, Ocean. *On Earth We're Briefly Gorgeous: A Novel*. New York: Penguin Press, 2019.

Wesley, Charles. "Idumea (Am I Born to Die?)." In *The Sacred Harp*. 1991 Edition. Carlton: Sacred Harp Publishing, 1991: 47.

Wirzba, Norman. *Food and Faith: A Theology of Eating*. Second Edition. Cambridge: Cambridge University Press, 2019.

———. "From Maieutics to Metanoia: Levinas' Understanding of the Philosophical Task", in *Emmanuel Levinas: Critical Assessments of Leading Philosophers, Vol 1: Levinas, Phenomenology and his Critics*. Ed. Claire Elise Katz and Laura Trout. Abingdon: Routledge, 2005: 385-401.

———. *From Nature to Creation: A Christian Vision for Understanding and Loving Our World*. The Church and Postmodern Culture. Ed. James K.A. Smith. Grand Rapids: Baker Academic, 2015.

———. "The Touch of Humility: An Invitation to Creatureliness." *Modern Theology* 24, no. 2 (April 2008): 225-244.

Zizioulas, John D. *Being as Communion: Studies in Personhood and the Church*. Contemporary Greek Thought. Christos Yannaros, Bishop Kallistos, Costa Carras eds. Crestwood: St. Vladimir's Seminary Press, 1985.

———. *Communion and Otherness: Further Studies in Personhood and the Church*. Ed. Paul McPartlan. London: T&T Clark, 2007.

Chapter 4
The Pursuit of Public Theology toward Women Under Confucian Society

Kyeo Re Lee[1]

Abstract

Over the centuries, Confucianism has greatly influenced East Asian societies. Western feminists criticized Confucianism as the leading cause of the oppression of women under Confucian society. This criticism is undeniable since the influence continues to exist down to the present. However, Confucianism is also an essential element that forms the identity of East Asian women. Taiwanese women have been active in environmental protection since the 20th century. They identify with the term, ecofamilism, that shows the connection between one's care for the environment and the care of one's family. This paper seeks to pursue a public theology toward women under Confucian society. As an Asian Christian woman, I seek to develop a deeper understanding of the identity of women under Confucian society through three theological lenses, salvation, incarnation, and trinity.

---

[1] Kyeo Re Lee was born in South Korea, and at nine month went to Taiwan with her parents, who were missionaries. She grew up in Taiwan and identifies herself as more Taiwanese than Korean. She received undergraduate education in Taiwan and graduate education in Korea and the United States. She is currently a student in the Doctor of Philosophy in Intercultural Studies program with a concentration in development studies at Asbury Theological Seminary.

Introduction

The dominating philosophy in East Asian countries, such as China, Japan, Korea, Vietnam, and Taiwan, is Confucianism or Ru Jia (儒家). It influences every aspect of life, such as the spheres of politics, social relationships, education, economics, and culture. The traditional Confucian society emphasizes the "familial virtue of filial piety, the continuity of the family name, and ancestor worship."[2] These three characteristics require a male heir in the family, and the obligations tied to Confucianism ultimately generated the "roots of women's oppression" in many Asian countries.[3]

Traditionally, not only are women in Confucian societies given specific tasks to do for the household, but they are also confined to a particular space known as the inner or the private realm (*nei*). While women in the 21st century are empowered through education and have gained economic independence, Confucian values are still heavily influencing. In this paper, I attempt to gain a deeper understanding of the women under Confucian society and engage in this conversation through public theology. I will first examine the influence of Confucianism toward women in both the traditional and modern Confucian society. Then I will focus on one specific region, Taiwan, to observe how women in Taiwan integrate the traditional culture and their own identity to manifest the ideal Confucian society.[4] The source of this section comes from Wan-Li Ho's *Ecofamilism: Women, Religion, and Environmental Protection in Taiwan*.[5] Despite knowing the danger of using broad theological concepts, I will make an effort to engage in the public theological discourse toward East Asian women through the

---

[2] Li-Hsiang Lisa Rosenlee, introduction to *Confucianism and Women: A Philosophical Interpretation* (Albany: State University of New York Press, 2006), 9.

[3] Ibid.

[4] Due to the broad nature of this topic, I will focus on one specific region. Taiwan is also known as the Republic of China (ROC) and Chinese Taipei in international sporting events. In this paper, I will refer to it as Taiwan. Considering Taiwan itself, there is a need to look at the political situation. Despite the importance of Taiwan's political situation, I acknowledge that this topic is a broad one, which is beyond the scope of this paper. Therefore, I will focus on seeking public theology for women within a Confucian society and will not be dealing with the political situation of Taiwan in this paper.

5 Wan-Li Ho, *Ecofamilism: Women, Religion, and Environmental Protection in Taiwan* (Florida: Three Pines Press, 2016).

lenses of salvation, incarnation, and the trinity. Lastly, I will expand on the concept of ecofamilism proposed by Ho and use that to generate agency for women living within a Confucian society.

Women Under a Confucian Society

To fully understand the influence of Confucianism toward women, it is vital to explore the history and philosophy of traditional Confucianism.[6] After that, I will focus on analyzing the role of women living in a traditional Confucian society. Lastly, I will look at the influence of Confucianism towards women in the modern Confucian society.[7]

History and Philosophy of Traditional Confucianism

Confucianism originated with a Chinese philosopher, Confucius (551-479 BCE), who traveled between different states of China during a period of constant warfare.[8] He gave political and military advice to the state's leaders and tried to convince them to adopt his philosophy in governing the state.[9] He believed that to bring harmony to a chaotic society, there were two critical aspects to follow. First, one has to go back and follow the traditions. Going back to the traditions meant to remember the tradition and history of the people; therefore, it was necessary to remember the ancestors. Secondly, harmony was formed through the ordering of proper social relationships.[10] In the ideal Confucian society, each member of the society "knows his or her own social position and conducts his or her life according to the rituals appropriate to it, though this does not entail the rigidity of one's social position."[11]

---

[6] Traditional Confucianism refers to the time that Confucius formed his philosophy until the seventeenth century.

[7] Modern Confucian society in this particular section, refers to the twentieth and twenty-first century in China and Taiwan.

[8] China was not united and did not form as the People's Republic of China until the Qin dynasty in 221 BCE.

[9] Robert André LaFleur, "The Hundred Schools of Thought (c. 500-200 B.C.E.)," in *China: A Global Studies Handbook* (Santa Barbara, CA: ABC-CLIO, 2003), 17.

[10] There are five central relationships that traditional Confucianism accentuates. They are between father and son, ruler and subject, husband and wife, old and young, and between friends.

[11] Peimin Ni, "Classical Confucianism I: Confucius," in *The Oxford Handbook of World Philosophy*, ed. Jay L. Garfield and William Edelglass (Oxford [England]: Oxford

Confucianism was further developed through later Confucian scholars such as Mencius (370-289 BCE) and Xunzi (310-220 BCE). Through the effort of these Confucian scholars, Confucianism rose to become the state ideology of the Han dynasty (206 BCE – 220 CE).[12] It collapsed after the Han dynasty's downfall but was revived during the Song dynasty (960-1279 CE) and exerted its influence again in the Ming dynasty (1368-1644 CE).

Role of Women within Traditional Confucian Society

Confucianism has centuries of influence on East Asian countries, and it has become the desired way of life. If observing traditions and forming proper relationships are two central aspects of Confucianism, what are the role and the task of women under these rules? First, observing traditions relates to the practice of ancestor worship. For Asian society, this automatically connects with the patriarchal lineage, since the ancestors are remembered only through the male heir. Male lineage suggests the importance of giving birth to a son. Secondly, individuals perform their social responsibilities to bring perfect harmony and peace to society; on the other hand, not fulfilling one's responsibilities means the destruction of the society. The desire to achieve a perfectly harmonious society, but at the same time, the fear of social pressure, motivates people to follow the rules of society.

These two ideologies have historically placed tremendous pressure on women. They were often oppressed if they could not fulfill the expected roles and tasks given by society. There were pressures for getting married, pregnancy, and giving birth to a male heir. These pressures exist for every woman, including newborn girls, since it was common to practice child concubinage, which placed women under marriage at a young age by her family. Before marriage, to be seen as more desirable or attractive to men, women in China deformed their feet by foot binding.[13] After the marriage, it was considered the "most

---

University Press, 2011), 33.

[12] The numerous philosophical schools in China were referred to as the Hundred Schools of Thought. Confucianism stood out as the dominant state ideology among these philosophies.

[13] The practice of foot binding was the sign of wealth because one cannot help with farming if their feet are bound.

unfilial deed" and even committing "the crime of being unfilial" if one failed to give birth to a son.[14] This expectation gave men reasons to marry concubines and even divorce their wives if they felt their wives were not meeting these expectations. The preference for a male heir rather than a female also led to the problem of female infanticide.

In a Confucian society, the proper role for women is limited to the realm inside the house. The inside (or private realm) of the household belonged to women, while and, the outside (or public realm) belonged to men. The public realm is where men express their political opinions, attain government jobs, and establish social relationships. Women's social relationships exist within the household, and their survival mainly depends on men.[15] Before marriage, women are considered the "temporary residents," and after marriage, they are viewed as the "outsiders" of the family.[16] They are the "spilt water" that can never become part of the maternal side of the family again once they are married.[17]

Influence of Confucianism Toward Women Under Modern Confucian Society

The heightened emphasis on marriage or the family for women in traditional Confucian society continues to exist in modern Confucian society. I will provide three examples to illustrate the experience of women within the Confucian society. Thw first is provided by an American anthropologist, Margery Wolf (1933-2017), who observed modern Confucian society in Taiwan. The second example introduces

---

[14] Rosenlee, "Chinese Sexism and Confucianism," in *Confucianism and Women*, 123.

[15] Before their marriage, they depend on their father. After marriage, they depend on their husband, and women depend on their son after becoming a widow.

[16] These phrases are used by Yoo Jin Deborah Park to describe the role of women in Confucian culture in the literature review section of her dissertation. Yoo Jin Deborah Park, "Women's Effective Leadership in Contemporary Taiwanese Churches" (Ph.D. diss., Biola University, 2014), 32.

[17] The Chinese allegory that says, "a married daughter is spilt water" is a figurative way to describe a daughter not being taken back to her natal family after marriage. It is often used negatively to refer to the broken relationship between the married daughter and her natal families. Park uses this allegory to describe the women in Confucian society as well. Ibid.

the negative terminology of Chinese society, referring to Chinese women in the 21st century. The last example demonstrates how Chinese women in churches within a Confucian society are not exempt from their social environment which still emphasizes women's marital status.

Wolf wrote a short excerpt about the development of young Taiwanese girls in the 1960s and indicated how women in a Confucian society have a distinctively different self-identity than men. Women have different identities because their identities are rooted in their married families instead of their natal family. Young Taiwanese girls realized they belong to "some unknown family in some unknown place."[18] Wolf described the girls perception of the knowledge of leaving the natal family eventually as if "it stands before her like a dark cloud on the horizon" from childhood.[19] She also noticed the young girls in Taiwan learn to "watch other people's faces," which means the girls master the skill of being sensitive to others' emotions early on to avoid punishments.[20] It is more likely that a girl would get punished by her mother if she disobeys by not doing her chores well or not keeping her male siblings happy. Ultimately, the girls find out that the skill of reading faces helps with the well-being of her marriage as well. Nonetheless, even after the marriage, the identity and the status of women is not fully recognized until they give birth to a male heir.[21]

In the 21st century, Chinese women are still primarily affected by Confucian society's values, which emphasizes the marital status of women. In 2007, the All-China Women's Federation, founded by China's government in 1949 to advocate the rights and interests of women, coined the term *shengnu* to describe unmarried women over the age of 27.[22] In the same year, the Chinese Ministry of Education described the reason for many older single women as being due to the women's "overly

---

[18] Margery Wolf, "Beyond the Pattilineal Self: Constructing Gender in China," in *Self as Person in Asian Theory and Practice*, ed. Roger T. Ames, Wimal Dissanayake, and Thomas P. Kasulis (Albany: State University of New York Press, 1994), 262. Pattilineal is the typo in the book, which should be patrilineal.

[19] Ibid.

[20] Ibid.

[21] Ibid., 263.

[22] Leta Hong Fincher, "China's Leftover Women," *The New York Times*: Opinion, October 11, 2012, https://www.nytimes.com/2012/10/12/opinion/global/chinas-leftover-women.html.

high expectations for marriage partners."[23] Leta Hong Fincher sees this term coined as the result of the State's policy toward sex-ratio imbalance and low population. Since 2007, the Women's Federation advertised to convince single and educated women to get married, and one of the methods was to cause fear and shame in single and unmarried women by labeling them as "leftovers." Another similar term given to unmarried women is "3S women," which marks Single, the Seventies (born in the seventies), and Stuck.[24] Either the "leftover" or "3S women" terms are used about women who are educated and financially independent. They are not viewed positively but negatively as "picky educated women," incomplete, selfish, disrespectful to parents, and shameful by the government-sponsored media and the society.[25] These phrases show the negative perception of society toward women who gain a higher education, salary, and independent single life. These terminologies also suggest that women can only attain real success or praise in society through marriage and not through higher economic or educational status. In other words, the status or the value of women is determined through marriage and not in oneself. Therefore, one understands that a Confucian society expects women to take their priority in seeking marriage partners and discourages women who find fulfillment outside of marriage.

The churches in such a Confucian society also adopt this social expectation toward women. Even more, these social pressures toward women are most visible in the leadership positions of the church. For example, if traditional Chinese churches can choose between a married female pastor or a single female pastor, one chooses the former. Although if there is a male candidate, then it is a different story, since the church still prefers to appoint a male to the leadership roles, such as the senior

---

[23] Sandy To, "Understanding *Sheng Nu* ('Leftover Women'): The Phenomenon of Late Marriage among Chinese Professional Women," *Symbolic Interaction* 36, no. 1 (2013): 2.

[24] Ben Schott, "Leftover Ladies & 3S Women," *The New York Times*: The Opinion Pages, Schott's Vocab Blog, last modified March 15, 2010, https://schott.blogs.nytimes.com/2010/03/15/leftover-ladies-3s-women/.

[25] Mary Kay Magistad, "China's 'leftover women,' unmarried at 27," *BBC News Magazine* (PRI's The World, Beijing), February 21, 2013, https://www.bbc.com/news/magazine-21320560.; Heather Chen, "Emotional advert about China's 'leftover women' goes viral," *BBC World News* (China), April 8, 2016, https://www.bbc.com/news/world-asia-china-35994366.

pastor.²⁶ Only if they do not have a possible male candidate, will they consider a female pastor. Therefore, it is hard, if not impossible, for single women to be appointed or invited to become the pastor or minister of a church.²⁷

Integration of Confucianism, Women, and Environmental Protection in Taiwan

While researching on the topic of women under Confucian society, I came across a book, *Ecofamilism: Women, Religion, and Environmental Protection in Taiwan*, written by a Taiwan scholar, Wan-Li Ho. This book shows how Taiwan women still live in Confucian society, and the deep root of Confucianism persists in their everyday lives. In this section, I examine Ho's book to understand the influence of Confucianism toward women further. Before the introduction of Ho's book, I hope to give a brief context to the contribution of the environmental protection movement in Taiwan to strengthen the effect of non-government organizations (NGOs) led by women.

Transformation of Taiwan Through Environmental Protection NGOs Movement

Taiwan is an island once called 'Formosa,' meaning 'beautiful island.' It is the name given by Portuguese in the sixteenth century. However, due to the rapid industrial development, it gained a nickname of 'garbage island' in the twentieth century.²⁸ It had one of the worst urban waste problems globally, and the garbage could be seen everywhere on the land. Moreover, the island is fully packed with 23 million citizens within the land size of 36,200 square kilometers, which is about the size of the Netherlands. Taiwan society blamed the government for its slow engagement in environmental protection, significant industries'

---

²⁶ However, the church is also more likely to appoint a married male pastor than a single male pastor.

²⁷ Mary Keng Mun Chung, "Women in Ministry in the *Chinese Diaspora*," in *Chinese Women in Christian Ministry*, Asian Thought and Culture, 48 (New York: Peter Lang, 2005), 161.

²⁸ Marcello Rossi, "Taiwan Has One of the Highest Recycling Rates in the World. Here's How That Happened," *Ensia*, (December 18, 2018), https://ensia.com/features/taiwan-recycling-upcycling/.

reluctance in taking responsibilities, and its own citizens' lack of concern toward nature. Taiwan citizens could not tolerate the problem of garbage anymore, so they decided to take action. After a few decades of work, Taiwan has developed one of the most effective recycling programs in the world. One program includes the purchase of government-approved blue bags by citizens for the disposal of mixed waste. Another exciting project is the community ritual in throwing away the trash. The classical music that plays on the yellow trash pickup truck alerts citizens that the trash truck is nearby; people come out of their house to throw trash. As a result, its recycling rate has exceeded over fifty percent.[29] Fifteen years ago, each Taiwan citizen produced an average of 2.6 pounds of waste, but the number has gone down to 1.9 pounds of waste produce per citizen.[30] The number of recycling companies in Taiwan has also grown from around 100 to more than 1,600 currently.[31] The decrease in waste and the increase of recycling companies in Taiwan could not have happened without the active collaboration between Taiwan citizens and its government to care for their homeland. The collaboration did not happen naturally, but it was the effort of many grassroots NGOs who protested and pressured the government to act in the waste management system.

Ecofamilism: Women, Religion, and Environmental Protection in Taiwan

Surprisingly, the most influential NGOs in the environmental care of Taiwan are led by women. It comes as a surprise since Confucianism accentuates in Taiwan, which the traditional role for women remains in the household. However, in her book, Ho shows the active involvement of women in the public sphere for the sake of environment protection, particularly the housewives, through advertising to the public, filing a lawsuit against powerful corporations, and protesting against the government policies. Nonetheless, Taiwan women view their activities in public as the extension of caring for private or the inner realm, the household, since the environment is a home that needs to be taken care of

---

[29] Kathy Chen, "Taiwan: The World's Geniuses of Garbage Disposal," *The Wall Street Journal* (May 17, 2016), https://www.wsj.com/articles/taiwan-the-worlds-geniuses-of-garbage-disposal-1463519134.

[30] Rossi, "Taiwan Has One of the Highest Recycling Rates in the World. Here's How That Happened," *Ensia*.

[31] Ibid.

for the benefit of the whole family. Ho uses the framework of ecofamilism to further expands on the perception of family and environment from the perspective of women.

Ho observes six NGOs that are led by women in Taiwan, which include the Buddhist Compassion Relief Foundation (Abbreviated as Tzu Chi by Ho),[32] Life Conservationist Association (LCA),[33] Taiwan Ecological Stewardship Association (TESA),[34] Homemakers Union and Foundation (HUF),[35] Conservation Mother's Foundation (CMF),[36] and Return Our Land Self-Help Association (ROL).[37] These six NGOs are diverse in religious beliefs, geographical location, and demographics, but they have one common feature: they are founded by women who saw the need for environmental protection in Taiwan. Also, most of the membership comes from women in these organizations. Tzu Chi, LCA, and TESA are motivated and built upon religious beliefs, such as Buddhism and Christianity. On the other hand, HUF, CMF, and ROL do not advocate specific religious beliefs. LCA, TESA, and HUF are based in the northern part of Taiwan, while Tzu Chi and ROL are on the eastern side and CMF on the southern part. The groups offer a variety of demographics. ROL is led by an aboriginal woman, representing a minority group in Taiwan. The rest of the NGOs are led by women from dominant groups of people in Taiwan, the Han-Chinese group. These organizations started after the lifting of martial law in Taiwan and have flourished since the 1990s.

---

[32] Started by a Buddhist nun called Dharma Master Cheng Yen, and eighty percent of her four million followers are women. It mainly focuses on the act of recycling.

[33] The founder is a Buddhist nun called Shi Chao Hwei. This organization is to prevent the killings of animals and to raise awareness of animal protection.

[34] It was started by an educated mother, Chen Tzu-Mei, who was concerned for her four children's health. This organization promotes awareness to eco-justice and the lifestyle of simple living. Most importantly, it provides environmental education to the churches.

[35] Began with a group of women who called themselves the homemakers. There are 1,200 members, and ninety percent are women in this group.

[36] Located in the southern part of Taiwan and found by Chou Chun-Ti. It advocates local environmental protection strategies and gives out education at families, schools, and community groups.

[37] This was started by Igung Shiban, an aboriginal woman that belongs to Taroko Tribe in Hualian County. She fought against the significant company, Asia Cement Company, to gain back the land of her people and ancestors.

After studying these six NGOs, Ho contrasts ecofeminism and ecofamilism. She sees the formal as the representation of the West and the latter as the East's representation. Ho identifies the women in six NGOs resonate better with ecofamilism than ecofeminism. Ecofeminism promotes ecological feminism, which identifies the suffering of nature as the suffering of women and the interconnection between the harmony of human beings and nature. However, when Ho conducted her interviews with men and women about ecofeminism, she sensed the tension from the respondents and only three out of forty-six people saw themselves as feminist.[38] Ho analyzes this result as the unfamiliarity of Taiwan participants' understanding of foreign concepts such as feminism. Another reason is that the respondents feared the term feminism automatically closes its door on the male participants. She argues that Taiwan respondents are more receptive to ecofamilism, which centers around the family, than ecofeminism.

Ecofamilism is a central terminology in Ho's book. It is a term first coined by a Taiwan sociologist Wang Juju Chin-shou in 2001.[39] Wang identifies ecofamilism similarly to Gaia theory, which sees human beings merely as one part of the environment; therefore, human beings have the responsibility to care for the entire ecological family.[40] Ho adopts this term and uses it as a central framework for the extensive work of Taiwan women in environmental protection. Ho emphasizes that ecofamilism does not limit oneself to one's own nuclear family; instead, it extends the concept of one's family to encompass the entire creation. Also, ecofamilism promotes the importance of "relationships, cooperation, and harmony" which can be found in Confucianism.[41]

Unlike women under traditional Confucian society, these NGO leaders have come out to the outer (public) realm – the realm traditionally belonging to the men – and immensely influenced society by raising public awareness of environmental protection and the bar of moral ethics. It certainly looks like Taiwan women have overcome the social structure of Confucianism. Although the traditional gender

---

[38] Ho conducted interviews that encompass forty-six women and men who led the environmental protection organizations in Taiwan. She conducted the interviews separately in 2000, 2007, and 2008.

[39] Ho, 6.

[40] Ibid., 7.

[41] Ibid., 177.

role of women has been restricted to the household, Ho believes Taiwan women have redefined the understanding of the household, and they have expanded their role as the caretaker of the whole environment, the universal household.

I agree with Ho that Taiwan women expanded their concept of an inner (private) realm, but the expansion of the inner realm does not equal freedom from the structure of Confucian society or freedom from the oppression caused by Confucian society. They still live under the Confucian society that values the structure of the family highly. Confucian society emphasizes familial relationships because it seeks the harmony and wellbeing of the whole society. The ultimate goal of Taiwan women in environmental protection is "improving the lives of people, and unifying people in their fight for environmental protection."[42] As proper citizens, it is everyone's responsibility to seek the flourishing of the community. However, it still seems that Taiwan women are confined to Confucian society that values the benefit of familial structure more than the woman herself, which has been the cause of women's oppression. I do not want Taiwan women or women under Confucian society to be content with being solely the caretaker of the whole creation. In the next section, I hope to use the lens of public theology to analyze the identity and the role of women under Confucian society.

Pursuit of Public Theology toward Women Under Confucian Society

In his book, *Theology in the Public Sphere: Public Theology as a Catalyst for Open Debate*, Sebastian Kim stresses the element of open conversation in public theology.[43] He writes that "Public theology is Christians engaging in dialogue with those outside church circles on various issues of common interest."[44] I agree with Kim on having open dialogue since it is the essential element in building a solid relationship. Without the conversation, it is difficult to know what others are thinking or to let others know about what one is thinking. One prerequisite in dialogue is to have a clear self-identity. If one does not know about oneself, one can only listen and not contribute to the conversation.

---

[42] Ibid., 183.

[43] Sebastian C. H. Kim, *Theology in the Public Sphere: Public Theology as a Catalyst for Open Debate* (London: SCM Press, 2011).

[44] Kim, introduction to *Theology in the Public Sphere*, 3.

As an Asian Christian woman pursuing a doctoral program, I set the primary goal throughout the program to search for the formation of my own identity and Asian women living under Confucian society. In this paper, I also pursue the same goal. Although I cannot represent all Asian women, I find Taiwan women's voice in Ho's book to represent women under Confucian society. I analyze and critique the voice of Taiwan women in Ho's book through three theological lenses, which are salvation, incarnation, and trinity.

Salvation for Women Under Confucian Society

Salvation relates to suffering, because salvation frees sinful human beings from the suffering or theological terms, from the effects of sin. However, salvation is about removing the suffering, and it is also "a relation of communion (koinonia) with God and other creatures in Christ."[45] This means the relationship with God, others, and even nature, are essential components of salvation. It is essential to dwelling in these relationships because every relationship teaches us about another aspect of God. Corrupted relationships can lead to suffering, but the right relationship can help us to participate in God's salvation history. God sent Jesus to the world, to indwell among creation, suffer for us, love, and save us. When we are set free from sin, we gain complete freedom through the love of God.

This concept of salvation focuses on the indwelling relationship with God, others, and nature. This salvation does not focus solely on individual salvation. Nimi Wariboko mentions the individualistic salvation is one of the foundations behind the Western economic system, and that individualistic salvation moves the focus away from the communal salvation.[46] Six NGO leaders and participants in Ho's book focus on communal or ecological salvation. However, despite the importance of salvation for the whole creation, I notice what is lacking

---

[45] S. Mark Heim, "Interfaith Relations and the Dialogue of Human Need" in *Public Theology for a Global Society: Essays in Honor of Max Stackhouse*, ed. Deidre King Hainsworth and Scott Paeth (Grand Rapids, MI: W. B. Eerdmans Pub. Co., 2010), 1766, Kindle.

[46] Nimi Wariboko, "The Moral Roots of the Global Financial Industry" in *Public Theology for a Global Society: Essays in Honor of Max Stackhouse*, ed. Hainsworth and Paeth, location 748, Kindle.

for Taiwan women is a personal relationship with God. Taiwan women seek the welfare of the family, society, and the universe, but how about the welfare of the women herself? Women should seek to restore the relationship with God first and seek relationships with others, creation, and even oneself, afterward.[47] Therefore, I suggest that while we emphasize the whole salvation, individual salvation still plays an essential part. The personal relationship with God is the foundation of understanding toward other relationships, such as God's relationship with others and nature. Women under Confucian society need to be aware of their relationship with God as their identity is often overshadowed by all of their social obligations.

The building block of the identity of East Asian women is their family. Many of them consider the value of family higher than their value. For this reason, they choose to sacrifice for the family. The ideal Confucian society was never entirely in balance for women, since it unequally leans toward men in a way that causes the oppression and sacrifice of women. One could say that Jesus demonstrated the sacrificial love for whole creation on the cross; likewise, we ought to follow the footsteps of Jesus Christ and sacrifice ourselves for others. However, Jesus was sent to the world because of God's love toward the creation. The source of Jesus' sacrifice for the salvation of creation comes from his relationship with Father, who "so loved the world, that he gave his one and only Son, that whoever believes in him shall not perish but have eternal life" (John 3:16 NIV). Therefore, sacrifice is not complete without love. In other words, the salvation of women under Confucian society does not come from the family, but it comes from a loving relationship with God. Through the love of God, women learn to love themselves, and it is through this love that they learn genuinely to love their families. I emphasize the difference between love and sacrifice because most women under Confucian society have not loved but only sacrificed for her family. Sacrificing for others does not equate the love toward others. I am not trying to disregard the sacrifice of women for the family. However, I am afraid that it is not enough to sacrifice for one's family or, according to ecofamilism, for the whole ecological family. One cannot truly love their family if they do not learn how to love themselves first.

---

[47] Tulo Raistrick, "The Local Church, Transforming Community," in *Holistic Mission: God's Plan for God's People*, ed. Brian E. Woolnough and Wonsuk Ma (Eugene, OR: Wipf & Stock, 2010), 138.

One can even ask, is it possible for resurrection to exist solely through the sacrifice of Jesus, but without the love from God? I believe God's love is the source of Jesus' sacrifice and the cause of the resurrection.

Incarnation for Women Under Confucian Society

Incarnation means the embodiment of a deity in human flesh. Here I am going back to the concept of God's love again because incarnation exists for the love of God. Incarnation tells the story of Jesus' love for creation, and Christians should become the witness to that love story. Christians can only love because they experience the incarnate love of Jesus. In the perspective of Christianity, the incarnate Son, who is Jesus Christ, "descended to our station 'under' the law, experiencing the pain, abuse, and temptation that are part and parcel of our fallen brokenness (Heb. 2:10-18 NIV)."[48] Jesus came down to earth as a worldly being. Instead of condemning the corrupted world, he carried all problems, sufferings, and sins onto his shoulder.

The incarnate Jesus saw the problems of this world as his own and suffered; therefore, he understood the sufferings of humans. From this perspective, Christians who are the witness of Jesus' life and death, should not avoid the problems of the world, but seek to view the problems of the society as their problems. This is different from viewing the problems of the society as non-relational to the self and pointing at others as the source of problems. Taiwan women have successfully recognized the environmental problem of society and brought positive changes to the environment. However, I want to challenge them to take an even more in-depth understanding of environmental problems, which is to view them as their problems. One cannot acknowledge the presence of God if one does not realize the brokenness in oneself. It is crucial to identify the difference between brokenness or sin and not meet the expectations of society. Many times, women under Confucian society have been blamed as the reason behind bad happenings. For example, from the perspective of marriage, if a woman remains single, which is unfortunate in Confucian society, then it is her problem since she has

---

[48] Richard J. Mouw, "Law, Covenant, and Moral Commonalities: Some Neo-Calvinist Explorations" in *Public Theology for a Global Society: Essays in Honor of Max Stackhouse*, ed. Hainsworth and Paeth (Grand Rapids, MI: William B. Eerdmans Publishing Company, 1513), Kindle.

high standards for men. On the other hand, if a woman faces divorce due to the husband's affair, then it is also the woman's problem since she is not pretty enough or does not manage the appearance of oneself well.[49]

These social pressures criticize the identity of women and cause the suffering of women. Contrarily, sin comes from the brokenness of the relationship between God and human beings. In Genesis 3:17, it shows that the correlation between men and the creation, since the sin of man caused the curse of the land. Ecofamilism also sees the co-dependent relationship of all creation. It sees the suffering of nature causes the suffering of human beings. Therefore, even though Taiwan women have an awareness of the environmental problems of society, but even more, they need to reflect on personal problems that cause the suffering of creation. It is a challenge that goes the same for men and women who pursue ecological care.

Trinity for Women Under Confucian Society

Jürgen Moltmann emphasizes the importance of rediscovering the triune nature of God.[50] This is because an individual's image of God reflects the being of God. The triune God refers to the community of Father, Son, and the Holy Spirit. The Persons of the Trinity continuously dwell in community and the relationships of love. Through this consistent, loving community of the triune God, human beings can also receive the love from God. At the same time, the community of human beings can reflect this loving relationship on earth as well.

In the loving relationship of the triune God, each Person is equal in this relationship. However, this seems complicated for the hierarchical Confucian society that requires people to perform proper relationships through obedience to a higher authority. There is always the one who is at a higher position than another in Confucian society. The one at the lower position needs to obey, and the one at the higher position needs to guide the lower through showing examples. The higher position can also refer to people who have more political, economic, or intellectual

---

[49] Fincher, "China's Leftover Women," *The New York Times*: Opinion.
[50] Jürgen Moltmann, "The Destruction and Healing of the Earth: Ecology and Theology," in *God and Globalization*, Vol. 2, The Spirit and the Modern Authorities (Harrisburg, Penn.: T & T Clark, 2001), 175.

power, and they are almost always men. However, this standard of the hierarchy is abolished in the triune God. One cannot boast about one's power; at the same time, one cannot look down upon the powerless. In the relationship of triune God, people are motivated to serve one another with love, instead of dividing people as higher or the lower classes of citizens.

Not only does the community love of the triune God seek to abolish the hierarchy system that human beings have constructed, it actively searches for the poor and weak in the community. It cares and loves the weak. The triune God rejoices when people find the weak in the community and love them. Taiwan women entered the trinity when they sought after the wellbeing of the weak and the suffering creation. They are considered as blessed in the eyes of God. The concept of blessing changes when one enters the relationship with triune God. People are not considered as blessed because they are wealthy, smart, talented, or from the women's perspective, because they are married and give birth to their son(s). In the eyes of the triune God, people are considered as blessed when they care for the weak in the community. God did not say blessed are the rich; instead, he said, "Blessed are those who have regard for the weak; the Lord delivers them in times of trouble. The Lord protects and preserves them—they are counted among the blessed in the land—he does not give them over to the desire of their foes. The Lord sustains them on their sickbed and restores them from their bed of illness" (Psalm. 41:1-3 NIV). The Lord blesses people who care for the weak. Therefore, the weak are no longer considered the people who do not deserve the blessing of God, but they are the people of God's favor.

Called to Love, Women Under Confucian Society

From the lenses of salvation, incarnation, and the trinity, I analyzed the strengths and weaknesses of women under Confucian society. Women under Confucian society seek the welfare of the whole community, instead of their own. They consider their responsibilities to care for the ecological family. They also willingly sacrifice for the benefit of the family. However, I found that women tend to search for their identity with the family. They might even try to find salvation in the family. However, as women under Confucian society, since they were born, they were considered outsiders of their nuclear family. Another weakness is the tendency to only see the problems in society and neglect to see women's internal problems.

Some might ask that if we are asking too much from women under Confucian society? I will answer that it is not asking too much because they have great potential and expect great things from them. Women under Confucian society are also called by God to love. The calling of love is the Greatest Commandment, and women and men are asked to obey this commandment. The Greatest Commandment, according to Jesus, is the law to "love the Lord your God with all your heart and with all your soul and with all your mind" and the second is "love your neighbor as yourself" (Matt. 22: 37-39 NIV). Even before the women under Confucian society were born, they belonged to God, and therefore, they were never "outsiders," but they have always been the insiders of triune God's family. They inherited the characteristics of caring and sacrificing from the triune God, and they have exhibited this influence on their society. However, it is never enough to do so with mere care and sacrifice since human beings have limitations.

On the other hand, the love of God is unlimited and great that God pours out his love for his creation and desires for them to thrive and flourish. He wants them to experience and receive the love from him entirely and to share that love with the entire world. The love of the triune God rejoices but also grieves for his creation. The whole body of Jesus Christ carries together with the suffering of the world. The deep love of God enables us to suffer with him, as well. Through the power of the triune God, women can search for the weak in the family and empower others and self with love. In the community of love, there is no more the separation of the inner and outer realm where one should be. One can exist anywhere and should seek to exist in places wherever the triune God is.

Conclusion

As an Asian woman, while living in different places in Asia, such as the Philippines, Japan, Korea, and Taiwan in the twentieth and the twenty-first century, I have seen, heard, and even personally experienced the negative attitude toward women. This phenomenon is also common in the churches of East Asia. I experienced the struggles of women under Confucian society even deeper after getting married recently to an Asian family. I say an Asian family because marriage in Asia is heavily influenced by the nuclear family of both women and men. It is harder to get married if there is no approval from the parents. My recent marriage experience enabled me to reflect more in-depth on the lives of women under Confucian society. I continuously face uncomfortable situations under the Confucian social structure, such as people concerned about my relationship status, and after the marriage, they are concerned about my plan for giving birth. These are the realities that I face as an East Asian woman. However, as much as I feel the community's tensions, I still love the community that I indwell.

Through writing the paper on the public theology for women under Confucian society, I have gained theological insights that gave me the hope and guidance for East Asian women. To understand East Asian women's public reality, I looked at the context of history and the philosophy of Confucianism. I also analyzed the role of women under both the traditional and modern Confucian society. Then I narrowed the focus to women of one region, which is Taiwan. After providing a brief introduction to the transformation of Taiwan society from a garbage island to one of the top recycling countries, I examined Ho's contribution. She integrates religion, women, and environmental protection in Taiwan. One of the most critical insights that she provides is the self-perception of Taiwan women and men toward environmental protection is different from the western ecofeminism perspective. They embrace the idea of ecofamilism better than ecofeminism. In the last section, I attempt to interpret the public reality of women under Confucian society with theological lenses, such as salvation, incarnation, and the trinity.

Even though Confucianism caused the oppression of women, it gave women a sincere desire to care for their families. This value of family led Taiwan women in the 20th century to further expand their concept of family to the whole ecological family. They immensely increased the awareness of environmental protection in Taiwan society and transformed the garbage island to one of the leading places in the world on environmental protection. In some ways, women were empowered through the value of Confucianism. However, women are still limited to the familial realm in the society, and I urge women first to form the loving relationship with God who loves and cares for them so that through the love from God, women can learn to love oneself, therefore exerts the true love in the family.

The concept of family in Confucianism functions as the central building block for the identity formation of women under Confucian society. However, there are other aspects of Confucianism, such as the cultivation of personality and education, that contribute to the formation of women's identity under Confucian society. The purpose of this paper is not to defend Confucianism but to identify the influence of Confucianism in women's lives. The preference of ecofamilism over ecofeminism in Taiwan shows Taiwan is built upon the family-centered structure of Confucian society. Taiwan women cannot fully represent the women under Confucian society; however, the ecofamilism framework can spark conversations in understanding the identity of women under Confucian society. Furthermore, ecofamilism can contribute to the public theology discourse as it invites more women under Confucian society to participate in this dialogue, not necessarily through their words but the simple act of picking up garbage on the street to show their care and love for the world, the extension of their family.

Works Cited

Chen, Heather. "Emotional Advert about China's 'Leftover Women' Goes Viral." *BBC World News* (China), April 8, 2016. https://www.bbc.com/news/world-asia-china-35994366.

Chen, Kathy. "Taiwan: The World's Geniuses of Garbage Disposal." *Wall Street Journal*, May 17, 2016. https://www.wsj.com/articles/taiwan-the-worlds-geniuses-of-garbage-disposal-1463519134.

Chung, Mary Keng Mun. "Women in Ministry in the Chinese Diaspora." In *Chinese Women in Christian Ministry*, 153-200. Asian Thought and Culture: v. 48. New York: Peter Lang, 2005.

Fincher, Leta Hong. "China's 'Leftover' Women." *The New York Times*: Opinion, October 11, 2012. https://www.nytimes.com/2012/10/12/opinion/global/chinas-leftover-women.html.

Heim, S. Mark. "Interfaith Relations and the Dialogue of Human Need." In *Public Theology for a Global Society: Essays in Honor of Max Stackhouse*, edited by Deirdre King Hainsworth and Scott R. Paeth, 139-157. Grand Rapids: W.B. Eerdmans Pub. Co., 2010.

Ho, Wan Li. *Ecofamilism: Women, Religion, and Environmental Protection in Taiwan*. St. Petersburg: Three Pines Press, 2016.

Kim, Sebastian C. H. Introduction to *Theology in the Public Sphere: Public Theology as a Catalyst for Open Debate*, 3-26. London: SCM Press, 2011.

LaFleur, Robert André. "The Hundred Schools of Thought (c. 500-200 B.C.E.)." In *China: A Global Studies Handbook*, 16-20. Global studies, Asia. Santa Barbara: ABC-CLIO, 2003.

Magistad, Mary Kay. "China's 'Leftover Women,' Unmarried at 27." *BBC News Magazine* (PRI's The World, Beijing), February 21, 2013. https://www.bbc.com/news/magazine-21320560.

Moltmann, Jürgen. "The Destruction and Healing of the Earth: Ecology and Theology." In *God and Globalization*, edited by Max L.

Stackhouse and Don S. Browning, 166–190. 2. Harrisburg: TPI, 2001.

Mouw, Richard J. "Law, Covenant, and Moral Commonalities: Some Neo-Calvinist Explorations" in *Public Theology for a Global Society: Essays in Honor of Max Stackhouse*, edited by Jay L. Garfield and William Edelglass, 103-122. Oxford: Oxford University Press, 2011.

Ni, Peimin. "Classical Confucianism I: Confucius." In *The Oxford Handbook of World Philosophy*, edited by Jay L. Garfield and William Edelglass, 26-36. Oxford: Oxford University Press, 2011.

Park, Yoo Jin Deborah. "Women's Effective Leadership in Contemporary Taiwanese Churches." Ph.D. diss., Biola University, 2014. ProQuest Dissertations & Theses.

Rosenlee, Li-Hsiang Lisa. Introduction to *Confucianism and Women: A Philosophical Interpretation*, 1-13. SUNY series in Chinese Philosophy and Culture. Albany: State University of New York Press, 2006.

_____. "Chinese Sexism and Confucianism." In *Confucianism and Women: A Philosophical Interpretation*, 119-147. SUNY series in Chinese Philosophy and Culture. Albany: State University of New York Press, 2006.

Rossi, Marcello. "Taiwan Has One of the Highest Recycling Rates in the World. Here's How That Happened." *Ensia*, December 18, 2018. https://ensia.com/features/taiwan-recycling-upcycling/.

Schott, Ben. "Leftover Ladies & 3S Women." *The New York Times*: The Opinion Pages, Schott's Vocab Blog, March 15, 2010.

To, Sandy. "Understanding *Sheng Nu* ('Leftover Women'): The Phenomenon of Late Marriage among Chinese Professional Women." *Symbolic Interaction* 36, no. 1 (February 2013): 1-20.

Wariboko, Nimi. "The Moral Roots of the Global Financial Industry." In *Public Theology for a Global Society: Essays in Honor of Max*

Stackhouse, edited by Deirdre King Hainsworth and Scott R. Paeth, 51-73. Grand Rapids: W.B. Eerdmans Pub. Co., 2010.

Wolf, Margery. "Beyond the Patrilineal Self: Constructing Gender in China." In *Self As Person in Asian Theory and Practice*, edited by Roger T. Ames, Wimal Dissanayake, and Thomas P. Kasulis, 251-268. Albany: SUNY Press, 1994.

Raistrick, Tulo. "The Local Church, Transforming Community." In *Holistic Mission: God's Plan for God's People*, edited by Brian E. Woolnough and Wonsuk Ma, 137-148. Regnum Edinburgh 2010 series. Eugene: Wipf & Stock, 2010.

Chapter 5:
Love Thy Ecological Neighbor: Christian Love as the Healing Balm For Our Broken World

Benjamin D. Foss[1]

Abstract

Does the Gospel relate to the present ecological crisis? If so, how does the Christian faith guide us as the Earth warms and climates change? In the following pages, I propose that the Christian ethic of love—specifically love of neighbor—has profound relevance for the current ecological crisis. Love of neighbor implies that we see and respond to the various ways in which all of our lives are deeply interconnected, including how we share our one common home. Love, then, must not only avoid negatively impacting my neighbor's ecological home, but must also repair and restore where damage has already been done or will be caused by the chain of events we have already set into motion.

---

[1] Benjamin Foss is a M.Div student at Asbury Theological Seminary in Wilmore, Kentucky. Having moved from Pentecostal pastor's kid to liturgy-loving Anglican, Benjamin has learned to love and enjoy many different parts of the body of Christ. He desires to serve the wider Church by bringing sound biblical exegesis and theology to current events.

Introduction

We are facing a global ecological crisis of our own making; the likes of which humanity has never faced before. The warning signs are inescapable, and the scientific data is overwhelming. In this paper I will argue that the Christian emphasis on love for neighbor serves as both a call to radical restorative action, and as a motivating force to make the necessary sacrifices in answering that call. The Christian call to love the Other serves as a powerful provocation to heal the earth, and a crucial point of engagement between climate science and public theology. I will argue that love is part of the Christian solution to the sin that has wrecked our world and our relationships with each other. Finally, I propose a two-fold practical call to action based on what I see as the responsibilities of the affluent to "stop the bleeding" and provide various kinds of aid to those who are the most vulnerable to the rapidly shifting climate. The voice of pubic theology is crucial for this topic, as it helps connect the power of Christian love with the kinds of sacrifices that are necessary in this hour of ecological crisis.

Part I - Our Shared Ecological Crisis

In the mountains of southeastern Kazakhstan high above Almaty sits the Tuyuksu glacier. It is massive, at over a mile and a half long, but is shrinking fast. When the Soviets built a research station near the glacier in 1957, it was only a few hundred feet away from the nearest edge of the Tuyuksu glacier. Now, researchers have to journey on foot for about an hour to reach the melting ice.[2] The Tuyuksu glacier, like hundreds of others around the world, is getting shorter and thinner as warmer temperatures lead to less ice accumulation in winter and more melting in summer. The Tuyuksu in particular has lost nearly half a mile of ice in just 60 years.[3]

This is a big problem for the people in Tien Shan, who rely on the Tuyuksu glacier as a steady supply of fresh water for drinking and irrigation. In the past, the people who live at the base of the mountains have been able to depend on the annual cycles of freezing and melting

---

[2] Henry Fountain, and Ben C. Sullivan. "Glaciers Are Retreating. Millions Rely on Their Water." *The New York Times* (January 16, 2019). https://www.nytimes.com/interactive/2019/04/17/climate/melting-glaciers-globally.html.

[3] Ibid.

to feed the Little Almaty river (their primary water supply) each year. As the Tuyuksu and other glaciers melt, the two million people in the lowlands of Almaty and elsewhere who depend on Little Almaty and other rivers will see a decline in fresh water flow, perhaps as soon as twenty years from now.[4] This is just one of many cities in Central Asia that are staring down a very serious decline in fresh water availability due to vanishing land ice in the coming decades.[5]

The effects of melting land ice can also be felt in Switzerland, which gets 60% of its electricity from hydro power plants that run off glacial melt. Almost all of Switzerland's 1500 glaciers have shrunk every year since 2001 and many will have disappeared altogether by the end of the current century.[6] The cruel irony is that the very energy source the Swiss have turned to is being threatened by the problem they were trying to help solve—global warming. In the absence of some other bold solution, they may have to turn to less-green sources of power to stay warm during the harsh winters, thus making the global warming problem even worse.

Melting land ice is just one of the many side effects of our warming planet and these effects can be found all over the globe. The northern part of the Great Barrier Reef outside Australia has experienced four bleaching events in the last twenty years,[7] including back to back bleaching in 2016 and 2017.[8] The trauma these events cause on the coral could lead to the death of one of the most biologically diverse ecosystems on the planet.

---

[4] Ibid.

[5] Ibid.

[6] Henry Fountain, and Ben C. Sullivan. "Where Glaciers Melt Away, Switzerland Sees Opportunity." *The New York Times* (February 14, 2019). https://www.nytimes.com/interactive/2019/04/17/climate/switzerland-glaciers-climate-change.html.

[7] "Bleaching" occurs when water temperatures get too warm for coral, causing heat stress. The plants lose their color and turn white (thus the name) in an effort to survive. The coral can recover, but it typically takes about a decade. The Great Barrier Reef has been averaging one bleaching event every five years since 1998. Albeck-Ripka, Livia. "The Great Barrier Reef Was Seen As 'Too Big to Fail.' A Study Suggests It Isn't." *The New York Times*, April 3, 2019. https://www.nytimes.com/2019/04/03/world/australia/great-barrier-reef-corals-bleaching.html.

[8] T.P. Hughes, J.T. Kerry, A.H. Baird, et al. "Global warming impairs stock-recruitment dynamics of corals." *Nature* 568 (2019):387–390 doi:10.1038/s41586-019-1081-y.

In Europe, summers have been getting increasingly hotter. In fact, the average summer temperature in Europe in 2005 matched the warmest summer of the 20th century.[9] August 2019 tied with 2015 and 2017 for second warmest since 1880, and all of the top five warmest Augusts have occurred since 2014.[10] Additionally, according to the National Oceanic and Atmospheric Administration (NOAA), Arctic sea ice coverage was 30.1% below average in August of 2019.[11] The warmer temperatures mean more ice melt, hotter summers, increased drought, and new challenges for people all around the world. Coffee farmers are especially vulnerable, as the various coffee bean plants tend to be quite sensitive to heat. It is estimated that global warming will render half of the land currently used for growing coffee useless by 2050.[12]

There is a general consensus that the earth has warmed around 1° C or more since 1850, the most common date given for the dawn of the Industrial Era.[13] That may not sound like a lot, but even this seemingly small change in global temperatures has generated the dramatic effects described above, and many, many others. The question is, are humans the cause, or is this just one of the Earth's natural cycles? After all, the earth has been warmer before than it is now, right?

---

[9] Mark Hertsgaard, *Hot: Living Through the Next Fifty Years on Earth* (Boston: Mariner Books, 2012), 9.

[10] NOAA, "Assessing the Global Climate in August 2019." National Oceanic and Atmospheric Administration (September 16, 2019), https://www.ncei.noaa.gov/news/global-climate-201908.

[11] NOAA, "Summer 2019 Was Hottest on Record for Northern Hemisphere." National Oceanic and Atmospheric Administration (September 16, 2019), https://www.noaa.gov/news/summer-2019-was-hottest-on-record-for-northern-hemisphere.

[12] C. Bunn, Läderach P., Ovalle Rivera O. et al. *Climatic Change* 129 (2015): 89, https://doi.org/10.1007/s10584-014-1306-x.

[13] Allen, M.R., O.P. Dube, W. Solecki, F. Aragón-Durand, W. Cramer, S. Humphreys, M. Kainuma, J. Kala, N. Mahowald, Y. Mulugetta, R. Perez, M. Wairiu, and K. Zickfeld, 2018: "Framing and Context." In: *Global Warming of 1.5°C. An IPCC Special Report on the impacts of global warming of 1.5°C above pre-industrial levels and related global greenhouse gas emission pathways, in the context of strengthening the global response to the threat of climate change, sustainable development, and efforts to eradicate poverty* [Masson-Delmotte, V., P. Zhai, H.-O. Pörtner, D. Roberts, J. Skea, P.R. Shukla, A. Pirani, W. Moufouma-Okia, C. Péan, R. Pidcock, S. Connors, J.B.R. Matthews, Y. Chen, X. Zhou, M.I. Gomis, E. Lonnoy, T. Maycock, M. Tignor, and T. Waterfield (eds.)]. In Press.

Time constraints limit our exploration of the scientific data, but a brief overview of some key material is necessary. The Intergovernmental Panel on Climate Change (IPCC), a group of 1,300 independent scientists gathered by the United Nations (UN) to collect and review studies on climate change, has issued a number of startling reports over the years. In 2013, the IPCC released a report to the UN stating that it determined that the observed warming in global temperatures since the pre-industrial era (typically defined as before 1850) was "very likely" due to human causes (namely, Green House Gas (GHG emissions).[14] But that "very likely" statement may be too conservative. A recent paper released by T. M. L. Wigley and B. D. Santer says the IPCC is not putting the case strong enough.[15] Not only is the likelihood that global warming is 95% anthropogenic, but human GHG emissions have actually offset natural factors that would otherwise be cooling the earth.[16]

One such natural factor is solar irradiance. The earth's temperature depends to a great degree on the amount of solar activity coming from the sun. If the sun was sending out more energy, we would expect to see a rise in global temperatures, and if solar irradiance declined, we would expect to see some cooling. But what we have instead is a divergence. While solar irradiance has dipped slightly in recent years, global temperatures have steadily increased decade after decade. Furthermore, it is estimated that the sun could account for no more than 10% of global warming in the 20th century.[17]

A comparison of the increase in carbon in the atmosphere alongside the increase in global temperatures shows this direct

---

[14] IPCC, 2013: Summary for Policymakers. In: *Climate Change 2013: The Physical Science Basis. Contribution of Working Group I to the Fifth Assessment Report of the Intergovernmental Panel on Climate Change* [Stocker, T.F., D. Qin, G.-K. Plattner, M. Tignor, S.K. Allen, J. Boschung, A. Nauels, Y. Xia, V. Bex and P.M. Midgley (eds.)]. Cambridge University Press, Cambridge, United Kingdom and New York, NY, USA.

[15] T.M.L Wigley, & Santer, B.D. Clim Dyn (2013) 40: 1087. https://doi.org/10.1007/s00382-012-1585-8

[16] Ibid.

[17] Mike Lockwood, "Solar Change and Climate: an update in the light of the current exceptional solar minimum," *Proceedings of the Royal Society A*, 2 December 2009, doi 10.1098/rspa.2009.0519; Judith Lean, "Cycles and trends in solar irradiance and climate," *Wiley Interdisciplinary Reviews: Climate Change* 1 (January/February 2010): 111-122.

correlation.[18] With no other plausible explanation available,[19] and the knowledge that increased carbon traps more heat from escaping into space, we are left with the conclusion that most of the climate science community reached some time ago: the earth is warming rapidly due almost entirely to human causes, and that is very bad news for all living creatures.

We have only begun to feel the effects of climate change and, even if we somehow could stop immediately all human GHG emissions, we would still have decades (and in some cases centuries)[20] of warming and climate change to deal with.[21] The climate system has its own kind of "inertia" and stopping it is comparable to stopping a moving train—even after the brakes are applied (in this case, reducing emissions).[22]

---

[18] G. P. Wayne, "Empirical Evidence That Humans Are Causing Global Warming." *Skeptical Science* (July 12, 2015), https://skepticalscience.com/empirical-evidence-for-global-warming.htm.

[19] "*This assessment concludes, based on extensive evidence, that it is extremely likely that human activities, especially emissions of greenhouse gases, are the dominant cause of the observed warming since the mid-20th century. For the warming over the last century, there is no convincing alternative explanation supported by the extent of the observational evidence.*" Wuebbles, D.J., D.W. Fahey, K.A. Hibbard, B. DeAngelo, S. Doherty, K. Hayhoe, R. Horton, J.P. Kossin, P.C. Taylor, A.M. Waple, and C.P. Weaver, 2017: *Executive Summary of the Climate Science Special Report: Fourth National Climate Assessment*, Volume I [Wuebbles, D.J., D.W. Fahey, K.A. Hibbard, D.J. Dokken, B.C. Stewart, and T.K. Maycock (eds.)]. U.S. Global Change Research Program, Washington, DC, USA: 1.

[20] Church, J.A., P.U. Clark, A. Cazenave, J.M. Gregory, S. Jevrejeva, A. Levermann, M.A. Merrifield, G.A. Milne, R.S. Nerem, P.D. Nunn, A.J. Payne, W.T. Pfeffer, D. Stammer and A.S. Unnikrishnan, 2013: "Sea Level Change." In: *Climate Change 2013: The Physical Science Basis. Contribution of Working Group I to the Fifth Assessment Report of the Intergovernmental Panel on Climate Change* [Stocker, T.F., D. Qin, G.-K. Plattner, M. Tignor, S.K. Allen, J. Boschung, A. Nauels, Y. Xia, V. Bex and P.M. Midgley (eds.)] (Cambridge, United Kingdom and New York, NY: Cambridge University Press), 1139-40.

[21] "*If greenhouse gas concentrations were stabilized at their current level, existing concentrations would commit the world to at least an additional 1.1°F (0.6°C) of warming over this century relative to the last few decades.*" Wuebbles, D.J., D.W. Fahey, K.A. Hibbard, B. DeAngelo, S. Doherty, K. Hayhoe, R. Horton, J.P. Kossin, P.C. Taylor, A.M. Waple, and C.P. Weaver, 2017: *Executive Summary of the Climate Science Special Report: Fourth National Climate Assessment*, Volume I [Wuebbles, D.J., D.W. Fahey, K.A. Hibbard, D.J. Dokken, B.C. Stewart, and T.K. Maycock (eds.)]. U.S. Global Change Research Program, Washington, DC, USA: 6.

[22] I borrowed the idea of climate "inertia" and the train metaphor from Mark Hertsgaard, *Hot: Living Through the Next Fifty Years on Earth* (Boston: Mariner Books,

Since completely eliminating human emissions is unrealistic with our current technology, the best we can hope for is mass reduction at a rapid rate, and, eventually, carbon neutrality. Even then, the biodiversity that is lost in the meantime due to rapidly changing ecosystems could take as long as millions of years to reemerge (albeit in new forms).[23] The longer humanity waits to act, the worse the damage will be.

So who is responsible for all this carbon in the air and the resulting warming? According to journalist Mark Hertsgaard in his acclaimed book *Hot*, the wealthiest 20% of the global population is responsible for about 80% of global emissions, while the bottom 20% have contributed just 1%.[24] Edward O. Wilson says that it would take four earths to bring and sustain the rest of the world at the standard of living that the US and other "developed" countries enjoy.[25] If the earth cannot sustain the "developed" nations;[26] how will it sustain those nations which attempt to reach the West's standard of living by using the same dirty power, fossil fuel-based transportation, and exploitative approach to natural resources that the West has been using for years?

Furthermore, it is those marginalized nations who contributed the least to the increase in greenhouse gasses in our atmosphere who are most vulnerable to the changing climate.[27] The lifestyles of the globe's affluent come at the ecological expense of the most vulnerable.[28] Wealthy nations have recourses for dealing with drought, shifting food supplies, flooding, rising oceans, deathly hot summers, and many of the other consequences of a rapidly changing climate. The most affluent in the wealthiest nations—those who have generated the most emissions through their lifestyles and consumerism—have the most means to mitigate the ecological crisis. But those at the bottom have no recourse, no advocate, no technological ability to subject nature to their will, and no resources to fall back upon once the rivers have dried up, or the

---

2012), 9, 25.

[23] Edward O. Wilson, *The Future of Life* (New York: Vintage, 2003), 150.

[24] Hertsgaard, *Hot*, 18.

[25] Wilson, *The Future of Life*, 150

[26] Pope Franziskus, *Encyclical on Climate Change and Inequality: On Care for Our Common Home* (Brooklyn: Melville House, 2015), 31.

[27] Ibid., 29.

[28] Ibid., 31; Jürgen Moltmann, *God for a Secular Society: The Public Relevance of Theology* (Minneapolis: Fortress Press, 2005), 93.

fish have migrated elsewhere, or massive flooding has washed all their homes away. Someplaces will experience severe drought, others will see increased rain and monsoons; the climate will change in different ways in different places. What we have is a dual inequality, which favor the wealthy and powerful over against the disadvantaged and vulnerable: an inequality of lifestyles (standard of living) which contribute to the problem, and an unequal capacity to ride the waves of rapid ecological change.

In summary, then, the farmers in southeast Kazakhstan are facing the same problem the global population as a whole is facing: namely, rapid global warming (and the resulting changes in climate) brought about by human emissions. Not only are humans the primary factor forcing this global change, but it is overwhelmingly the wealthiest people, companies, and nations which have contributed the most to the problem. However, those who did the most damage also tend to have the most resources to ride out the storm and survive, while those most likely to suffer the effects of a warming planet are the least responsible for global warming.

Does the Christian faith, or more specifically public theology, have anything to say about all this? In the following section, I will present a few key theological themes that profoundly speak into our shared ecological crisis, with a particular emphasis on the Second Commandment as a divine mandate to care for the poor by caring for our shared earth.

Part II - Love Thy Ecological Neighbor

Before exploring theology of love for our neighbor – the primary theological focus on this paper – I will briefly explore some of the broad biblical and theological issues that speak directly to ecotheology and humanity's relationship to the world.

A Conversion Back to the World

In the beginning, God created the cosmos and called it "good" (Gen. 31). The world as God made it was fundamentally good, and humanity was created to "tend" and "keep" it (Gen. 2:15). This language of cultivation and stewardship[29] implies a harmonious relationship between humanity and the world. But humanity rebelled against God (Gen. 3) and introduced sin into the world. This "moral disease"[30] broke humanity's relationship with God,[31] other humans, and with the earth itself.[32] Due to the poisonous effects of sin on human hearts, we as a species exchanged "dominion" with creation (Gen. 1:26-28) for domination over creation.[33]

Patriarch Bartholomew reminds us that to view the world God made as an object to be used and exploited leads us into domination (instead of biblical dominion) and grave ecological sin. His somber words are worth quoting in length:

> We have traditionally regarded sin as being merely what people do to other people. Yet, for human beings to destroy the biological diversity in God's creation; for human beings to degrade the integrity of the earth by contributing to climate change, by stripping the earth of its natural forests or destroying its wetlands; for human beings to contaminate the

---

[29] The concept of "stewardship" may be tainted in Evangelical circles and may need to be replaced with "keeping" or some other language that emphasizes our connected relationship with and responsibility for the good of the earth. See Brunner, Daniel L., Jennifer L. Butler, and A. J. Swoboda. *Introducing Evangelical Ecotheology: Foundations in Scripture, Theology, History, and Praxis* (Grand Rapids: Baker Academic, 2014), 150-1.

[30] Howard A. Snyder, and Joel Scandrett. *Salvation Means Creation Healed: the Ecology of Sin and Grace: Overcoming the Divorce Between Earth and Heaven* (Eugene: Cascade Books, 2011), 55-6.

[31] Due to the limited focus of this paper, I will be focusing exclusively on repairing the human-creature and human-to-human relationships and will not give attention to the human-God relationship. Despite how essential and central that relationship is to Christian theology, time and space limitations do not permit me to explore it in depth here.

[32] Franziskus, *Encyclical on Climate Change and Inequality*, 42; Daniel L. Brunner, Jennifer L. Butler, and A. J. Swoboda. *Introducing Evangelical Ecotheology: Foundations in Scripture, Theology, History, and Praxis* (Grand Rapids: Baker Academic, 2014), 100.

[33] Brunner, Butler, and Swaboda suggest that God's wrath toward Moses after he struck the rock (Num. 20) could be an example of how God feels when humans treat the environment and natural resources as something to be dominated and exploited rather than respected and responsibly used. Is striking the rock a "transgression of both divine and ecological boundaries"? Brunner, Butler, and Swoboda, *Introducing Evangelical Ecotheology*, 95-6.

earth's waters, land and air – all of these are sins… We are treating our planet in an inhuman, godless manner precisely because we fail to see it as a gift inherited from above. Our original sin with regard to the natural environment lies in our refusal to accept the world as a sacrament of communion, as a way of sharing with God and neighbor on a global scale. It is our humble conviction that divine and human meet in the slightest detail contained in the seamless garment of God's creation, in the last speck of dust.[34]

Sin has wide ranging effects on the way humans have thought about the world and responded to it, even in the church. Too often in Protestant theology the "image of God" (Gen. 1:26-28) has been seen and presented as a clear distinctive given to human beings over and against the created world—it allows us to see the natural world as a thing to be used rather than a garden to be tended. Alongside this there has been a tendency in Protestant circles to overemphasize God's transcendence from nature, rather than His immanence.[35] Our view of what it means to be made in the image of God has lost its earthiness precisely because our view of God Himself has suffered the same neo-Gnostic fate. But the immanence of God reminds us to love and care for the earth and its creatures.[36] Pope Francis reminds us that "the human environment and the natural environment deteriorate together."[37] This world is the bed we lie in.[38] When human beings hurt and degrade the earth we harm ourselves. In this way, the image of God which has often been leveraged as justification for the mechanistic cosmology of the West is actually undermined. Instead, we would do well to listen to our African brothers

---

[34] Patriarch Bartholomew, "Environmental Justice and Peace." The Ecumenical Patriarchate, 2011. https://www.patriarchate.org/bartholomew-quotes.

[35] Brunner, Butler, and Swoboda, *Introducing Evangelical Ecotheology*, 100-2.

[36] This is not to juxtapose God's immanence and transcendence as two irreconcilable perspectives, but to emphasize the healthy relationship with Creation that emerges when proper balance between these two realities is restored. Ibid., p.102.

[37] Franziskus, *Encyclical on Climate Change and Inequality*, 29.

[38] This and other powerful images can be found in Chief Seattle's famous 1855 letter to the President in response to his request to purchase land from his people and relocate them. Seattle, Chief. "Letter From Chief Seattle." Álex Rovira. Accessed December 12, 2019. http://www.alexrovira.com/en/sensaciones/articulo/carta-del-jefe-indio-seattle.

and sisters who stress the interconnectedness of all living things through the "bondedness of life."[39]

Sin has broken humanity's relationship with the earth. Humanity's sinfulness has meant a conversion to the Self at the expense of the Other—and especially: God, our neighbor, and our shared world. Sadly, much of the Western worldview (including elements of Western theology) has exacerbated this divide, and the misuse of the image of God outlined above is just one of the many examples that could be given. Thankfully, many prominent leaders in the wider Church have been calling for a conversion back to the earth.[40] Twenieth century German theologian Dietrich Bonhoeffer gives us firm theological ground to stand on when he emphasizes that following Christ is a conversion back to the true humanity, one that is "worldly" and incarnate.[41] Christian conversion does not turn us inward to ourselves, or upward to an immaterial heaven, but outward to the world. God, in His infinite and matchless love, is reconciling all things to Himself (Col. 1:20), including the entire created order. If we are to participate in God's loving, reconciling work, it will necessarily include rethinking humanity's relationship to the earth and thus proactively working to heal the damage that has been done. This is essential to loving the world as God does.

To love in this way involves a crucial worldview shift away from "Earth as dominated tool" to "Earth as God's good creation that He loves." How we join God's reconciling work will depend on what we perceive as our relationship with the earth. And this is connected to our view of God Himself, and His involvement in His creation. Jürgen Moltmann emphasizes that countering the ecological crisis from our current point of view, which sees the natural world as property that we own (with God far away in some immaterial Heaven), will simply lead to more reliance

---

[39] See Harvey Sidima's chapter on how the African perspective of the interconnectedness, or "bondedness" of all life can contribute to Christian ecotheology. Harvey Sidima, *Liberating Life: Contemporary Approaches to Ecological Theology*. Edited by Charles Birch, William R. Eakin, and Jay B. McDaniel (Eugene: Wipf & Stock, 2007), 137-48.

[40] See esp. Franziskus, *Encyclical on Climate Change and Inequality*.

[41] See Bonhoeffer's definition of the word "metanoia" as becoming "the human being Christ creates in us", and "walking the path that Jesus walks." Dietrich Bonhoeffer, *Letters and Papers From Prison* (Minneapolis: Fortress Press, 2015), 466.

on technology as a dominating tool to craft the world into *our* image.[42] Our broken relationship with the world is a symptom of our broken relationship with God, just as our distorted view of our relationship to nature mirrors our distorted overemphasis of God's transcendence at the expense of immanence. A biblical ecology that focuses on healing and restoration is a prerequisite for arriving at necessary God-honoring solutions to our shared ecological crisis. If God-who-is-Love walks among us in the forest, that changes how we relate to both the Creator and the trees.

The Ecological Implications of the Second Commandment

Sin has not only broken the human-creature or human-earth relationship, it has also fractured the human-to-human relationship in profound and devastating ways. One of the first things we read in Genesis after Adam and Eve sinned and were judged is the story of Cain killing his brother Abel (Gen. 4:1-15). The story of the human race from that point forward has frequently been characterized by violence, exploitation, deception, coercion, slavery, theft, sexual violence, racism, bigotry, oppressions of the poor, murder, genocide, war, and more. The entrance of sin into God's good world has led to the shedding of blood in perpetuity. The marginalized in history have often groaned with the Creation itself, crying out for salvation.

Much could be said about the divine solution to this global problem, but I want to focus on love—specifically the Second Commandment—and its profound ecological implications in this time of global environmental crisis.

When Jesus is asked by one of the Jewish religious leaders what the greatest commandment is, He answers thus:

> "You shall love the Lord your God with all your heart, and with all your soul, and with all your mind." This is the great and foremost commandment. The second is like it, "You shall love your neighbor as yourself." On these two commandments

---

[42] Moltmann, *God for a Secular Society*, 100.

depend the whole Law and the Prophets. (Matt. 22:37-40, NASB)

The primacy of love for the Other is a premiere theme in the Christian Scriptures, and it comes into particular focus in the New Testament. Christ serves as an example of sacrificial love for the Other (Jn. 3:16), even for His enemies (Rom. 5:10). The greatest love one can possess is to lay one's very life down for the Other (Jn. 15:13; Rom. 5:7-8). The sign that someone really belongs to God is that s/he loves well (1 Jn. 2:9-11), which is the very command of Christ to His disciples (Jn. 15:12). God Himself is love (1 Jn. 4:8) and He desires that we reflect that love in the way we conduct our lives (1 Jn. 2:5-6; 4:7, 11).

There is little dispute over the primacy of love in Christian theology. But who are the neighbors Jesus would have us love? In the story of the Good Samaritan (Lk. 10:25-37), Jesus destroys all notions of ethnic, political, or geographic boundaries between human beings (cf. Eph. 2:11-16). The one who really is a neighbor to the victim in this parable does not share ethnicity, nationality, or land (immediate physical space) with the one he helps. What makes him a neighbor is their shared humanity and their shared placement in the world. What makes him a good neighbor is his generous aid in a time of grave need. Jesus then turns to His audience and says, "Go and do the same" (Lk. 10:37, NASB). What makes this Samaritan "good" is his recognition that the neglected man on the side of the road is his neighbor simply because he is human, and the Samaritan's actions reflect that understanding.

When we examine the profound implications of Jesus' lesson in light of the ecological crisis, it is clear that there are no real boundaries between neighbors in our shared earthly home. Our national borders—even the vast stretches of ocean that separate continent from continent—vanish in the global environment so that all of us in the one global community share the same backyard. The carbon dioxide emitted in North America contributes to melting the Tuyuksu glacier in southeast Kazakhstan, just as the warming generated by China—currently the world's heaviest emitter of GHGs[43]—is putting the coffee farms in Central

---

[43] BP, *BP Statistical Review of World Energy 2019*, London, 2019, https://www.bp.com/content/dam/bp/business-sites/en/global/corporate/pdfs/energy-economics/statistical-review/bp-stats-review-2019-full-report.pdf: 54.

America in jeopardy. Everyone is my ecological neighbor who Christ commands me to love. As Pope Francis said, "We need to strengthen the conviction that we are one single human family" that shares one common home.[44]

However, part of the challenge of our modern world is that our ecological neighbors are distant and invisible to us. Those of us in the West are called upon by the Gospel to love our ecological neighbors—people we have often unwittingly and unknowingly wronged—must do the work of identifying and humanizing those neighbors who live thousands of miles away, often on different continents, in different cultures—nearly in different worlds. We need to see the faces of the children in southeast Kazakhstan who could be without fresh water in their lifetime. It is not enough to identify the number of people who will suffer, or even where. Statistics don't often move human hearts. We need to humanize the problem by giving the victims of climate change names and faces so that our neighbor is no longer an abstract theological concept, but a flesh and blood human being bearing God's holy image, just like ourselves. Christlike love for neighbor—the kind of love that gives everything for the sake of the Other—will be nearly impossible so long as the Other remains nameless and faceless.

"A Universal Communion"

Pope Francis, in his profound *Encyclical On Climate Change and Inequality*, speaks of the relationship between humans and the natural world as "a universal communion."[45] Pope Francis and others have pointed to the interdependent relationship between humanity and the created world, in part, by emphasizing that humanity itself is part of Creation. Christian Scriptures teach us that humanity was formed out of the dust (Gen. 2:7) and will someday return to dust (Gen. 3:19). We must break down many of the ideological and theological barriers we have erected between ourselves and the river, the wombat, and the fir tree.[46] We are all part of the same "universal communion" of life which depends upon God's gracious upholding for its very existence (Heb. 1:3).

---

[44] Franziskus, *Encyclical on Climate Change and Inequality*, 32.
[45] Ibid., 55-6.
[46] Brunner, Butler, and Swoboda, *Introducing Evangelical Ecotheology*, 151, 100-2. Even as pastors and theologians fight to reclaim the immanence of God, we must also

Pope Francis says that our connection with the earth is so deep that one can almost physically feel the afflictions of the natural world.[47] Furthermore, the injustices we inflict upon the earth by dominating it as an object to be exploited leads to the objectification and abuse of our neighbor as well.[48] The same sinful disease in human hearts that pushes us to over-fish, over-farm, and over-hunt also pushes us to over-work, under-pay, and otherwise exploit our neighbor. The inverse is also true. If we learn to regain our intimacy with the land, we will be led back to each other as well. Pope Francis goes even further, however. Not only does one lead to the other, but caring for creation and caring for people are nearly indistinguishable since "human dignity finds its roots in our common Creation."[49] They are two sides of the same coin.

For this reason, Pope Francis says, "a true ecological approach always becomes a social approach," and framing the problem in this way allows us to "hear both the cry of the earth and the cry of the poor."[50] To hear (and respond to) one cry is to hear (and respond to) the other, especially since the groanings of creation are often heard loudest in the places where the poor are most plentiful.[51] But how can those of us in the West who through technology and affluence have become so isolated from the afflicted (both man and beast) become open to hearing their cry?

I would argue that the task of Christian theology and the Church is to call for a return to love in our view of Creation and each other. Public theology is indispensable here, as it helps the Church speak meaningfully and profoundly into the conversations happening in the public square. The Church of Jesus Christ, with its unique perspective centered on

---

do the difficult work of maintaining the transcendent "otherness" of God as well, lest we fall into the error of pantheism.

[47] Franziskus, *Encyclical on Climate Change and Inequality*, 55-6.

[48] Ibid., 57; Moltmann reverses this order, but still emphasizes direct relationship between the two. Moltmann, *God for a Secular Society*, 94.

[49] Franziskus, *Encyclical on Climate Change and Inequality*, x.

[50] Ibid., 30.

[51] I interpret the "groaning" of creation in Rom. 8:22, at least in part, as natural disasters, droughts, and other climate-related problems that arise from sin's contamination of God's good world. As mentioned earlier, these kinds of effects are felt most profoundly by the poorest since they have the least means of mitigating their effects and the fewest amount of resources and supporting infrastructure to fall back on.

the Gospel and informed by two thousand years of reflection, has an irreplaceable role to play in shaping the way humans relate to the natural world. For example, we have already spoken of the primacy of love in the human-to-human relationship. Given the profound interconnectedness of humans and the natural world, we can no longer speak of restoring human relationships without also speaking of repairing our relationship with the earth. If love is the divine reparative virtue for human-to-human relationships, it seems only fitting then that holy affection for the earth is the antidote to sin's poisonous influence on how humans interact with the natural world.[52] It is not only fitting, but I would argue that it is necessary.[53] If we learn to love Brother River and Sister Tree, we will also love our brothers and sisters on distant continents.[54] If we learn to enjoy long walks in the woods we will also learn what it means to listen long to the voices that have been drowned out by the noise of our affluence. For some, the order may be reversed, but it is the re-centering of love in our relationship to all of life that matters, for "we cannot be in relationships of stewardship and solidarity with the unloved."[55]

In sum, sin has broken our relationship with God, each other, and the natural world. The brokenness of the human-creature relationship can be seen through our dominating exploitation of nature as an object to be used, rather than a garden to be kept and watched over. Our human-to-human relationships are also broken due to sin, and this has manifested itself in exploitation of the Other. The command to "love your neighbor as yourself" is the divine answer to this human brokenness, and it has profound ecological implications. As we reflect on the command to love, we see that obedience involves loving the earth itself, for we cannot really love one without loving the other in our modern, globalized world. Therefore, restoring the human-creature relationship and the human-to-human relationship requires the same self-sacrificing love that Christ displayed on the cross to transform our orientation to all living things (Eph 1:10).

---

[52] Brunner, Butler, and Swoboda, *Introducing Evangelical Ecotheology*, 150-1.
[53] See Moltmann's negative example of this interconnected relationship. Violence towards human and nature flow from the same inner, sinful disposition. Moltmann, *God for a Secular Society*, 94-6.
[54] Franziskus, *Encyclical on Climate Change and Inequality*, 58.
[55] Brunner, Butler, and Swoboda, *Introducing Evangelical Ecotheology*, 151.

Part III - Love As Ecological Action

As we move from the abstract and into the concrete, we move more explicitly into the discipline commonly called "public theology." This is the practice of examining the data and relevant materials on a given topic (in this case, global climate change), examining Christian theology and values to see how the Church could or should speak into that topic, and then bringing the two together in an interactive way. Having performed the first two steps in the first two sections above, I will now move onto the third. In light of the data above, and in light of the Christian call to love your neighbor, what ought to be done? This is the kind of question that a public theologian explores, and it is the question I will attempt to begin answering below.

I have already proposed that we see the command to love as a call to sacrifice, and it is here, in reflecting on the practical outworking of the second commandment, that Christlike love shows itself to be a double-edged sword. "For God so loved the world *that He gave…*" (Jn. 3:16 NKJV, emphasis mine). Love motivates *and* compels radical, concrete, sacrificial action. If humanity regains its holy affections for the wilderness and the foreigner, the unavoidable result will be reconciliatory action. Christlike love is the subversive force that declares war on our self interest and redirects our affections. It is both challenge and motivation; command and desire.

Having argued for the importance of Christian love for framing our response to the ecological crisis, and clarifying that the restoration of divine affections for neighbor and wilderness go hand in hand, I would now like to argue (as I have already begun to argue) that Christian theology is a powerful voice not only in restoring our love and value for our "universal communion" of life, but that restoration necessarily leads to radical, ecological, reparative action for the sake of our human and non-human neighbors. My treatment of the practical side will by no means be exhaustive, but I believe the two areas I am focusing on below will give us a good place to start.

Stopping the Bleeding

I have already mentioned that the wealthiest populations in the world contribute the most to global warming. It seems natural, then, that various pressures to move toward a more eco-friendly lifestyle (religious, cultural, economic, and so on) should be applied to those for whom that pressure is most relevant. This will be a difficult task, however, since the wealthy and powerful—nations, corporations, and individuals—are the ones with the greatest ability to exempt and insulate themselves from the "rules" everyone else is expected to follow. Here the call of Christ to the rich man rings as loud and clear as ever: "Jesus said to him, 'If you wish to be complete, go and sell your possessions and give to the poor, and you will have treasure in heaven; and come, follow Me'" (Matt. 19:21, NASB). Christian theology takes the burden off of the poor and powerless and places the biggest (but not sole) responsibility for sacrificial action on those who have the greatest means.

The challenge, however, is that, at the individual level, the impact any one individual can have on global emissions is minuscule. It is hard for those in the West to see and measure their direct responsibility in the changing climate, and so it is difficult for us to really care.[56] The sacrifices required to adopt a sustainable lifestyle feel much more real than the consequences of continuing with business as usual, at least for now.[57] We desperately need to stop the bleeding (by dramatically reducing global emissions), but how do we motivate vast populations to make concrete sacrifices, beyond simply telling them to love better?

First, I think ours is largely a problem of information. A lot of people do not know how bad things really are, or how their day-to-day decisions generate ripple effects across the entire global community. As I said before, the affluent are often isolated from the problem. The Western woman's old clothes seem to vanish in the donation bin. America's trash is picked up and people don't know where it goes. And who has even heard of the Tuyuksu glacier? The problem of global warming needs to be "humanized." Retooling our moral intuitions is only part of the task; feeding those intuitions with the right information that propels

---

[56] Fleming Rutledge, *The Crucifixion: Understanding the Death of Jesus Christ* (Grand Rapids, MI: Eerdmans Publishing Company, William B., 2017), 122.

[57] Franziskus, *Encyclical on Climate Change and Inequality*, 36.

informed action is just as necessary. People will not be motivated to solve a problem they don't know about or don't believe in.

That being said, the dissemination of raw scientific data is not likely to convince many people, to the chagrin of scientists all over. Jonathan Haidt, in his book *The Righteous Mind* emphasizes the need for appealing to a variety of moral "taste buds"—such as care, fairness, loyalty, and sanctity—in order to reach a broad range of people of varying moral and political stripes.[58] The case for radical ecological action must be presented in a variety of ways in order to engage the broadest possible group of people. Combining the right information with a multi-varied effort to renew our love for creature and neighbor could yield powerful results.

What does adopting a "sustainable" lifestyle look like for the affluent? That is an incredibly complex question with varying answers for a broad spectrum of contexts and situations. However, a few general starting points can be given.[59]

The most popular and visible emitter of GHGs are our fossil-fuel burning automobiles and other carbon-based forms of transportation (such as planes). While these do matter, the transportation sector only accounts for about 14% of global GHG emissions. Some of the most impactful changes the top 20% globally can make are some of the less visible. For example, electricity and heat production makes up an astounding 25% of global emissions.[60] Simple lifestyle changes like switching to LED bulbs, reducing one's use of climate control, installing more energy efficient windows and insulation, unplugging electronics that aren't being used, and installing solar panels (when possible) can all have substantial impacts on emissions, especially when scaled to hundreds of millions of people.

---

[58] Jonathan Haidt, *The Righteous Mind: Why Good People Are Divided by Politics and Religion* (New York: Vintage Books, 2013), chs.6-8, esp. p. 214-16.

[59] For more practical ideas, see Brunner, Butler, and Swoboda, *Introducing Evangelical Ecotheology*, chs. 8-9.

[60] EPA, "Global Greenhouse Gas Emissions Data." EPA. Environmental Protection Agency, 2014. https://www.epa.gov/ghgemissions/global-greenhouse-gas-emissions-data#Reference 1.

Consumerism is a massive driving factor in global emissions. The manufacture of popular items like jeans uses massive amounts of energy and fresh water, as does the raising of animals for meat such as cows and pigs. Simple decisions to eat less meat, wear clothes for longer, wash them less often, and buy less "stuff" all add up (again, especially when scaled) to greatly reduced emissions. Changes in consumer habits also powerfully shape capitalist markets with profound ecological implications. If consumers buy fewer jeans, the ecologically costly manufacturing process will shrink in response. If the globally affluent eat less meat and more vegetables, the respective industries will follow. Demand shapes production, and if consumers make individual decisions from an ecologically friendly perspective, the market will have no choice but to follow.

Finally, members of wealthy nations have a responsibility to speak out with their voices and their votes, demanding their governments exert their power to curtail national and global emissions as much as possible. There are some things only governments have the power to do. Therefore, citizens must demand "green" policies, regulation of emissions from mega-corporations, and new standards for environmental protections and stewardship. Love means advocacy on behalf of those who suffer the most from global warming.

Dealing With "Climate Inertia"

Stopping the bleeding will not be enough, however. The effects of climate change will be felt for decades, perhaps even centuries. I agree with Pope Francis that the affluent owe a great "ecological debt" to the rest of the world (human and otherwise).[61] Nations, organizations, and individuals must adopt "differentiated responsibilities" to not only stop contributing to the problem, but to help those who are and will suffer from a crisis they did not create.[62] Justice demands the West and the affluent to not simply say "sorry," stop their emissions, and leave the poor to suffer while the earth slowly recovers (assuming she does recover). The mother in rural India cannot be expected to "forgive and forget"[63] as she starves of famine, or watches her home wash away in a

---

[61] Franziskus, *Encyclical on Climate Change and Inequality*, 31-2.
[62] Ibid., 32.
[63] Rutledge, *The Crucifixion*, 114.

monsoon.[64] Justice demands that steps be taken toward practical healing of our relationships, and of the land itself. To do this is to do the very work of God.[65]

Practically, this means that wealthy nations in particular must use their resources to give practical aid to the most vulnerable. In the case of the melting Tuyuksu glacier and the people who depend on its water, nations like the U.S. or China have a responsibility to help them implement more efficient irrigation and plumbing technologies so they use less fresh water, and perhaps create stores of water for the future. Countries like Australia may need some financial aid as their tourism industry—a large portion of their economy—dwindles in response to the bleaching and death of the Great Barrier Reef. Many places will need food and water supplies, new homes, relocation help, technological assistance, and more. The primary weight of this responsibility to care for the global community should fall on those who have contributed the most to the crisis, and who have the most resources to spare. All of this will involve many sacrifices for the rich and poor alike, but is that not what love is all about?

I have offered an all-too-brief overview of how Christlike love compels us to take concrete action; however, it is a start. In my view, the biggest challenge lies not in finding work to do; it is in getting the affluent to open their ears and eyes in order to hear and see the mutual cries of the earth and her poor. Once we are awake to the severity of the problem and willing to allow Christlike love to propel us toward radical action, the path forward readily presents itself with an overwhelming number of necessary steps. This does not imply that a comprehensive transformation of modern society into a new, sustainable form will be easy, or that the pathway to get there will be obvious. I am confident that once the attention and affections of humanity are re-directed through a conversion back to our human and creaturely neighbors, we will have (or will invent) the tools to return to a state of equilibrium with the natural world.[66] The church can play a crucial role here by making ecotheology a central part of catechesis, and through political

---

[64] Some places will become drier while others will see increased rainfall. Climate change takes different forms in different places, even on the same continent.

[65] Ibid., 125, 109; cf. Isa. 10:1-2; 11:4; Jer. 5:27-9.

[66] Moltmann, *God for a Secular Society*, 97.

activism to encourage governments (local and national) to enact eco-friendly policies. In nations like the US where the Church still retains influence and large numbers in the population, her unified voice has the potential to generate large amounts of cultural and political change for the betterment of our common home.

Conclusion

The human race is facing a global crisis of its own making. The warning signs are all around us. The luxurious lifestyles enjoyed primarily by the West over the last 170 years cannot be universalized nor sustained. What has been enjoyed so far by the First World has largely come at the expense of the Third World (to borrow language from Moltmann). Not only that, but this standard of living has also come at the expense of future generations, and the earth itself.[67]

From a theological perspective, the primary disease is sin, which has broken our human-creature and human-to-human relationships in complex and devastating ways. The theological answer to this complex brokenness is, in part, the primacy of restoring love in all of our relationships, including our relationship with Creation itself. Given the deep interconnectedness of the human race with nature itself, especially in the context of our global ecological crisis, loving one's neighbor and loving the earth are two sides of the same coin.

Christian love is not only a call to action. It also acts as the primary motivator to sustain such action. We do not guilt people into sacrificial change and call it love. We stir up divine affection for land and brother alike so that we fight for the good of the Other out of a desire for communion, not guilt or shame.

Love then moves us into concrete action which, in terms of the ecological crisis, means that the affluent must shoulder the primary burden of reducing emissions and supporting and helping the vulnerable adapt and survive a global ecosystem that will be changing for decades to come, at the very least.

---

[67] Ibid., 93.

If humanity does all this—if love wins in our hearts and propels us to radical ecological action—we have an opportunity to join God's ministry of reconciliation for the whole created order. We can be part of making the current earth look more like the New Earth, one that is green, sustainable, and just.[68]

---

[68] Rutledge, *The Crucifixion*, 131.

Works Cited

Albeck-Ripka, Livia. "The Great Barrier Reef Was Seen As 'Too Big to Fail.' A Study Suggests It Isn't." *The New York Times*. April 3, 2019. https://www.nytimes.com/2019/04/03/world/australia/great-barrier-reef-corals-bleaching.html.

Allen, M.R., O.P. Dube, W. Solecki, F. Aragón-Durand, W. Cramer, S. Humphreys, M. Kainuma, J. Kala, N. Mahowald, Y. Mulugetta, R. Perez, M. Wairiu, and K. Zickfeld, *Framing and Context. In: Global Warming of 1.5°C. An IPCC Special Report on the impacts of global warming of 1.5°C above pre-industrial levels and related global greenhouse gas emission pathways, in the context of strengthening the global response to the threat of climate change, sustainable development, and efforts to eradicate poverty* [Masson-Delmotte, V., P. Zhai, H.-O. Pörtner, D. Roberts, J. Skea, P.R. Shukla, A. Pirani, W. Moufouma-Okia, C. Péan, R. Pidcock, S. Connors, J.B.R. Matthews, Y. Chen, X. Zhou, M.I. Gomis, E. Lonnoy, T. Maycock, M. Tignor, and T. Waterfield (eds.)]. In Press, 2018.

Bartholomew, Patriarch. "Environmental Justice and Peace." *The Ecumenical Patriarchate*, 2011. https://www.patriarchate.org/bartholomew-quotes.

Bonhoeffer, Dietrich. *Letters and Papers From Pirson*. Minneapolis: Fortress Press, 2015.

BP, *BP Statistical Review of World Energy 2019*, London, 2019 https://www.bp.com/content/dam/bp/business-sites/en/global/corporate/pdfs/energy-economics/statistical-review/bp-stats-review-2019-full-report.pdf.

Brunner, Daniel L., Jennifer L. Butler, and A. J. Swoboda. *Introducing Evangelical Ecotheology: Foundations in Scripture, Theology, History, and Praxis*. Grand Rapids: Baker Academic, 2014.

Bunn, C., Läderach, P., Ovalle Rivera, O. et al. Climatic Change, 2015, 129: 89. https://doi.org/10.1007/s10584-014-1306-x

Church, J.A., P.U. Clark, A. Cazenave, J.M. Gregory, S. Jevrejeva, A. Levermann, M.A. Merrifield, G.A. Milne, R.S. Nerem, P.D. Nunn, A.J. Payne, W.T. Pfeffer, D. Stammer and A.S. Unnikrishnan. *Sea Level Change. In: Climate Change 2013: The Physical Science Basis. Contribution of Working Group I to the Fifth Assessment Report of the Intergovernmental Panel on Climate Change* [Stocker, T.F., D. Qin, G.-K. Plattner, M. Tignor, S.K. Allen, J. Boschung, A. Nauels, Y. Xia, V. Bex and P.M. Midgley (eds.)]. Cambridge University Press, 2013.

EPA, "Global Greenhouse Gas Emissions Data." Environmental Protection Agency, 2014. https://www.epa.gov/ghgemissions/global-greenhouse-gas-emissions-data#Reference 1.

Franziskus, Pope. *Encyclical on Climate Change and Inequality: On Care for Our Common Home.* Brooklyn: Melville House, 2015.

Fountain, Henry, and Ben C. Sullivan. "Glaciers Are Retreating. Millions Rely on Their Water." *The New York Times*, January 16, 2019. https://www.nytimes.com/interactive/2019/04/17/climate/melting-glaciers-globally.html.

Fountain, Henry, and Ben C. Sullivan. "Where Glaciers Melt Away, Switzerland Sees Opportunity." *The New York Times*. February 14, 2019. https://www.nytimes.com/interactive/2019/04/17/climate/switzerland-glaciers-climate-change.html.

Haidt, Jonathan. *The Righteous Mind: Why Good People Are Divided by Politics and Religion.* New York: Vintage Books, 2013.

Hertsgaard, Mark. *Hot: Living Through the Next Fifty Years on Earth.* Boston: Mariner Books, 2012.

Hughes, T.P., Kerry, J.T., Baird, A.H. et al. "Global warming impairs stock–recruitment dynamics of corals." *Nature*, 2019, 568: 387–390, doi:10.1038/s41586-019-1081-y.

IPCC, Summary for Policymakers. In: *Climate Change 2013: The Physical Science Basis. Contribution of Working Group I to the Fifth Assessment Report of the Intergovernmental Panel on Climate*

Change [Stocker, T.F., D. Qin, G.-K. Plattner, M. Tignor, S.K. Allen, J. Boschung, A. Nauels, Y. Xia, V. Bex and P.M. Midgley (eds.)]. Cambridge University Press, 2013.

Lockwood, Mike. "Solar Change and Climate: an update in the light of the current exceptional solar minimum," *Proceedings of the Royal Society A*, 2 December 2009, doi 10.1098/rspa.2009.0519; Lean, Judith. "Cycles and trends in solar irradiance and climate," *Wiley Interdisciplinary Reviews: Climate Change*, vol. 1, January/February 2010.

Moltmann, Jürgen. *God for a Secular Society: The Public Relevance of Theology*. Minneapolis: Fortress Press, 2005.

NOAA, "Assessing the Global Climate in August 2019." National Oceanic and Atmospheric Administration, September 16, 2019. https://www.ncei.noaa.gov/news/global-climate-201908.

NOAA, "Summer 2019 Was Hottest on Record for Northern Hemisphere." National Oceanic and Atmospheric Administration, September 16,2019.https://www.noaa.gov/news/summer-2019-was-hottest-on-record-for-northern-hemisphere.

Rutledge, Fleming. *Crucifixion: Understanding the Death of Jesus Christ*. Grand Rapids: Eerdmans Publishing Company, William B., 2017.

Seattle, Chief. "Letter From Chief Seattle." *Álex Rovira*. Accessed December 12, 2019. http://www.alexrovira.com/en/sensaciones/articulo/carta-del-jefe-indio-seattle.

Sidima, Harvey. *Liberating Life: Contemporary Approaches to Ecological Theology*. Edited by Charles Birch, William R. Eakin, and Jay B. McDaniel. Eugene: Wipf & Stock, 2007.

Snyder, Howard A., and Joel Scandrett. *Salvation Means Creation Healed: the Ecology of Sin and Grace: Overcoming the Divorce between Earth and Heaven*. Eugene: Cascade Books, 2011.

Wayne, G. P. "Empirical Evidence That Humans Are Causing Global Warming." *Skeptical Science*, July 12, 2015. https://

skepticalscience.com/empirical-evidence-for-global-warming.htm.

Wigley, T.M.L. & Santer, B.D. Clim Dyn (2013) 40: 1087. https://doi.org/10.1007/s00382-012-1585-8.

Wilson, Edward O. *The Future of Life*. New York: Vintage, 2003.

Wuebbles, D.J., D.W. Fahey, K.A. Hibbard, B. DeAngelo, S. Doherty, K. Hayhoe, R. Horton, J.P. Kossin, P.C. Taylor, A.M. Waple, and C.P. Weaver, *Executive Summary of the Climate Science Special Report: Fourth National Climate Assessment, Volume I* [Wuebbles, D.J., D.W. Fahey, K.A. Hibbard, D.J. Dokken, B.C. Stewart, and T.K. Maycock (eds.)]. Washington, DC: U.S. Global Change Research Program, 2017.

Chapter 6
Who Owns The Land? Zimbabwean Traditional Leaders' Use of African Traditional Customs And Religion Contrasted with Biblical Approaches

Dwight S.M. Mutonono[1]

Abstract

Traditional chiefs have been co-opted into the Zimbabwean government in various ways by the ruling politicians. Whether in the previous Rhodesian or present Zimbabwean government, the chiefs have been used as political pawns. For more than a decade, the chiefs have publicly sided with the ruling party in Zimbabwe. They have entered into a patronage relationship with the government and have become channels of coercive manipulation of their constituents. The Zimbabwean church has generally not been supportive of government coercive methods and some have spoken out against it. There is an antagonistic relationship between the church and the government backed by the chiefs. The government and chiefs' religious response is that Christianity is not authentically African and they are advocating for a return to African traditional religious practices linked to the ancestral spiritual ownership of land. The assertion that Christianity is not authentically African and therefore it is not the religion that is practiced by true African people is questioned. So too is the assertion that land ultimately belongs to the ancestors.

---

[1] Dwight S.M. Mutonono is the past Executive Director of Africa Leadership and Management Academy in Zimbabwe. He holds a Doctor of Ministry in Transformational Leadership degree from Bakke Graduate University and is currently working on a Ph.D at Asbury Theological Seminary.

Abbreviations

Central Intelligence Agency   CIA
Movement for Democratic Change   MDC
United States Department of State   USDOS
Zimbabwe African National Union - Patriotic Front   ZANU-PF
Zimbabwe National Traditional Healers Association   ZINATHA

Introduction

Land in African traditional cosmology belongs to the departed ancestors. Though physically dead, their spirits are understood to be very active and involved in what goes on in the lives of their descendants.

In an article co-authored with Mautsa, we highlight that traditionally land belonged to the whole community and could not be owned by an individual.[2] The chiefs were custodians of the land in each area, allocating it to people according to custom. The community were stewards, nurturing and ensuring that it would look after everyone. Chiefs would be wealthier than the community, but there was a purpose. Elizabeth Mutambara explains,

> The accumulation of wealth by the chief is made on behalf of the tribe. For example, the Shona chief designates a piece of land called *zunde ramambo* that is cultivated collectively by his subjects. The produce from this portion of land is stored in granaries at the chief's compound for future use by people in his community. The *zunde* practice is a food security measure.... In Shona traditional society, the wealth of the chief benefits everybody. This is captured in the Shona expression, *Panodya ishe varanda vanodyawo* translated as "When the chief eats the subjects eat as well."[3]

Zimbabwean chiefs' modern use of land and the links with political party structures has become questionable however. The chiefs have highlighted that land belongs to the ancestors, but have linked Christianity with some of the natural disasters and different

---

[2] Dwight Simpson Munyaradzi, Mutonono, and Makoto L Mautsa, 'Land', in *Africa Bible Commentary* (Nairobi, Kenya: WordAlive Publishers, 2006), 290; David Goodwin, 'Whatever It Takes: Strategies by Communal Land Right - Holders in Zimbabwe for Enhancing Tenure Security." *Africa: Journal of the International African Institute* 83, no. 1 (2013): 177–79.

[3] Mutambara Maaraidzo Elizabeth, "Towards a Land Conservation Ethic in Zimbabwe: An Ethical and Religio -Cultural Analysis of Land Conservation Policies and Practice in Communal Areas." (Ph.D., University of Denver, 2008), 54–55.http://search.proquest.com/pqdtglobal/docview/230691200/abstract/D242BDBB89344A3DPQ/.

social maladies that happen in Zimbabwe.[4] They blame the malaise on the imposition of a foreign people and foreign faith on the land of the ancestors. They recommend promoting the traditional religious veneration of ancestors and the corresponding rejection of Christianity.

I would like to highlight here that in traditional Zimbabwean customs, departed (dead) ancestors were linked to newborn babies through ritual. The part of the umbilicus that remains attached to the baby and dries up and subsequently drops off after birth was taken and buried in the family home. This is the burial of the umbilicus, *rukuvute* (Shona) or *inkaba* (Ndebele) ceremony.[5] One of the ways in which the Shona (the dominant tribe) refer to themselves is *mwana wevhu* (the son of the soil) which literally refers to this ceremony whereby the departed ancestors, buried in the soil, are introduced to the new child, thereby physically and spiritually uniting them with the child. Land therefore has a transcendent relationship with the living and the dead and perpetually belongs to the community which always includes the departed ancestors.

While this continues to guide how Zimbabweans think of the land, the government and the chiefs have collaborated to create a narrative that is antagonistic to the Zimbabwean Church; positing it as an imposition of the white person's religion. Christianity is therefore seen as the religion of colonial elements that forcibly took the physical land and replaced traditional religion with white people's religion. Christianity is therefore seen as not authentically African and the government is working to return the land to the black people and restore traditional religion to receive the ancestral blessing. This study interrogates that narrative in two ways. First, by asking questions about whether present day Zimbabweans can truly claim that they are the owners of the land; and second by interrogating the assertion that Christianity is not authentically African.

Land is one of the most public areas of life. Everyone has some relation to land and it affects life in all-encompassing ways. It is therefore

---

[4] John Chitakure, *African Traditional Religion Encounters Christianity: The Resilience of a Demonized Religion* (Wipf and Stock Publishers, 2017:), 23–24; Gwaze Veronica, "Disasters: What Is Wrong?" *The Sunday Mail* (21 April 2019), https://www.sundaymail.co.zw/disasters-what-is-wrong.

[5] Goodwin, "Whatever It Takes," 177.

important to grapple with a public theology of land, which is the focus of this study.

In the next section, this chapter will consider the socio-cultural context of Zimbabwe in relation to the question of land ownership. The section that comes after will engage with the issue from biblical and Christian perspectives. I will then conclude with a section that proposes how theology can provide a way forward.

Socio-Cultural Context

For more than a decade (beginning in the early 2000s) and in the latest Zimbabwean 2018 general elections, the president of the chiefs, Fortune Charumbira, has publicly said that the chiefs have agreed to endorse Zimbabwe National African Union – Patriotic Front (ZANU-PF) and its incumbent president. This is according to several reports.[6] This endorsement has not just been vocal, it has often been coercive, and chiefs have manipulated the vote in their area to be in ZANU-PF's favor. The Australian government report just cited quotes a 2007 communication from the United States Department of State (USDOS):

> The USDOS reports that in 2007 (prior to the last round of elections), Chief Charumbira ordered traditional leaders to expel villagers who supported the opposition [MDC][7] and to withhold food aid from them. Also in 2007, and in relation to denying MDC supporters access to subsidised [*sic*] maize, the

---

[6] Australian Government Refugee Review Tribunal, "Country Advice Zimbabwe: Treatment of MDC Members by Zanu PF Election Related Violence, Masvingo West-MDC History" (2011). https://www.justice.gov/sites/default/files/eoir/legacy/2014/01/06/election_violence.pdf; Anti-Corruption Trust of Southern Africa;

See also: "Capture of Zimbabwean Traditional Leaders for Political Expediency." Harare, Zimbabwe "Anti-Corruption Trust of Southern Africa," 2017: http://kubatana.net/wp-content/uploads/2017/11/Actsa-Report-Capture-of-Zimbabwean-Traditional-Leaders-for-Political-Expediency.pdf;

See also: *Newsday*, "The Unholy Matrimony between the Chiefs and Zanu PF," *NewsDay Zimbabwe* (9 May 2018), https://www.newsday.co.zw/2018/05/the- unholy-matrimony-between-the-chiefs-and-zanu-pf/.

[7] Movement for Democratic Change (MDC)

chief reportedly stated that [w]e cannot continue to feed our enemies as they are sell outs [sic].⁸

The chief described the MDC as enemies and sell-outs. Any Zimbabwean outside ZANU-PF is seen as the enemy and is treated as such. The term "sell-out" is very derogatory in Zimbabwe. It was used during the war against colonial rule to denote those black people who cooperated with or worked with white enemies. The "them" and "us" divide at that time of the colonial conflict was between black and white people. The ZANU-PF government and chiefs have re-invented the divide and used it for their own political purposes. By way of contrast, the MDC has more international sympathy and is more open to interracial membership. This makes them "sell-outs".

The chiefs have been accused of instructing villagers in their areas to vote ZANU-PF (the ruling party). If their area went to the opposition, villagers would fear possible reprisals. The history of state-sponsored violence against areas that voted for the opposition in past elections is filled with inducing fear amongst the people through coercive power.

The chiefs have been given special privileges by the government and compared to colonial structures which took their land, sidelining and disenfranchising them, the chiefs have been treated very well. They therefore feel obligated and beholden to the ZANU-PF party. However, the link goes even deeper, for the war of liberation through which ZANU-PF gained political leadership was fought on the premise that the liberation fighters were working to restore land that was taken from the ancestors. The ancestors were therefore invoked by spirit mediums that worked with traditional leaders (chiefs). The liberation fighters often referred to themselves as *mwana wevhu* (son of the soil) an allusion to the *rukuvute/ inkaba* ceremony that is mentioned in the introduction. Thus, the links between the people of the land, the chiefs, and the ruling elite go beyond simple patronage or vote-buying to a deep-seated understanding of how the land is to be restored to its original pre-colonial state, both physically and spiritually.

---

⁸ Australian Government Refugee Review Tribunal, Country Advice Zimbabwe, 8.

From here, this section will focus on the relationship between the government and chiefs in Zimbabwe before critically considering the accusations against Christianity.

Chiefs and the Zimbabwean Government: A Patrimonial Relationship?

The literature about patrimonial relationships is varied with a lack of consensus on exactly what constitutes a patron-client structure.[9] I would describe a patrimonial relationship as one in which a patron has control of resources of some kind and gives access to these in exchange for loyalty from the recipients, often described as clients. Broadly in the context of this study the patron presents himself/herself as a benefactor and of course the recipients of this beneficence are supposed to reciprocate by showing love and respect for their leader. Political Scientist Kate Baldwin in her dissertation describes the relationship between politicians and traditional leaders (chiefs) in Africa:

> In rural Africa, traditional leaders, chiefs or emirs are generally the most important patrons within their communities, often overseeing the allocation of land, the administration of key rituals, and the adjudication of local disputes. In places as diverse as Burkina Faso, Cameroon, the DRC,[10] Ghana, Malawi, Mozambique, Senegal, Zambia and Zimbabwe, these leaders continue to dominate social and economic activities within rural communities, and they play a key role in linking their communities to elected politicians.[11]

In the Zimbabwean context, there are some relational similarities between chiefs and the political systems derived from colonial structures before and after independence. In the Rhodesian, pre-independence context, "The colonial state wanted to bolster the powers of chiefs as part of a system of indirect rule...the emphasis on chiefly power was

---

[9] Susan C. Stokes, "Political Clientelism," *The Oxford Handbook of Political Science* (7 July 2011), https://doi.org/10.1093/oxfordhb/9780199604456.013.0031.

[10] Democratic Republic of Congo.

[11] Kate Baldwin, "Big Men and Ballots The Effects of Traditional Leaders on Elections and Distributive Politics in Zambia" (Ph.D., Columbia University, 2010), 3. http://search.proquest.com/pqdtglobal/docview/750045479/abstract/6CF528A9F8EB4BE0PQ/28.

essential for the colonial state during the 1960s and 1970s because the state wanted chiefs to impose agricultural and conservation measures on rural communities."[12] The Rhodesian government, led by Ian Smith, tried to privilege the chiefs and thereby use them to control the rural communities. They created a narrative that the state-controlled media promoted. They tried to demonize the liberation fighters, calling them terrorists and working with the chiefs to make it difficult for the liberation fighters to operate in their areas. When it became clear that the political landscape was shifting and independence with black control of government was inevitable, the Rhodesians sponsored a chief in the hopes that they could influence the future government through him if he succeeded. A Central Intelligence Agency (CIA) communication is revealing:

> Chief Jeremiah Chirau has the least support of any of the Rhodesian leaders who have been involved in the settlement process, largely because he owes his political position almost entirely to Prime Minister Smith. In December, 1976, Chirau and fellow Chief Kayisa Ndiweni announced the formation of the Zimbabwe United People's Organization. It appears almost certain that Smith's white minority regime encouraged the creation of ZUPO [sic], and has since given financial support to the organization.[13]

Chief Chirau was one of the people that Smith tried to work with in an alliance (the bi-racial transitional government) that involved others like Bishop Abel Muzorewa and the Reverend Ndabaningi Sithole. When independence came, the relationship of the new, Zimbabwean government with the chiefs was understandably initially strained. They were labelled as puppets of the previous regime. So originally, as far as the government was concerned, at least some of the chiefs had become "sell-

---

[12] Nyambara Pius S., "Immigrants, 'Traditional' Leaders and the Rhodesian State: The Power of 'Communal' Land Tenure and the Politics of Land Acquisition in Gokwe, Zimbabwe, 1963–1979," *Journal of Southern African Studies* 27, no. 4 (December 2001): 780, https://doi.org/10.1080/03057070120090736.

[13] CIA Document, "CIA Document 'Chief Chirau's Position' Pdf," 5 October 1978, 1. https://www.cia.gov/library/readingroom/docs/CIA- RDP80T00634A000400010029-1.pdf.

outs." They presently have a key ally status. However, as Hansungule[14] points out, de-colonization in Africa was a let-down to the people. The average Zimbabwean remained poor, landless and without dignity. Independence was little more than a change from white oppressors to black oppressors, the system remained unchanged, it was a copy and paste of the colonial regime practices. The biggest shift in attitude to the chiefs was when the incumbent ZANU- PF party realized that it was losing power and the populace was shifting its support to the opposition MDC party.

To counteract that, they initiated a wave of forceful land invasions and co-opted the chiefs by giving them several personal benefits, according them a new status as the national custodians of traditional religion. Ezra Chitando, a Zimbabwean religious studies professor outlines the process through which the new relationship was established:

> The co-option of traditional leaders and chiefs by the state also facilitated the subservience of indigenous religions to the interests of the ruling party. Although the chiefs had been denounced as stooges during the liberation struggle and had been marginalized in the early 1980s, their fortunes were dramatically transformed in the late 1990s. ... When the urban vote swung to the MDC, it [ZANU PF] moved quickly to win over chiefs to its side. It gave them a sense of importance, maintaining that it had 'restored' their powers, awarded them salaries, electrified their rural homes and increased their visibility... the chiefs were transformed into guardians of ancestral traditions. In turn the chiefs became partners who sealed off the rural areas from the MDC. With very few exceptions, they declared their territories 'liberated zones' where only ZANU-PF could operate. They also harnessed their status as ritual specialists to proclaim Mugabe as the sole legitimate leader of the country. However, it is important to

---

[14] Hansungule Michelo, "Who Owns Land in Zimbabwe? In Africa?," *International Journal on Minority and Group Rights* 7, no. 4 (2000): 305–40, https://doi.org/10.1163/15718110020908070.

acknowledge that some chiefs refused to be used as pawns in the political game.[15]

The linkages between traditional religion, land, traditional leaders (chiefs) and the ZANU-PF government can be clearly seen in the cited process. It became a deeply entrenched system with roots in the rural areas that the chiefs controlled. The urban influence of chiefs is very limited. The MDC opposition party is stronger in the urban centers, but the ZANU-PF party maintains control of the rural areas through the chiefs. Without the rural areas ZANU-PF would not presently be in power.

Baldwin[16] identifies various ways in which the relationship between traditional chiefs and political authorities plays-out. The first is what she describes as a traditional patrimonial relationship which operates according to the patron-client system and exercises control through coercive means. The second is what she describes as an institutionalist view on secret elections. Elections in the traditional patrimonial scheme would be nothing more than window dressing, the outcome is predetermined through the deep patron-client network. In the institutional view, however, elections through secret ballot once understood as free and fair, and truly adopted, will minimize the chiefs' influence because of the institutionalization of that free and fair democratic system. The elections would truly reflect the wishes of the people.

My personal observation is that in Zimbabwe, the population has moved to a position which is more in line with the institutionalist view. In 2008, the population voted overwhelmingly for the opposition, but the sitting president, Mugabe, refused to relinquish power. After controversially delaying the announcement of presidential election results for three weeks, he managed to manipulate a run-off election against Morgan Tsvangirai. The violence unleashed by the ZANU-PF government against the opposition, especially in rural areas that had voted for Tsvangirai was vicious and unprecedented. State-sponsored

---

[15] Chitando Ezra, "'In the Beginning Was the Land:' The Appropriation of Religious Themes in Political Discourses in Zimbabwe," *Africa: Journal of the International African Institute* 75, no. 2 (2005): 227.

[16] Baldwin, "Big Men and Ballots."

militia used coercion to manipulate the rural population. The traditional patrimonial system from which they had moved was now backed by a state-sponsored machinery of violent coercion in the case of non-compliance. This was all done under the veneer of a war to restore the land of the ancestors. The state wanted to give the impression that a new liberation war was being fought against colonialists. Whereas in the past it was fought with white colonists, now it is being waged against MDC "sell-outs" who would put the land under white people's control and allow the dominance of Christian worship (white people's religion) in the land.

Baldwin describes a third way in the continuum of the relationship between politicians and chiefs. She refers to this as the "chiefs as informational cues" perspective, in which the chief is seen as a respected leader and guiding voice by the community. She then proposes what she calls a co-operative interaction approach in which the chief lobbies politicians for the interests of the community and backs the candidate who will best benefit him (in rare instances "her") and the community. The politician in turn needs the chief's support and co-operation to implement envisaged development projects. It becomes a win-win scenario.

What Baldwin describes is the ideal situation, and while useful in the Zambian context, is not accurate here. Instead, the relationship between the chiefs and politicians in Zimbabwe could best be described as a mafia-like patrimonial environment. Lack of compliance leads to very severe and unwelcome consequences. Left to itself, the country was moving towards the more open and free environments that Baldwin envisages. But, after reading Baldwin's work on Zambia, I would say in her typology, Zimbabwe is being dragged back to a heightened traditional patrimonial relationship, with all coercion necessary to accomplish envisaged goals.

The chiefs and traditional leaders have been co-opted into a narrative that says indigenous religions need to be re-adopted and Christianity needs to be rejected as a European religion. The land needs to be returned to the ancestors, the rightful owners according to African cosmology. This narrative requires interrogation and this study will now begin to critique the arguments which are at the foundations of this system. The political leaders are playing a clever game here. To the international world, Zimbabwe is a modern democracy with elections and other bureaucratic structures that go with Western style systems of governance. The political leaders project themselves in that way to the world. To the rural communities, however, they present themselves as a part of traditional governance systems that have been there since pre-independence times. The rural people see the chief as their leader; whatever the chief says is accepted and obeyed. The chiefs therefore instruct their communities that they are desirous of fair, democratic elections, but behind-the-scenes, the people must make sure to vote ZANU-PF. If their area does not go to ZANU-PF, there will be consequences. And sure enough, a history of state-sponsored violence against communities that voted wrongly[17] ensues. The next part of this section will critically consider this perspective.

A Critical Assessment of Chiefs' Claims About Land and African Traditional Religions

To try to objectively understand the issue of Zimbabwean land ownership it is necessary to go back to the historical record and attempt to analyze the demythologized version of the narrative being currently offered. The mythological narrative that ZANU-PF is presenting is that Zimbabwe belongs to the ancestral spirits and Christianity is incompatible with the land called by that name. The land needs to be restored to black people and re-dedicated to their ancestors. In describing the danger of public myths that seek to steer popular opinion, Ramachandra sees that through myths, "…entire societies are held captive to the merchants of fear and death."[18] History is almost always told with an agenda: the narrator plays a big part, first in what does and does not get into the narrative and second how it is told, or the slant that it is given. Good

---

[17] One of the Shona sayings that people have recently learnt from this context of chiefs and elections is the saying "*Mono vota zvakanaka.*" Which can be translated "Vote well" or "Vote in a good or right way." When the chief calls his community a day before elections and addresses them, these words can be received as a veiled threat. The community better make sure they vote in a good way, which means voting for ZANU-PF.

[18] Vinoth Ramachandra, *Subverting Global Myths: Theology and the Public Issues Shaping Our World* (Downers Grove, Il: IVP Academic, 2008), 10.

historical research is triangulated.[19] Triangulation is gained through considering the same event from different sources so that commentary can be separated from fact.

The original inhabitants of Zimbabwe are likely not the present so-called indigenous people who are mostly of Bantu origin and migrated from the north.[20] Human beings through the centuries are in constant state of movement and whole people groups move from country to country through various forms of migration. It should be kept in mind that several Zimbabweans, including me, are presently in diaspora. White people who were born in Zimbabwe are legally just as much Zimbabweans as I am. Some have migrated to Zimbabwe from other countries and some have migrated out of Zimbabwe and become citizens of other countries. Statistics are many and their veracity is difficult to establish, but the International Organization of Migration report of 2018 quotes one source as saying there are a total of 1,253,100 Zimbabwean emigrants. However, at the same time, they also mention another source whose estimates they question, that says, "…over 3 million Zimbabweans live in South Africa alone…"[21] According to the World Population Review, Zimbabwe has a population of 14,740,828.[22] Conservative estimates would therefore indicate that 9 percent of Zimbabweans live outside the country, but if the bigger estimate for South Africa alone is to be believed the figure is more than 20 percent.

In the modern world people frequently migrate from rural to urban environments and into regional and global destinations. In traditional Africa, the Bantu migration is a known phenomenon. Various migrations are identified and though uncertain, some events are agreed upon: "The earliest history of the Bantu-speaking people of Zimbabwe may not be discussed with certainty because very little is

---

[19] Leedy Paul D., and Jeanne Ellis Ormrod, *Practical Research: Planning and Design* (Boston: Pearson, 2013), 102,142,162, 259.

[20] A. T. Bryant, *Bantu Origins: The People & Their Language* (Capetown, South Africa: Struik, 1965).

[21] Admire Chereni, and Paradzayi P Bongo, "Migration in Zimbabwe: A Country Profile 2010-2016." (Harare, Zimbabwe: International Organization of Migration, 2018), 34, https://publications.iom.int/system/files/pdf/mp_zimbabwe_2018.pdf.

[22] World Population Review, "Zimbabwe Population 2019 (Demographics, Maps, Graphs)," accessed 7 December 2019, http://worldpopulationreview.com/countries/zimbabwe-population/.

known. However, it is generally agreed that about the fifth century A.D. there began a southward migration from the north across the Zambezi River by the Bantu-speaking pastoralists."[23]

The Bantu people have been historically traced as originally coming from Cameroon.[24] Archaeological excavations at the Great Zimbabwe monument have resulted in the following analysis from Hufmann: An initial influx called Period I occurred in the Early Iron Age, ending about A.D. 400. The next influx, or Period II began soon after this and a new population can be discerned, this lasted until A.D. 1100. The final influx or Period III immediately followed and lasted till the 15th century. In the 1800s the Nguni speakers or Ndebele peoples came back to Zimbabwe after originally migrating to South Africa.[25]

The original inhabitants of Africa were the Bantu and Nilotic peoples.[26] Arabic peoples also have a long history in the north of the continent. Though there probably was some previous interaction, many would have come in during the Islamic invasions which happened after A.D. 670. Islam started around A.D. 610 when Muhammad was forty and first said he saw the angel Gabriel, thereby launching the faith. After his death, the movement spread into other parts of the world and entered Africa around A.D. 670. Archaeologists generally agree that the earliest inhabitants of Zimbabwe were the San people or Bushmen as they are colloquially called in the literature, "Later the Bushmen were joined by the Bantu, who migrated from the north of the continent."[27] After indicating that historically the Shona people, who are the predominant present day Zimbabwean Bantu descendants, are said to have entered Zimbabwe sometime after A.D. 1000, Mudenge, an academic and former minister of state points to possible ways in which the present day Shona either displaced or integrated with the original inhabitants:

---

[23] Zebron Masukume Ncube, "Ancestral Beliefs and Practices: A Program for Developing Christian Faith among Adventists in Zimbabwe" (D.Min., Andrews University, 1988): 27, http://search.proquest.com/pqdtglobal/docview/287995286/abstract/68EDDA3A09F64E59PQ/1.

[24] A. T. Bryant, *Bantu Origins*.

[25] T. N. Huffman, 'The Rise and Fall of Zimbabwe', *The Journal of African History* 13, no. 3 (July1972): 355, https://doi.org/10.1017/S0021853700011683.

[26] Hansungule, "Who Owns Land in Zimbabwe?," 306.

[27] Ibid.

> Some go further to claim that the later Iron Age people were a better-armed and better-fed horde of invaders who absorbed, dominated or wiped out the previous 'Early Iron Age' population....They found other iron-using agricultural communities known to archeologists as the 'Gokomere' group....But the weight of evidence at present would seem to suggest that both the so-called 'Early' and 'Later' Iron Age peoples were Bantu-speakers.[28]

I would like to highlight here that present day Zimbabwean inhabitants can all be shown to have come into the land from somewhere else and many of these have moved on and are no longer living in Zimbabwe. The legitimate owners or dead ancestors of the land would therefore strictly speaking be the ancestors of the displaced original San people and not the present predominantly Shona and Ndebele people who are in the land. A.D. 1000 is the first entrance of the Bantu peoples from the north.

Christianity first came to Zimbabwe through the Portuguese and 1560 is the recorded date of the conversion of the first *Munhumutapa* (named Negomo Mupunzagutu) to become a Christian.[29] Mudenge goes into detail about the Jesuit's relationship with the Mutapa kings (literally *Munhumutapa* or *Mwenemutapa* or as the Portuguese rendered it *Monomotapa*) who inhabited the houses of stone (*dzimbabwe*)[30] that were built at Great Zimbabwe, the court, palace and capital city of the Mutapa state. The Mutapa kingdom which was said to have been founded by Prince Mutota[31] covered the territory that is modern day Zimbabwe but stretched further into parts of modern day Zambia, Mozambique, Botswana and South Africa. The Portuguese encountered Arab and Swahili traders when they first landed at the Beira coast in Mozambique. From there they went inland to look for the inland source from which the traders were coming. That is how they found the Great

---

[28] S. I. G. Mudenge, *A Political History of Munhumutapa c.1400-1902*, First Edition edition (Harare, Zimbabwe: Zimbabwe Pub. House, 1988), 22.

[29] S. I. G. Mudenge, *Christian Education at the Mutapa Court: A Portuguese Strategy to Influence Events in the Empire of Munhumutapa*. Harare, Zimbabwe: Zimbabwe Pub. House, 1986: 3.

[30] The name Zimbabwe is derived from Great Zimbabwe which literally means house of stone. This is the historic stone structure found in Masvingo, a city that is south of Harare, the capital.

[31] Mudenge, *A Political History of Munhumutapa*, 37.

Zimbabwe which was at the heart of the trade, and the Mutapa dynasty which was housed there.

It is noteworthy that some of the Mutapa kings converted and became Christians. Mudenge chronicled how some of them were trained in Doa, India to become priests and one even ended up in China.[32] Mudenge has a strong anti-colonial and anti-missionary tone to his writings about the Christian influence on the Mutapa kings. He is right to highlight that some missionaries worked in cahoots with colonial authorities to disenfranchise Africans, but that is only telling a partial story. Despite the trappings that come with trying to preach the gospel in the context of managing church-state relations and all the complexities of Christian public life, it cannot be denied that some from the Mutapa lineage willingly embraced Christianity. Isichei shows that centuries later, after the original interaction with the Portuguese had long ended, David Livingstone encountered a Christianity with Roman Catholic influences when he first came to the area. "In southern Africa, several Mutapa princes became friars, and when Livingstone travelled on the Zambezi, he encountered a Catholicism that had never entirely died out."[33]

If some of the Mutapa kings who are the great *mhondoro* ("a spirit medium, especially guardian spirit of a tribe; a lion")[34] of Zimbabwe became Christians; it indicates that perhaps the original relationship between Zimbabwean traditional religion and Christianity was not as polarised or antithetical as the conveyors of the modern narrative would want us to believe.

The strongest proponent and advocate for the restoration of Zimbabwean traditional religion in our generation was Professor Gordon Chavunduka. Chavunduka was the holder of a PhD from the University of London and a strong academic, to the extent of being appointed Vice Chancellor of University of Zimbabwe from 1992-1996. His father was an Anglican priest. He was brought up as an Anglican, and when he died, his funeral was conducted by the Anglican Church. However,

---

[32] Mudenge, *Christian Education at the Mutapa Court*.
[33] Elizabeth Isichei, *A History of Christianity in Africa: From Antiquity to the Present* (Grand Rapids: Lawrenceville, N.J: Eerdmans, 1995), 45.
[34] Mudenge, *A Political History of Munhumutapa*, 15.

Chavunduka was also a traditional healer and served as the president of the Zimbabwe National Traditional Healers Association (ZINATHA). He was very conversant with, and an authority in the area of traditional religion, to the extent of becoming a traditional healer which would very likely mean he was a spirit-medium. His views on Christianity are therefore highly dynamic with regards to traditional religion. He bemoaned the missionary attempt to destroy African indigenous religions but then went on to explain how indigenous religion is not exclusivist, arguing that it could accommodate other faiths. He explains:

> The African religion is a hospitable religion which accepts the fact that other religious systems may be equally valid, or even more so. The African religion is prepared to embrace other beliefs and practices as long as the necessary cultural adjustments are made to accommodate them. The African religion can therefore facilitate inter-religious dialoge [sic].[35]

This position is not as polemic as one would expect from the president of the traditional healers. Perhaps this view is influenced by Chavunduka's Anglican background. In the same document, Chavunduka further explains that in the African traditional religion cosmology, the ancestors are concerned with problems of social life at a lower level. They will help in maintaining social stability through controlling rainfall and fertility on the land and creating good social order. God[36] operates at a higher level: "Ultimate dominion over the whole world is in the hands of God. God is for everyone. It is believed that God takes very little interest in individuals in their day-to-day life. He is concerned mainly with matters of national and international importance."[37] My co-authored article on land in the *Africa Bible*

---

[35] Gordon L. Chavunduka, "Dialogue Among Civilisations: The African Religion in Zimbabwe Today." Crossover Communication, 2001: 4, http://www.ewfi.de/Text/African%20Religion.pdf.

[36] Zimbabweans believe in one creator God called *Mwari*. People do not talk directly to God but their issues are communicated to the spirit world by their dead ancestors who are now part of that world and can communicate to God. *Mwari* is the name used for God in Zimbabwe, whether from the traditional religion or a Christian perspective. Zimbabwean traditional religion is open to the concept of one creator God as presented in Christianity.

[37] Ibid., 4.

Commentary[38] alludes to the same idea. Ultimately, from biblical and African traditional religious perspective, it is God who owns the earth and allows people to move from one place to the other according to his sovereign control. African traditional culture and religious practices are very closely aligned to biblical laws, especially as found in the Old Testament. Some of the laws in the Pentateuch like the requirement for a bride price on the discovery of pre-marital sex (Ex 22: 16-17) and the similarities of ritual practice between the scapegoat (Lev 16:22-24) and what the Shona call *kurasira* (literally to throw away), a ritual in which a goat or chicken (usually black) is sent into the wilderness after being given the community or family's sins, indicate close commonalities.

Despite public political rhetoric that would seem to support a polarized and antagonistic relationship with no middle ground between African traditional religion and Christianity, past-President Mugabe's private life and personal practice was more ambivalent on this issue. He was a devout Catholic who would be in church every Sunday. He was brought up and educated by Catholic priests at a Catholic mission.[39] In his most difficult hour when the whole nation, including his trusted military, turned against him and staged a coup in November 2017, he turned to the church.[40] It was Father Fidelis Mukonori, and only him that Mugabe would trust and talk to at that time. He announced his resignation as President while holding the rosary, silently reciting a prayer.[41] Furthermore, he died with a priest by his bedside to say the last rites. Mugabe was cared for and influenced by the Catholics from childhood. The public posturing of a divide between Christianity and traditional religion is therefore clearly about political expediency and not a true expression of religious beliefs in the country. The political leaders do not truly believe that Christianity is a white person's religion

---

[38] "Mutonono and Mautsa, "Land," 290.
[39] "Robert Gabriel Mugabe," South African History Online' (20 February 2017), https://www.sahistory.org.za/people/robert-gabriel-mugabe.
[40] "The Impact of Religion on Robert Mugabe," *The Economist* (20 November 2017), https://www.economist.com/erasmus/2017/11/20/the-impact-of-religion-on-robert-mugabe; Reuters, "Zimbabwe's Mugabe Cried When He Agreed to Step down - Report," *The Irish Times*, accessed 7 December 2019, https://www.irishtimes.com/news/world/africa/zimbabwe-s-mugabe-cried-when-he-agreed-to-step-down-report-1.3305794.
[41] Ibid.

and they do accept and acknowledge that not all white people are their enemies. Having white benefactors does not make a person a "sell-out."

The true commitment to the religious views on land that are often peddled in public would therefore need to be interrogated. The more authentic or traditionally religious orthodox position is that though Africans believe that land belongs to the ancestors, they are not the ultimate owners; instead, God is the owner and allocates to different people at different times as he wills. I accept that historic versions of Christianity were partners with and agents of colonialism; however, despite all those failings, Africans have been able to relate with God through Christianity. Recently, strong African contextualizing theologies have emerged. These contextual theologies are debunking the myth that Christianity is not African. One such theologian, Kwame Bediako has proposed an integrative African theology that presents Jesus as the ultimate ancestor for the African.[42] He is the one who takes us to God the Father. Jesus would therefore become the ultimate *mhondoro* or lion spirit over the land of Zimbabwe. The next section will provide a biblical and Christian perspective on Zimbabwean land. Land is central to the African understanding of public life. Everything revolves around the Zimbabwean land that was bequeathed to the present generation by their ancestors.

Biblical and Christian Perspectives

The argument that links Zimbabwean land to the ancestors presupposes that Christianity is not an authentically African religion and was imported from the European colonists and missionaries. This view is based on Christian history traced from the original Portuguese encounters with the *Munhumutapa* kingdom (c. A.D. 1506)[43] and the later encounters with Protestant missions. It assumes that the Bantu would have had no previous knowledge of or contact with Christianity, an assumption that may not be entirely true. The next section will focus on the period before the entrance of the Portuguese to understand if there was any previous Zimbabwean link with Christianity or other related faiths like Judaism or Islam. It is important to keep in mind

---

[42] Kwame Bediako, *Christianity in Africa: The Renewal of Non-Western Religion* (Edinburgh; Maryknoll, N.Y: Orbis Books), 1996.

[43] Mudenge, *A Political History of Munhumutapa*, 52.

the research that has been previously alluded to which indicates that the present-day Bantu inhabitants of Zimbabwe arrived in the country around A.D. 1000. They were coming from the north, most likely from the region of present day Cameroon.

Zimbabwean Encounter with Christianity and Other Religions Before the Portuguese

As mentioned previously, the Portuguese found Swahili and Arab traders who were interacting with the *Munhumutapa* kingdom before they came. This means that, if not Christianity, the Shona were at least aware of Islam before the arrival of the Portuguese Mudenge provides a written record of a speech that a Muslim *Quasis* (priest)[44] named Mingame made to Muslim leaders when the Portuguese came. His biggest fear was that the *Mukarangas*[45] "…motivated by the example of their Emperor and of their elders, will follow the law of the crucified with such haste and excitement that in no time all the cities of Mocranga [Mukaranga] and all the places [villages?] of Botonga will pay Him homage."[46] This Muslim priest feared that once exposed to Christianity, the emperor or *Munhumutapa* would convert to the faith, as would his kingdom. Islam is not Christianity, but it is a faith that came after and is founded on Jewish and Christian history. Burton[47] shows that when Muhammed started Islam he saw it as an Arabic expression of Christianity. Though some would argue against Burton's understanding, his assertion is that Islam from inception is an attempt by Arabs to adopt Christianity and it is a syncretized (with Arabic religion and culture) form of Christianity. Muhammad claimed to have received the Quran from the angel Gabriel; interpreters do however see that much of the revelation he presented is contained in the Jewish and Christian scriptures.

What the Islamic priest probably feared is that the Christian faith would be attractive to the Shona. The Shona were not Arabs, and once

---

[44] Mudenge says the *Quasis* was an Arabic priest. I could not find other documents that confirm this, but since Mudenge uses original sources I choose to defer to his expertise and research in this area.

[45] The other way in which the Shona (Zimbabwean Bantu grouping) were described, also a designation for one Shona tribe.

[46] Mudenge, *Christian Education at the Mutapa Court*, 6.

[47] Keith Augustus Burton, *The Blessing of Africa: The Bible and African Christianity* (Downers Grove, IL: IVP Academic, 2007).

exposed to the original template from which Islam is formed, would likely accept it. He could also have feared the possibility of the African historical roots of Christianity becoming apparent to the *Munhumutapa* kingdom. This would likely ignite the excitement of the Shona because they would see Christianity as authentically African and they would be following the faith of their ancestors.

Research into the early African links with Christianity is growing. For example, Thomas Oden wrote significant scholarship illuminating the whole North African landscape in as far as early Christianity (from biblical times) is concerned.[48] Other authors have also helped bring understanding of this period, highlighting how, from about three hundred years before Christ, a strong Jewish community lived in areas like modern day Egypt, Libya, Tunisia and Algeria, probably going down to at least Sudan and Ethiopia. This community was the catalyst for first Jewish and then early Christian faith presence in Africa.[49] In fact, if we go back to New Testament times, of the three people who laid hands to Barnabas and Saul, sending them with the gospel to Europe, at least two were African, one possibly even being called black (Acts 13:1). Both Nilotic and Bantu people groups were in these areas.

Isichei traces the original encounter of the North African Berbers with the Greek empire to almost seven hundred years before Christ. "Cyrenaica lies West of Egypt, in what is now eastern Libya. The Arabs were to call it 'the Green Mountain', for its hills attracted sufficient rain for pastoral farming. Greek colonists settled among the Berbers; tradition dates this to 639 BC..."[50] The Berbers were the original inhabitants of areas to the west of Egypt (Lybia, Tunisia, North Africa). It was only after the Arab invasions beginning A.D. 670 that the Berbers mixed with Arabs and became Muslim. Up to then they were Christian. Initially that region was a strong center of early Christianity. However, Christianity

---

[48] Thomas C. Oden, *How Africa Shaped the Christian Mind: Rediscovering the African Seedbed of Western Christianity* (Downers Grove, Ill.: IVP Academic, 2010); Oden, Thomas C., *The African Memory of Mark: Reassessing Early Church Tradition* (Downers Grove, IL: IVP Academic, 2011); Thomas C. Oden, *Early Libyan Christianity: Uncovering a North African Tradition* (Downers Grove, IL: IVP Academic, 2011).

[49] Isichei, *A History of Christianity in Africa*; See also Ogbu U. Kalu, ed., *African Christianity: An African Story* (Trenton, NJ: Africa World Press, Inc., 2007).

[50] Isichei, *A History of Christianity in Africa*, 15.

there was weakened due to several schisms and confinement of the faith to towns by the time of the Islamic invasions. Ischei again says,

> Gradually, the Berbers of the north-west became, first *mawali*, then Muslims. There were economic inducements to conversion: the chance of joining the armies that conquered Spain, and freedom from poll tax. The Maghrib lacked the monastic tradition that did so much to preserve Christianity in Egypt and Ethiopia. There was a process of desertification, the causes of which are debated, and the vast olive groves of inland Numidia gradually gave way to steppe…[51]

The point of this discourse is to highlight that the original Bantu who migrated from the North of Africa were likely influenced by the early Christian world.[52] Christianity at that time moved from Africa to Europe. In fact, Europe came into the biblical history picture very late. Most of the events of scripture happened in the Fertile Crescent area and going down the Mediterranean into Egypt and North Africa. Joseph was in Africa and the twelve tribes of Israel developed there, spending at least four hundred years between the book of Genesis and Exodus in Egypt before coming out as a nation. In my book, *Stewards of Power: Restoring Africa's Dignity*[53] I highlight that Joseph was married to an African woman. That means at least two tribes in Israel (Ephraim and Manasseh) had African blood. It can be argued that the original Israelites had a good amount of African blood. They were not prohibited from marrying Africans. Even Moses had a Cushite wife (Numbers 12:1). The original inhabitants of that area (Egypt and North Africa) were not predominantly Arabic until after the Arab invasions of A.D. 670. Egypt and North Africa likely had inhabitants who were closely related to the Nilotic and Bantu peoples of Africa.[54]

---

[51] Isichei, *A History of Christianity in Africa*, 44.

[52] Desertification and over-population of that area has been attributed as a possible reason for the Bantu migrations.

[53] Dwight Mutonono, *Stewards of Power: Restoring Africa's Dignity* (Carlisle, U.K.: Hippobooks, 2018).

[54] A. T. Bryant, *Bantu Origins*. Gonzalez in his book *Faith and Wealth* (Justo L. Gonzalez, *Faith and Wealth: A History of Early Christian Ideas on the Origin, Significance, and Use of Money* (Eugene, OR: Wipf and Stock Publishers, 2002), 44–47.) shows how the social stratifications that were created in Egypt because of the invasion

This means that several early Christian leaders who shaped the direction of the Church from its foundations, people like Augustine of Hippo, Tertullian, and Origen were close in ethnicity to the Bantu, if not Bantu themselves. They lived centuries before the Arab invasions. Islam is a copy of the faith they believed.

If the Shona in Zimbabwe understood this history, no thinking leader would make the assertion that Christianity is not an African religion. The idea that African traditional religion was the only homogenous and exclusive religion of Zimbabwe becomes untenable. Even forms of Judaism were likely within the Zimbabwean environment at that time. The Shona tribe called *Varemba* or *Lemba* of South Africa claim descent from a Jewish lineage and their traditional practices are too closely linked to Judaism for their claims to be easily dismissed.[55] In summary, though the Shona predominantly practiced African traditional religion, it was in a context where elements of Judaism and Islam were present. Christianity, though not practiced in any recorded way, might not have been an entirely unknown concept. It can also be demonstrated that at least in the North Africa area from where the Bantu migrated up to about A.D. 670, Christianity was present. According to archeology, the Bantu ancestors of Zimbabweans arrived c. A.D. 1000.

This section will end with a brief consideration of land from a biblical perspective.

Biblical Perspective on Land

The nation of Israel is closely linked with the land that God promised them. This, of course, is a major source of present day global contention and up to now remains a cause of conflict. However, despite the controversy around it, there are broad lessons for all people that can be learned through a study of Israel and the land. Brueggemann's book

---

of Greeks, Romans and Jews who dominated the Egyptian world of that time reduced the original inhabitants to servitude causing them to leave their lands to go into the wilderness or migrate southwards. The likelihood is also apparent from other authors like Ischei and Kalu who are cited in this study.

[55] Steve Vickers, "Lost Jewish Tribe "Found in Zimbabwe," *BBC News*, (8 March 2010), http://news.bbc.co.uk/2/hi/8550614.stm.

The Land: Place as Gift, Promise, and Challenge in Biblical Faith[56] gives great insight into this issue, for as he explains, the biblical Israel started off as a people without a land, then they were promised a geographical region as theirs. At some point, they were a landed people and then they became an exiled people who were expelled from it. Eventually after the exile, they returned, but largely under foreign domination. Brueggemann highlights that, "Land is a central, if not *the central theme* of biblical faith."[57] God is the creator and ultimate owner of everything in the world, "The earth is the Lord's, and everything in it, the world, and all who live in it" (Ps 24:1). Human conduct on the earth is therefore not independent of God's approval or censure.

The universal biblical principles that govern life on any part of the earth are summarized in the following way:[58]

1. God owns the land (Ps 24:1; Gen 1:9-10; Lev 25:23; Ps 50:12; Gen 3:23-24; 4:11; Deut 2:5, 9; Ps 125:3)
2. God's laws govern life on the land (Gen 6:7; Lev 18:25-28; Deut 4:25-27; 11:8-25; Josh 23:12-16, 15; 1 Kgs 9:6-7; 2 Kgs 17:7-23)
3. God desires that land benefits its inhabitants (Lev 25:8-34; Isa 1:17; 3:14-15; 10:1-4; 11:4; 25:4; 58:1-14; Jer 2:34; 7:5-7; 22:13; 25:4; Ezek 9:9; 16:49; 18:5-9, 16; 22:29; Hos 12:7; Amos 2:6-8; 4:1-2; 5:11-12; 8:4-8; Mic 2:2; Zech 7:10)

Israel was promised land on the basis that God wanted them to live according to his laws once on it. The Canaanites were driven out of the land on the same principle. They violated the creator's universal laws which govern life on the land, and the land vomited them out (Lev. 18:25). The land was not created to be the ground on which wickedness would be practiced. It was rather supposed to be used in conformity with God's laws, it was a conditional gift. Israel found out that they would be treated no better. After living in the land for many years and violating the Lord's commands while in it, they too were expelled. The broad principles remain: land should serve and benefit all its inhabitants, especially the

---

[56] Walter Brueggemann, *The Land: Place as Gift, Promise, and Challenge in Biblical Faith*, Second edition (Minneapolis, MN: Augsburg Books, 2002).

[57] Ibid., 3.

[58] Mutonono and Mautsa, "Land," 290. There are several scriptures in the original source that buttress the three points captured in this article.

poor and the alien. Bloodshed, injustice, immorality, impunity and general lawlessness will eventually result in God's judgment.

Kwame Bediako's previously alluded to thinking is paradigmatic.[59] The accepted narrative believed by many in Zimbabwe is that Christianity represents a European religion that came with the colonialists; therefore, like colonialism, Christianity should be rejected as a white person's religion. However, the truth is Christianity is much more African than it is European. It is truly for all people; a universal faith. Bediako walked a theological tight rope that African Christian thinkers need to follow. African liberators want to co-opt African Christian thought leaders, as do some Western leaders. Balcomb's chapter in a book written in honor of Bediako says,

> On the one hand, he had to counter the strident critique of his fellow African scholars who would have seen him as a 'sell out' to the cause of African liberation and on the other, he had to counter the whispered innuendos of those seeking to perpetuate the 'civilising' [sic] myth of Western Christianity in what they continue to see as the 'dark continent'.[60]

The biblical context has very close synergies with African culture. Bediako theorizes that the reason why Christianity is finding such ready acceptance on the continent today is that in it, Africans find something that is deeply and authentically African.[61] As previously mentioned, African traditional culture and religious practices are very closely aligned to biblical laws, especially as found in the Old Testament. Biblical teaching on land as summarized in the three points above fully expresses traditional ideals concerning the land. The African would say, "Yes, God owns the land! Yes, his laws govern life on it! And yes, he desires that it benefit all its inhabitants!"

---

[59] Bediako, *Christianity in Africa*; See also: Bediako, Kwame, *Theology and Identity: The Impact of Culture upon Christian Thought in the Second Century and in Modern Africa* (Eugene, OR: Wipf & Stock Pub, 2011).

[60] Gillian Mary Bediako, *Seeing New Facets of the Diamond: Christianity as a Universal Faith - Essays in Honor of Kwame Bediako*. Edited by Bernhardt Quarshie and J. Kwabena Asamoah-Gyadu (Eugene, OR: Cascade Books, 2015), 69.

[61] Bediako, *Christianity in Africa*.

Having considered the socio-cultural context around the traditional leader's use of African traditional worldview and religion, as well as understanding some theological perspectives that can help guide thinking, the paper will conclude by proposing a way forward that is theologically informed.

Conclusion - How Theology Can Provide a Way Forward

The collaboration between Zimbabwe's traditional leaders and the ruling party to influence public opinion and behavior on land issues is based on the narrative that Christianity is a European faith. African traditional religion is presented as the authentic cultural way to worship and an African world view that is derived from this view is seen as the basis for conduct related to Zimbabwean land.

For various reasons this position is disputable:

First, the sincerity of the protagonists of this view is doubtful. This whole view is the creation of a narrative by politicians who are exploiting patrimonial culture for their own benefit. The fact that they are active members of Christian churches and turn to them in times of crisis indicates a heart allegiance to Christianity. For example, even the late president of the Zimbabwe Traditional Healers Association was not at all exclusivist in his views on Christianity and African traditional religion. The highly-polarized relationship between the faiths that is being peddled is therefore not reflective of practice on the ground.

Second, the earliest records on the entrance of Christianity into Zimbabwe through the Portuguese at the Munhumutapa court and their interaction with the Mutapa kings points to a historical acceptance of the faith by the Mutapa lineage. This was the most powerful kingdom in Zimbabwean history covering the whole present day territory and extending into South Africa, Botswana, Zambia and Mozambique. Not only did they become Christians, some of them became Catholic priests. To say this was forced on them is an untenable position. Mudenge[62] alleges that there was a grand scheme by the Portuguese to gain control of the Mutapa court through Christian education. If that was the case, then they had some success. In the next point of dispute below I will

---

[62] Mudenge, *A Political History of Munhumutapa*.

address Mudenge's allegation. For now, it is important to think about the implications of the Mutapa lineage embracing Christianity. If they, who are the great ancestors, the *mhondoro* or lion spirit over the land to whom the ancestral spirit mediums speak, accepted Christianity, the modern-day assertions become undermined.

The allegation that one of the western powers' strategy to gain control of colonial territories was to use Christianity to pacify and soften the colonized, making them accommodating is commonly held. I do not deny the historical efforts to politicize Christianity. Politicians throughout history have tried to use Christianity for their own ends. This does not just apply to Christianity, but religion in general. Politicians' concerns are motivated by the desire to gain control. Everything and anything in society that can be used towards that end will be utilized. The Portuguese may have tried it with the Mutapa kingdom. It should be kept in mind that even Zimbabwean politicians do this today. However, this narrative does not adequately explain the phenomenon of the explosive growth of Christianity after colonization. The efforts and proliferation of African Initiated Churches[63] that mix African traditional religious beliefs with Christianity are another phenomenon that is not adequately explained by this perspective. Bediako's proposal that Christianity is the renewal of non-western religion can better explain this. Perhaps the enthusiastic acceptance of Christianity by Africans is because Christianity is profoundly African in ways that resonate with the people.

Third, Church history reveals that for the first three or four hundred years the African church was dominant in world Christianity, shaping Christianity for all generations after. From the catechetical schools of Alexandria to the early influence of Cyrene (Simon of Cyrene carried Jesus cross, Lucius of Cyrene sent Barnabas, who himself was likely from Cyrene[64] and Saul to the Europeans), to the great minds of the Latin fathers like Augustine and Tertullian in the early Western Church and Origen in the Eastern Church, the African voice was strong. Instead of Christianity coming to Africa from the Europeans as some would have it, historically, it actually was coming back home. It went to Europe, then came back home.

---

[63] Some refer to them as African Independent Churches
[64] Oden, *The African Memory of Mark*.

In light of these areas of dispute, I conclude with the way forward that theology can provide to this issue:

1. The church needs to actively educate its members on the true history and contribution of Africans to Christianity from antiquity, before the modern appearance of Europeans on the continent. Theological institutions need to make this an important part of the formal training of future Christian leaders. All formal and informal means of communication need to be mobilized to get the message out until the child playing in the field sings it. More energy needs to be placed in the development of a theology of land in Africa. A clearer understanding of biblical ideals on land use can help to more effectively use land as God intended and embellish not only the African continent, but the rest of the world as well.

2. Chiefs, as customary custodians of the land need to be encouraged to operate on good moral principles. They may not accept Christianity, but they should uphold the moral principles that come from a fear of the God who owns the land and to whom they are ultimately accountable. They should not let political expediency overrun prudence and make them violate the moral values that underpin their trust as custodians of the land. Whether it be custodians on behalf of the ancestors who are under God (*Mwari* in Shona) or under a Christian belief system, the moral obligations remain. Shedding of innocent blood and injustice are an abomination. They also should respect themselves and the dignity of their office by refusing to be played with as political pawns by whatever new system or party that comes into power, whether white or black, Rhodesian or Zimbabwean.

Work Cited

Anti-Corruption Trust of Southern Africa. "Capture of Zimbabwean Traditional Leaders for Political Expediency." Harare, Zimbabwe: Anti-Corruption Trust of Southern Africa, 2017. http://kubatana.net/wp-content/uploads/2017/11/Actsa-Report-Capture-of-Zimbabwean-Traditional-Leaders-for-Political-Expediency.pdf.

Australian Government Refugee Review Tribunal. "Country Advice Zimbabwe: Treatment of MDC Members by Zanu PF Election Related Violence, Masvingo West - MDC History," 2011. https://www.justice.gov/sites/default/files/eoir/legacy/2014/01/06/election_violen ce.pdf.

Baldwin, Kate. "Big Men and Ballots The Effects of Traditional Leaders on Elections and Distributive Politics in Zambia." Ph.D., Columbia University, 2010. http://search.proquest.com/pqdtglobal/docview/750045479/abstract/6CF528A9F8E B4BE0PQ/28.

Bediako, Gillian Mary. *Seeing New Facets of the Diamond: Christianity as a Universal Faith - Essays in Honor of Kwame Bediako*. Edited by Bernhardt Quarshie and J. Kwabena Asamoah-Gyadu. Eugene, OR: Cascade Books, 2015.

Bediako, Kwame. *Christianity in Africa: The Renewal of Non-Western Religion*. Edinburgh : Maryknoll, N.Y: Orbis Books, 1996.

———. *Theology and Identity: The Impact of Culture upon Christian Thought in the Second Century and in Modern Africa*. Eugene, OR: Wipf & Stock Pub, 2011.

Brueggemann, Walter. *The Land: Place as Gift, Promise, and Challenge in Biblical Faith*. Second edition. Minneapolis, MN: Augsburg Books, 2002.

Bryant, A. T. *Bantu Origins: The People & Their Language*. Capetown, South Africa: C. Struik, 1965.

Burton, Keith Augustus. *The Blessing of Africa: The Bible and African Christianity*. Downers Grove, IL: IVP Academic, 2007.

Chavunduka, Gordon L. "Dialogue Among Civilisations: The African Religion in Zimbabwe Today". Crossover Communication, 2001. http://www.ewfi.de/Text/African%20Religion.pdf.

Chereni, Admire, and Paradzayi P Bongo. "Migration in Zimbabwe: A Country Profile 2010-2016." Harare, Zimbabwe: International Organization of Migration, 2018. https://publications.iom.int/system/files/pdf/mp_zimbabwe_2018.pdf.

Chitakure, John. *African Traditional Religion Encounters Christianity: The Resilience of a Demonized Religion*. Eugene, OR: Wipf and Stock Publishers, 2017.

Chitando, Ezra. "'In the Beginning Was the Land': The Appropriation of Religious Themes in Political Discourses in Zimbabwe." *Africa: Journal of the International African Institute* 75, no. 2 (2005): 220–39.

CIA Document. "CIA Document 'Chief Chirau's Position'. Pdf," 5 October 1978. https://www.cia.gov/library/readingroom/docs/CIA-RDP80T00634A000400010029-1.pdf.

Gonzalez, Justo L. *Faith and Wealth: A History of Early Christian Ideas on the Origin, Significance, and Use of Money*. Eugene, OR: Wipf and Stock Publishers, 2002.

Goodwin, David. "Whatever It Takes: Strategies by Communal Land Right - Holders in Zimbabwe for Enhancing Tenure Security." *Africa: Journal of the International African Institute* 83, no. 1 (2013): 164–87.

Gwaze, Veronica. "Disasters: What Is Wrong?" *The Sunday Mail*, 21 April 2019. https://www.sundaymail.co.zw/disasters-what-is-wrong.

Hansungule, Michelo. "Who Owns Land in Zimbabwe? In Africa?" *International Journal on Minority and Group Rights* 7, no. 4 (2000): 305–40. https://doi.org/10.1163/15718110020908070.

Huffman, T. N. "The Rise and Fall of Zimbabwe." *The Journal of African History* 13, no. 3 (July 1972): 353–66. https://doi.org/10.1017/S0021853700011683.

Isichei, Elizabeth. *A History of Christianity in Africa: From Antiquity to the Present*. Grand Rapids, MI: Lawrenceville, N.J: Eerdmans, 1995.

Kalu, Ogbu U., ed. *African Christianity: An African Story*. Trenton, NJ: Africa World Press, Inc., 2007.

Leedy, Paul D, and Jeanne Ellis Ormrod. *Practical Research: Planning and Design*. Boston, MA: Pearson, 2013.

Mudenge, S. I. G. *A Political History of Munhumutapa c 1400-1902*. Harare, Zimbabwe: Zimbabwe Pub. House, 1988.

———. *Christian Education at the Mutapa Court: A Portuguese Strategy to Influence Events in the Empire of Munhumutapa*. Harare, Zimbabwe: Zimbabwe Pub. House, 1986.

Mutambara, Maaraidzo Elizabeth. "Towards a Land Conservation Ethic in Zimbabwe: An Ethical and Religio -Cultural Analysis of Land Conservation Policies and Practice in Communal Areas." Ph.D., University of Denver, 2008. http://search.proquest.com/pqdtglobal/docview/230691200/abstract/D242BDBB89344A3DPQ/6.

Mutonono, Dwight. *Stewards of Power: Restoring Africa's Dignity*. Carlisle, U.K.: Hippobooks, 2018.

Mutonono, Dwight Simpson Munyaradzi, and Makoto L Mautsa. "Land." In *Africa Bible Commentary*. Nairobi, Kenya: WordAlive Publishers, 2006.

Ncube, Zebron Masukume. "Ancestral Beliefs and Practices: A Program for Developing Christian Faith among Adventists in Zimbabwe." D.Min., Andrews University, 1988. http://search.proquest.com/pqdtglobal/docview/287995286/abstract/68EDDA3A09F64E59PQ/1.

Newsday. "The Unholy Matrimony between the Chiefs and Zanu PF." *NewsDay Zimbabwe*, 9 May 2018. https://www.newsday.co.zw/2018/05/the-unholy-matrimony-between-the-chiefs-and-zanu-pf/.

Nyambara, Pius S. "Immigrants, 'Traditional' Leaders and the Rhodesian State: The Power of 'Communal' Land Tenure and the Politics of Land Acquisition in Gokwe, Zimbabwe, 1963–1979." *Journal of Southern African Studies* 27, no. 4 (December 2001): 771–91. https://doi.org/10.1080/03057070120090736.

Oden, Thomas C. *Early Libyan Christianity: Uncovering a North African Tradition*. Downers Grove, IL: IVP Academic, 2011.

———. *How Africa Shaped the Christian Mind: Rediscovering the African Seedbed of Western Christianity*. Downers Grove, IL: IVP Academic, 2010.

———. *The African Memory of Mark: Reassessing Early Church Tradition*. Downers Grove, IL: IVP Academic, 2011.

Ramachandra, Vinoth. *Subverting Global Myths: Theology and the Public Issues Shaping Our World*. Downers Grove, IL: IVP Academic, 2008.

Reuters. "Zimbabwe's Mugabe Cried When He Agreed to Step down - Report." *The Irish Times*. Accessed 7 December 2019. https://www.irishtimes.com/news/world/africa/zimbabwe-s-mugabe-cried-when- he-agreed-to-step-down-report-1.3305794.

South African History Online. "Robert Gabriel Mugabe." 20 February 2017.https://www.sahistory.org.za/people/robert-gabriel-mugabe

Stokes, Susan C. "Political Clientelism." *The Oxford Handbook of Political Science*, 7 July 2011. https://doi.org/10.1093/oxfordhb/9780199604456.013.0031.

The Ecomunist. "The Impact of Religion on Robert Mugabe." *The Economist*, 20 November 2017. https://www.economist.com/erasmus/2017/11/20/the-impact-of-religion-on-robert-mugabe.

Vickers, Steve. "Lost Jewish Tribe 'Found in Zimbabwe.'" *BBC News*, 8 March 2010. http://news.bbc.co.uk/2/hi/8550614.stm.

World Population Review. "Zimbabwe Population 2019 (Demographics, Maps, Graphs)." Accessed 7 December 2019. http://worldpopulationreview.com/countries/zimbabwe-population/.

Chapter 7
A Theological Response to Growing "Vaccine Hesitancy" in American Evangelical Churches
Samuel J. Hood[1]

Abstract

While vaccine development has largely been viewed by society and the medical community as an indispensable asset to American public health, recent years have seen a rise in a more critical narrative within the American evangelical community. Termed by health professionals as "vaccine hesitancy," this wariness has been listed by the World Health Organization (WHO) as "one of the top ten threats to global heath in 2019," contributing to a universal increase in the spread of vaccine-preventable diseases.[2] However, there is no clear evidence that evangelical beliefs are contributing to increase in vaccine hesitancy seen within the American evangelical community. In this paper, I propose that the theological doctrines of creation and new creation are helpful for evangelicals to see how stewarding public health is part of our created design and a meaningful way we participate in God's coming kingdom. Moving to practice, I encourage Christian ministers to foster healthy trust in the medical community and implement practical church policies that reinforce public health — from making public statements to requiring vaccinations within their childcare.

---

[1] Samuel J. Hood is currently an M.Div. student at Asbury Theological Seminary. He plans to further his theological education and pursue a career in both pastoral ministry and Christian academia.

[2] World Health Organization, "Ten Threats to Global Health in 2019" (2019), https://www.who.int/emergencies/ten-threats-to-global-health-in-2019(accessed 12/05/19).

Introduction

Vaccinations are undoubtedly one of the greatest medical achievements of the modern world.[3] Few medical technologies have been as successful at improving the quality and duration of human life globally than vaccines. Before the measles vaccine was developed in 1963, it is estimated that over four million American children contracted the disease, hospitalizing over a hundred thousand and killing five hundred a year.[4] However, in 2000, just thirty-seven years after the first implementations of the vaccine, measles was declared eradicated from the United States.[5] While vaccine development has largely been viewed by society and the medical community as an indispensable asset to American public health, recent years have seen a rise in a more critical narrative related to vaccination.

A small minority of the population—labeled by the media as the "anti-vaccination movement"[6]—claims that vaccines are unsafe for children, some even asserting that immunizations are behind the societal increase of developmental disorders, including autism.[7] Nonetheless, in this climate of competing voices, a majority of parents resisting child vaccinations are not ideologically opposed to vaccines but are simply cautious due to the surrounding debates. Termed by health professionals as "vaccine hesitancy,"[8] this wariness has been listed by the World Health Organization (WHO) as "one of the top ten threats to global health in 2019, contributing to a universal increase in the spread of vaccine-preventable diseases.[9] Specifically, the WHO reported a 30%

---

[3] Harvard Library: Office for Scholarly Communication, "Mandatory Vaccination: Why We Still Got to Get Folks to Take Their Shot" (2006), http://nrs.harvard.edu/urn-3:HUL.InstRepos:8852146 (accessed 12/05/19).

[4] Paul A. Offit, *Deadly Choices: How the Anti-Vaccine Movement Threatens Us All* (New York, NY: Basic Books, 2011), xxvi.

[5] George Washington University Public Health Online, "A History of Measles in the United States" (March 9, 2019), https://publichealthonline.gwu.edu/blog/measles-history-in-the-united-states/ (accessed 12/05/19).

[6] See Offit, *Deadly Choices*, xvii-xxiv.

[7] Sarah Geoghegan, Kevin P. O'Callagan, and Paul Offit, "Vaccine Safety: Myths and Misinformation," *Frontiers in Microbiology* 11, Article 372 (2020): 1-7, https://doi.org/10.3389/fmicb.2020.00372.

[8] Geoghegan, "Vaccine Safety: Myths and Misinformation," 1.

[9] World Health Organization, "Ten Threats to Global Health in 2019" (2019), https://www.who.int/emergencies/ten-threats-to-global-health-in-2019(accessed

global increase in measles cases in 2019."[10] This data correlates with the disease's surge within the United States' population as well. According to the US Center for Disease Control (CDC), there were 1,249 cases and 22 outbreaks of measles in 2019, the most cases reported since the eradication of the disease in 2000.[11] Notably, one of the most widespread measles outbreaks of 2019 took place within the Orthodox Jewish community of New York.[12] These case studies, among others, demonstrate that under-vaccinated, close-knit communities are particularly susceptible to heightened transmission of vaccine-preventable disease.

In this paper, I seek to explore the rising phenomenon of vaccine hesitancy and its relationship to the American evangelical community. In this first section, I ask how the ever-increasing prevalence of vaccine hesitancy affects American evangelicalism and in what unique ways the community may be contributing to the growth of the practice. In the second section of the essay, I will attempt to develop a theological framework that integrates the doctrines of creation and new creation into the issues of public health and immunization. Finally, in the third section of my essay, I will briefly propose ideas for how evangelical church leadership can utilize their response to growing vaccine hesitancy to effectively steward public health within their faith communities.

"Vaccine Hesitancy" & Its Relationship to American Evangelicalism

One particular nuance of the "anti-vaccine movement" often unaddressed in today's media and cultural conversation is the difference between vaccine refusal and vaccine hesitancy. This leads to the question: what exactly is vaccine hesitancy? According to the Strategic Advisory Group of Experts (SAGE) on Immunization, vaccine hesitancy "refers to the delay in acceptance or refusal of vaccination despite availability of vaccination services."[13] This constitutes a spectrum of parents who either

---

12/05/19).

[10] Ibid.

[11] Manisha Patel, et al, "National Update on Measles Cases and Outbreaks — United States, January 1-October 1, 2019," *Morbidity and Mortality Report* 68 (2019): 893-896.

[12] Ibid., 893.

[13] Noni E. MacDonald, "Vaccine Hesitancy: Definition, Scope and Determinants," *Vaccine* 33 (2015): 4161–64, https://pdfs.semanticscholar.org/bcb3/bc5e6cb4477e23d1387945d8eaae9fbe75f8.pdf.

(1) refuse all vaccines but are unsure about their decisions or (2) accept some vaccines but are delayed in getting their children vaccinated.[14]

It might be surprising but in my experience most parents who choose to not vaccinate their children or delay vaccinations do not consider themselves "anti-vaxxers." Similar to persons who identify as pro-life rather than anti-abortion, this self-description is more than an intentional rhetorical decision; it provides a window into their psychology and decision-making. When I have discussed this issue, many "vaccine-hesitant" parents will admit that vaccines have been globally effective and will often admit their decision might be different if they lived outside the United States. What becomes clear is that their confidence in immunization has been majorly undermined because of predominant misinformation.

The WHO EURO Vaccine Communication Center has highlighted three main categories that determine vaccine hesitancy: (1) complacency, (2) convenience, and (3) confidence.[15] Social standing is one major determinant on this issue. Middle-class and upper-class families more frequently fall into patterns of complacency due to lower risk of disease and greater ability to attain proper medical care. However, lower-class families tend to be less complacent because they feel the threat of diseases. Furthermore, lower-class parents, specifically mothers, have difficulty taking time off of work to ensure their children get their required vaccinations.

An erosion of confidence related to vaccinations is becoming more prevalent today across all strata of social class. Vaccine confidence, according to SAGE, is "trust in (1) the effectiveness and safety of vaccines; (2) the system that delivers them, including the reliability and competence of the health services and health professionals and (3) the motivations of policy-makers who decide on the needed vaccines."[16] Trust in vaccine safety, administration, and policy are compromised in the current cultural dialogue surrounding immunization. Even at a more macro level, we are living in a time of increasing institutional distrust. According to a 2019 poll done by the Pew Research Center, trust in the

---

[14] Ibid., 4162.
[15] Ibid., 4164.
[16] Ibid., 4162.

government, media, and one another is declining in the United States.[17] Roughly three-fourth of Americans believe public trust in government is diminishing, and two-thirds of the population believe trust in other citizens is in decline as well. Trust in our medical institutions is no exception.[18] The government and media play a central role in fostering trust in our health policies and perceptions. As trust in them wains, so do public health norms.

Paul A. Offit, chief of the Division of Infectious Diseases and the director of the Vaccine Education Center at the Children's Hospital of Philadelphia, has chronicled the history of vaccination opposition in his book *Deadly Choices: How the Anti-Vaccine Movement Threatens Us All*. While there has been opposition within the United States to vaccines since their inception, the modern anti-vaccine movement began in the early 1980s.[19] A documentary titled *DTP: Vaccine Roulette* claimed that the pertussis vaccine in the combination DTP (diptheria, tetanus, and pertussis) shot was responsible for causing brain damage in children. This documentary caused great controversy and was a catalyst for a congressional hearing in Florida.[20] Even though the hearing ruled that the benefits of the pertussis vaccine far out-weighed any potential safety risks, the group of parents that testified before Congress started an organization called Dissatisfied Parents Together (DPT). Later this organization renamed itself the Vaccine Information Center, which has become the most influential anti-vaccine, activist organization in America today.[21]

If the *Vaccine Roulette* documentary aired in 1982 kick-started the modern vaccine opposition movement, then surely Andrew Wakefield's 1988 paper reawakened the movement. In the British medical journal *The*

---

[17] Pew Research Center, "Key Findings about Americans' declining trust in government and each other," *Pew Research* (July 22, 2019), https://www.pewresearch.org/facttank/2019/07/22/key-findings-about-americansdeclining-trust-in-government-and-eachother/ (accessed 12/05/19).

[18] As one study concluded, "Distrust of the health care system is relatively high in the United States." Katrina Armstrong, et al. "Distrust of the Health Care System and Self-Reported Health in the United States," *The Journal of General Internal Medicine* (2006): 292-297, https://www.ncbi.nlm.nih.gov/pmc/articles/PMC1484714/pdf/jgi021-0292.pdf.

[19] Offit, *Deadly Choices*, 1-12.

[20] Ibid., 9.

[21] Ibid., 8.

Lancet, Wakefield and a team of twelve other co-authors "claimed to find a link between the measles, mumps, and rubella (MMR) vaccine and the symptoms of autism in children."[22] The media sensationalized Wakefield's findings, causing its quick dissemination to the public. Since then the international medical community has criticized the study extensively. Wakefield himself made claims contradictory to their reported findings. As the original article states, "We did not prove an association with the measles, mumps, and rubella vaccine and the syndrome described."[23] In 2004, ten of the original twelve co-authors retracted their support of the study because of Wakefield's misrepresentation of their research. Even the medical journal *The Lancet* retracted the study from publication. Later in 2007, the General Medical Council, which oversees doctors in England, investigated Wakefield. They ruled that he was guilty of dishonest medical conduct and suspended his medical license.[24]

Beyond all this, the findings in Wakefield's study have not been replicated by any other peer-reviewed studies. In 2019, the Danish government released an eleven-year study that included over 650,000 child-participants. The study confirmed dozens of past reports, maintaining that the MMR vaccination did not increase the risk of autism among the children they observed.[25] Nonetheless, the effects of Wakefield's paper linger in society. For example, even in 2011 the *Denver Post* reported that parents in Colorado — a state having one of the highest vaccine refusal rates in the country — were citing the supposed link between the MMR vaccine and autism as their major reason for refusing to vaccinate their children.[26]

---

[22] Stacy Metzinger Herlihy and E. Allison Hagood, *Your Baby's Best Shot: Why Vaccines are Safe and Save Lives* (Lanham, Maryland: Rowman & Littlefield Publishers), 81.

[23] A.J. Wakefield et al. "Ileal-Lymphoid-Nodular Hyperplasia, Non-Specific Colitis, and Pervasive Developmental Disorder in Children," *The Lancet* 351 (February 28, 1998): 647–41, https://www.thelancet.com/action/showPdf?pii=S0140-6736(97)11096-0.

[24] Sarah Boseley. "Andrew Wakefield found 'irresponsible' by GMC over MMR vaccine scare," *The Guardian* (January 28, 2010), https://www.theguardian.com/society/2010/jan/28/andrew-wakefield-mmr-vaccine.

[25] Anders Hviid et all, "Measles, Mumps, Rubella Vaccination and Autism: A Nationwide Cohort Study," *Annals of Internal Medicine* 170 (2019): 513-520, https://doi.org/10.7326/M18-2101.

[26] Michael Booth, "Colorado parents rank second in nation for vaccine refusals," *The Denver Post* (November 28, 2011), https://www.denverpost.com/2011/11/28/

This is where the anti-vaccine movement and vaccine hesitancy intersect. Many of the parents that are vaccine hesitant are hesitant precisely because of the misinformation they are receiving from anti-vaccine activists and organizations.[27] Social media gives the anti-vaccine movement a distinct advantage it did not have in 1982 or 1998. Many parents that are against vaccinations spread content on social media created by anti-vaccine activists and groups. In my personal research at my home evangelical church, I discovered that many family members and friends have become vaccine hesitant specifically because of things they have read on their Facebook feed. This where the connection between vaccine hesitancy and American evangelicalism comes into play.

While religion acts a social determinant within American public health and holds an interesting connection to immunization,[28] studies have shown that vaccine hesitancy is on the rise regardless of religion, political affiliation, or geographic location.[29] Within the forty-five states that allow for vaccine exemptions, the surge in vaccine hesitancy has caused an increase in parents choosing religiously-based exemptions.[30] While it is tempting to attribute religious belief to this behavior, there are studies that indicate this correlation is doubtful.

The American Association of Pediatrics put out a study in 2018 that maintains, "States with religious and personal belief exemptions were one-fourth as likely to have kindergartners with religious exemptions as states with religious exemptions only."[31] This infers that parents typically request "religious exemptions" when they do not have

---

colorado-parents-rank-second-in-nation-for-vaccine-refusals/ (accessed 12/05/19).

[27] Talha Burki, "Vaccine Misinformation and Social Media," *The Lancet Digital Health* 1, Issue 6 (2019), https://doi.org/10.1016/S2589-7500(19)30136-0.

[28] Ellen L. Idler, *Religion as Social Determinant of Public Health* (New York, NY: Oxford University Press, 2014).

[29] Gordana Pelčić, et al, "Religious exception for vaccination or religious excuses for avoiding vaccination." *Croatian Medical Journal* 57 (2016): 516–521, https://www.ncbi.nlm.nih.gov/pmc/articles/PMC5141457/.

[30] Jacqueline K. Olive, "The state of the antivaccine movement in the United States: A focused examination of nonmedical exemptions in states and counties," *PLOS Medicine* 15 (2018): e1002578, https://doi.org/10.1371/journal.pmed.1002578.

[31] Joshua T.B. Williams, et al, "Religious Vaccine Exemptions in Kindergartners: 2011-2018," *Pediatrics* 144 (2019): e20192710, https://pediatrics.aappublications.org/content/pediatrics/144/6/e20192710.full.pdf.

the option to choose a "personal belief exemption" (whether related to the safety or ethics of vaccinations). A global study that looked at religious beliefs and immunization confirms this as well. The author of this study, John D. Grabenstein, concluded that "religious reasons to decline immunization actually reflected concerns about vaccine safety or personal beliefs among a social network of people organized around a faith community, rather than theologically based objections per se."[32] While more studies need to be done on this issue, there does not seem to be a strong connection between religious beliefs and vaccine refusal within evangelical faith communities.

On the other hand, there is evidence that "white evangelicals" tend to be more supportive of parental choice for vaccines compared to other Christian traditions.[33] In a 2017 poll, 22% of white evangelical Protestants supported the rights of parents to not vaccinate their children even if that put the health of others at risk.[34] That rate was 5% higher than the national average (17%), 9% higher than black Protestants (13%), 11% higher than Catholics (11%), and 12% higher than white mainline Protestants (10%).[35] While research is lacking to link parental choice with the practice of vaccine refusal, it speaks for itself that evangelical Protestants were over two times more likely than mainline Protestants to support parental choice.

In sum, the evidence indicates that vaccine hesitancy and vaccine refusal are on the rise independent of religion, political affiliation, and geographic location. In the case of evangelical Christianity, it appears there are no core evangelical beliefs that are antithetical to immunization. However, there is evidence that evangelical Christians are more likely to support parental choice and oppose school-based vaccine requirements than other Christian traditions. It is likely this has more to do with political beliefs related to the role of government and

---

[32] John D. Grabenstein, et al, "What the World's religions teach, applied to vaccines and immune globulins," *Vaccine* 31, issue 16 (2013): 2011-2023, https://doi.org/10.1016/j.vaccine.2013.02.026.

[33] Pew Research Center, "Public Opinions about childhood vaccines for measles, mumps, and rubella," *Pew Research* (February 2, 2017), https://www.pewresearch.org/science/2017/02/02/public-opinion-about-childhood-vaccines-for-measles-mumps-and-rubella/ (accessed 12/05/19).

[34] Ibid.
[35] Ibid.

religious freedom than any particular theological belief. Whatever it is, it seems that evangelicalism falls into a more general trend related to vaccine hesitancy and vaccine refusal.

From Eden to the New Jerusalem: How A Theology of Creation and New Creation Functions as a Framework for Public Health and Immunization

Critically acclaimed author Eula Biss wrote the book *On Immunity: An Inoculation* about her experience as a mother wrestling with the issue of vaccination.[36] Despite her fears, the reality of social immunity, or herd immunity, caused her to change her mind and vaccinate her son.[37] Herd immunity arises when populations reach high-enough rates of immunity that the spread of disease is limited due to the lack of potential carriers.[38] The reality of herd immunity is one of the reasons why operating with an individualistic framework when approaching the issue of vaccinations — like supporting parental choice or opposing school-based vaccine requirements — is problematic.

When Eula concludes her book, she invites us to envision our social body as a garden. For her, when we adopt this metaphor, we begin to see how "immunity is a shared space —a garden we tend together."[39] Eula's perspective inspires me because of the biblical significance of gardens, permeating the first and final pages of scripture, from Eden to the New Jerusalem. Even the resurrected Lord, outside the empty tomb, is supposed by Mary Magdalene to be a gardener.[40] In scripture,

---

[36] In the following section, I will be pulling from a previous essay I wrote entitled "On Immunity: Tending the Garden of Public Health" in Dr. Gregg Okesson's class MS 627: Public Theology for Global Development at Asbury Theological Seminary in the fall of 2019.

[37] Eula uses the language of social immunity interchangeably with the language of "herd immunity."

[38] Social immunity is another term for "herd immunity."

[39] Eula Biss, *On Immunity: An Inoculation* (Minneapolis, MI: Graywolf Press, 2014), 163.

[40] On this G.K. Chesterton writes, "On the third day the friends of Christ coming at day-break to the place found the grave empty and the stone rolled away. In varying ways, they realized the new wonder; the world had died in the night. What they were looking at was the first day of a new creation, with a new heaven and a new earth; and in a semblance of a gardener God walked again in the garden, not in the cool of the

the garden is a symbolic representation of creation and new creation. It is a picture that yields fruitful for Christians wanting to develop a more robust theology of public health and immunization.

Long before tending a garden was evidence of human civilization or employed as a metaphor for human interdependence, it was a mark of humanity's created design. Jewish scripture begins with the story of creation. The Creator God transforms the chaos of the cosmos into a habitable order. The heavens are filled with stars. The sea is brimming with fish. The sky has its birds, and the earth its creatures. The pinnacle of these creatures are human beings, men and women, who collectively bear the image of their Creator God (Gen. 1:26).

One way human beings mirror their Creator to the world is that they rule on behalf of God. The language used in Genesis is of "dominion" over God's creation (Gen. 1:28).[41] Dominion, in the Hebrew scriptures, is not about domination; rather, it is a call to be faithful stewards of God's good creation. Part of the way humanity embodies this vocation of stewardship is tending and keeping the garden God placed them in. What makes a garden unique is that it is a physical manifestation of bringing habitable order out of the chaos of nature. Tending the garden is intended as a parallel for the work of God's creation. As the Old Testament scholar John Walton writes, "These roles bring humanity into partnership with God as continuing his creative work of bringing order."[42] In summary, Genesis 1 is about the good world God created, and Genesis 2 is about humanity's vocation to steward that good world with and on behalf of God. This is what the doctrine of creation is all about.

Now, as we know, the story takes a dramatic turn with the fall of humanity in Genesis 3. The fall produces the disintegration of

---

evening, but in the dawn." — G.K. Chesterton, *The Everlasting Man* (Oxford City Press, 2011), 138.

[41] Walter Brueggemann writes, "The human person in the image of God, like the image of a sovereign on a coin, is a representative and regent who represents the sovereign in the midst of all other subjects where the subject is not directly and personally present. Thus, the human person is entrusted with 'dominion' (Gen. 1:28; Ps. 8:5-8)." Walter Brueggemann, *Theology of the Old Testament: Testimony, Dispute, Advocacy* (Minneapolis, MN: Fortress Press, 1997), 450.

[42] John Walton, *Old Testament Theology for Christians: From Ancient Context to Enduring Belief* (Downers Grove, IL: InterVarsity Press, 2017), 86-87.

human relationship. Violence and greed become defining characteristics of human life. The fall also leads to the disordering of God's world. Humanity is not only afflicted by its own sin and injustice but also suffers at the hands of a chaotic, fallen world. It is here in scripture where the whole drama of redemption begins. Through the story of Israel and the story of Jesus, God enacts a plan to bring salvation to the world.[43]

As theologians have pointed out, the Greek word for salvation (σῴζω) includes the idea of healing within it.[44] God's plan of salvation is about bringing healing to humanity's relationship with God, one another, and to creation. At the end of salvation history in the book of Revelation, the New Jerusalem descends from heaven. Planted in this garden-city, flowing with water and blossoming with all kind of fruits, is the tree of life that contains leaves for "the healing of the nations," (Rev. 22:17). It is a picture of a renewed Eden and a renewed humanity. This is salvation.

Recovering a more robust doctrine of creation and new creation is vital for evangelical Christians to engage issues related to public health like immunization. Howard A. Snyder has written extensively on the need for this recovery in his book *Salvation Means Creation Healed*.[45] I propose three main reasons why evangelicals need to recapture a more robust doctrine of creation and new creation. First, the doctrine of creation informs how we should think of institutions —from the government to the medical community. While human institutions are stained by the fall, they also reflect humanity's divine vocation to steward creation and bring forth order and life. While we should not have a naïve optimism about human institutions that ignores the seriousness of the fall, we should also not embrace an exaggerated cynicism about human institutions that ignores the reality of our created design. In fact, when politicians and pediatricians do their jobs with integrity and excellence, they participate in God's new creation in the world.

---

[43] N.T. Wright uses the language of "story of Israel" and "story of Jesus" as a shorthand for the whole redemptive drama — N.T. Wright, *Simply Good News: Why the Gospel is News and What Makes It Good* (New York, NY: Harper One Publishers, 2015).

[44] Gregg A. Okesson, "Public Theology for Global Development: A Case Study Dealing with 'Health' in Africa," *The Asbury Journal* 67 (2012): 56-76.

[45] Howard A. Snyder, *Salvation Means Creation Healed: The Ecology of Sin and Grace: Overcoming the Divorce between Earth and Heaven* (Eugene, OR: Cascade Books, 2011), 52-55.

Second, the doctrines of creation and new creation reminds us that sickness and disease are not part of God's intention for the world. They are part of the fallen world that has been "subjected to futility" (Rom. 8:20). One reason vaccine opposition exists is because of a theological confusion between the doctrine of creation and doctrine of the fall. Christians that oppose vaccinations often see them as byproducts of our fallen world where corrupt, economic interests prioritize financial profit over and against the well-being of humanity. Often their medical substitutes for vaccines are naturopathic prescriptions as well (e.g., vitamin A as a substitute for the MMR vaccine, etc.), where nature is used to heal corrupted humanity. The problem is that the evidence better supports the opposite theologically as it pertains to immunization. The natural world is the source of disease, inflicting humanity with great suffering and death. In response to the fallen nature of the world, humanity has created medical technologies that not only protect people from these diseases but has also led to eradication of disease. By engaging in such medical work, we mirror the image of God — innovating, advancing life, and bringing order to the chaos of the world.

Third, the doctrine of new creation gives the church a vision for actively participating with God as an effective agent of healing in the world. Our call to steward "public health" goes beyond our call "to love our neighbors as ourselves," (Mt. 22:36-40). Stewarding public health is part of what it means to bring about God's new creation in the world and to show God's love for his creation. While sickness and disease will persist until Christ brings the kingdom of God in fullness at the end of the age, humanity has the opportunity to continue eradicating diseases, ameliorating human suffering, and fostering human flourishing before Christ returns. I particularly love what N.T. Wright says about this in *Surprised by Hope*:

> What we do in the Lord is "not in vain," and that is the mandate we need for every act of justice and mercy, every program of ecology, every effort to reflect God's wise stewardly image into his creation. In the new creation the ancient human mandate to look after the garden is dramatically reaffirmed, as John hints in his resurrection story, where Mary supposes Jesus is the gardener. The resurrection of Jesus is the reaffirmation of the goodness of creation, and the gift of the Spirit is there

to make us the fully human beings we were supposed to be, precisely so that we can fulfill that mandate at last.[46]

Through these words, we are reminded that our labors for 'public health' are not in vain. Such labors are, indeed, proleptic signposts of what is coming in fulness when Christ comes again.

How Evangelical Churches Can Respond to Growing Vaccine Hesitancy & Help Steward Public Health

So how can American evangelical churches respond to the issue of growing vaccine hesitancy? First, Christian ministers must own their responsibility to safeguard the physical health of their congregants. John Wesley's example is helpful on this issue. Randy L. Maddox reminds us that "offering health advice and care was a central dimension of Wesley's ministry and his model for the ministry of early Methodists."[47] This is evidenced by Wesley's book *Primitive Physick* on wellness advice, which was one of the most popular books in England during the eighteenth century. Healthcare has become exceedingly more professionalized since Wesley's day. Nonetheless, it is challenging to envision Wesley *not* publicly addressing an issue like vaccine hesitancy today, with its significant medical and ethical implications.

Second, I would encourage evangelical churches to think through ways they can reinforce healthy forms of institutional trust, specifically as it pertains to the medical community. Are churches honoring healthcare workers in the faith community — from doctors to nurses to researchers? Are we discipling our congregants to think about the medical industry as a means of fulfilling humanity's creation mandate and bringing about new creation? An admirable thing about Wesley was his refusal to pit divine healing and medical healing against each other.[48] Not pitting the two is particularly necessary within charismatic evangelical churches.

---

[46] N.T. Wright, *Surprised by Hope: Rethinking Heaven, the Resurrection, and the Mission of the Church* (New York, NY: Harper Collins Publishers, 2008), 210-11.

[47] Randy L. Maddox, "Reclaiming the Eccentric Parent: Methodist Reception of John Wesley's Interest in Medicine," In *Inward and Outward Health: John Wesley's Holistic Concept of Medical Science, the Environment, and Holy Living*. Edited by Deborah Madden (London: Epworth, 2008),15-50.

[48] Ibid., 40.

While there is much talk about "health" today, the word "health" tends to refer to physical realities and "healing" tends to refer to supernatural ones. Churches can make an intentional effort to apply the language of healing to healthcare functions, thereby affirming the holistic value, both physical and spiritual, of medical workers in the faith community.

Third, evangelical churches should consider the ways they can practically protect their communities from potential outbreaks and help safeguard public health. Many churches may want to leave this up to the regulations of the state government and the public school systems. That will surely be more convenient for families within the faith community that are vaccine hesitant or refuse vaccines. Nonetheless, churches may want to be preventative in their approach. A reasonable policy for churches to adopt is the requirement of vaccinations for their Sunday morning children's program, with the exceptions of medical exemption or first-time visitors. This change would involve a partnership between church leadership and medical professionals within the congregation to create and implement ethical church policies related to public health. While requiring children's vaccinations could come with initial complications, it would offer additional support to the state as well as the school systems that are fulfilling such public health functions. Practical approaches like these also model to church families who affirm vaccines that church leadership values their health and safety.

Since most states still allow for religious exemptions related to public school attendance, adopting church policies that require vaccinations for a children's program might be too stringent for some churches at this juncture. That being said, a supplemental practice that can reinforce those policies is releasing an official statement expressing why the church encourages vaccinations. In addition to this, pastors can also consider preaching on Christian responsibility to care for public health, including immunization. Churches should be warned that parents ideologically opposed to vaccinations will rarely be persuaded by such statements. However, parents that are vaccine hesitant are likely to heed such encouragements from their pastor or church staff.

Conclusion

In summary, vaccine hesitancy is a primary global health concern. A major impetus for growing vaccine hesitancy is diminishing confidence in the safety of vaccines and the competence of health professionals. As it pertains to the American evangelical community, there is not a significant connection between evangelical beliefs and growing vaccine hesitancy. Nonetheless, since there is a general trend of vaccine hesitancy within American evangelical communities, it is necessary for evangelical churches to wrestle through how they can better steward public health related to immunization.

In the second section of this essay, I proposed that the doctrines of creation and new creation are helpful for framing a theology of public health and immunization. The doctrine of creation helps inform us that when humans cultivate, create, and bring order to the world, they are fulfilling their vocation to bear God's image. Because of the fall, sin and disease entered the world. Nonetheless, through the story of Israel and the story of Jesus, God enacted a plan of salvation, which is connected to the reality of healing. I applied this to the area of public health and maintained that immunization is not only an area where humanity is fulfilling its creation mandate but also is a way we are participating in God's new creation. In other words, stewarding public health is an eschatological, kingdom reality.

In my final section, I attempted to blend this eschatological vision with an ecclesiological praxis. What exactly does it look like for evangelical churches to be positive agents of public health? More specifically, what does it look like for the church to properly respond to the issue of vaccine hesitancy growing in this country? First, I argued that Christian ministers can learn from John Wesley's example in caring for the physical health of their congregants. Second, I encouraged churches to foster healthy trust in the medical community by valuing health professionals within the church and framing their service as furthering God's healing in the world. Last, I discussed how churches can take practical steps to reinforce social and ethical norms related to vaccination — actions that range from requiring vaccinations for their Sunday morning children's program to putting out a church statement encouraging parents to vaccinate their children.

All in all, the crucial invitation, as Eula Biss so eloquently writes, is to see how "Immunity is a shared space — a garden we tend together." And though it may not feel this way, Jesus is with us as the gardener. A garden is where it all began, and a garden is where it is all going. Christ is beckoning his church to tend the garden of the world, so we can be like leaves from the tree of life that are "for the healing of the nations."

Work Cited

Armstrong, Katrina, Abigail Rose, et al. "Distrust of the Health Care System and Self-Reported Health in the United States." *The Journal of General Internal Medicine* 2006: 292-297. https://www.ncbi.nlm.nih.gov/pmc/articles/PMC1484714/pdf/jgi021-0292.pdf.

Augustine. *Confessions*. New York, NY: Oxford University Press, 2008.

Biss, Eula. *On Immunity: An Inoculation*. Minneapolis, MI: Graywolf Press, 2014.

Booth, Michael. "Colorado parents rank second in nation for vaccine refusals." *The Denver Post*. November 28, 2011. https://www.denverpost.com/2011/11/28/colorado-parents-rank second-in-nation-for-vaccine-refusals/.

Boseley, Sarah. "Andrew Wakefield found 'irresponsible' by GMC over MMR vaccine scare." *The Guardian*. January 28, 2010. https://www.theguardian.com/society/2010/jan/28/andrew-wakefield-mmr-vaccine.

Brueggemann, Walter. *Theology of the Old Testament: Testimony, Dispute, Advocacy*. Minneapolis, MN: Fortress Press, 1997.

Burki, Tahla. "Vaccine Misinformation and Social Media." *The Lancet Digital Health*. Volume 1, Issue 6 (October 01, 2019). https://doi.org/10.1016/S2589-7500(19)30136-0.

Chesterton, G.K. *The Everlasting Man*. Oxford City Press, 2011.

George Washington University Public Health Online. "A History of Measles in the United States." March 9, 2019. https://publichealthonline.gwu.edu/blog/measles-history-in-the-united-states/.

Geoghegan Sarah, O'Callagan, Kevin P, and Paul Offit. "Vaccine Safety: Myths and Misinformation." *Frontiers. Microbiology*

Volume 11, Article 372 (2020): 1-7. https://doi.org/10.3389/fmicb.2020.00372.

Grabenstein, J. D., et al. "What the World's religions teach, applied to vaccines and immune globulins." *Vaccine.* Volume 31, issue 16 (2013): 2011-2023. https://doi.org/10.1016/j.vaccine.2013.02.026.

Harvard Library: Office for Scholarly Communication. "Mandatory Vaccination: Why We Still Got to Get Folks to Take Their Shot." 2006. http://nrs.harvard.edu/ur3:HUL.InstRepos:8852146

Herlihy, Stacy Metzinger and E. Allison Hagood. *Your Baby's Best Shot: Why Vaccines are Safe and Save Lives.* Lanham, MD: Rowman & Littlefield Publishers, 2012.

Hviid, A., Hansen, J. V., Frisch, M., et al "Measles, Mumps, Rubella Vaccination and Autism: A Nationwide Cohort Study." *Annals of Internal Medicine.* 2019; 170; 513-520. https://doi.org/10.7326/M18-2101.

Idler, Ellen L. *Religion as Social Determinant of Public Health.* New York, NY: Oxford University Press, 2014.

Kim, Sebastian. "Editorial." *International Journal of Public Theology.* Vol. 2 (2017): 135-139. https://doi.org/10.1163/15697320-12341490.

Lewis, C.S. *The Problem of Pain.* San Francisco, CA: Harper Collins, 1940.

MacDonald, Noni E. "Vaccine Hesitancy: Definition, Scope and Determinants." *Vaccine.* Vol. 33 (2015): 4161–64. http://doi.org/10.1016/j.vaccine.2015.04.036.

Maddox, Randy L. "Reclaiming the Eccentric Parent: Methodist Reception of John Wesley's Interest in Medicine." In *"Inward and Outward Health": John Wesley's Holistic Concept of Medical Science, the Environment, and Holy Living,* 15–50. Edited by Deborah Madden. London: Epworth, 2008.

Mnookin, Seth. *The Panic Virus: A True Story of Medicine, Science, and Fear.* New York, NY: Simon & Schuster, 2011.

Offit, Paul A. *Deadly Choices: How the Anti-Vaccine Movement Threatens Us All.* New York, NY: Basic Books, 2011.

———. *Bad Faith: When Religious Belief Undermines Modern Medicine.* New York, NY: Basic Books, 2015.

Okesson, Gregg A. "Public Theology for Global Development: A Case Study Dealing with 'Health' in Africa." *The Asbury Journal.* Vol. 67 (2012): 56-76.

Olive J. K., Hotez, P. J., Damania, A., Nolan, M.S. "The state of the antivaccine movement in the United States: A focused examination of nonmedical exemptions in states and counties.:" *PLOS Medicine.* Vol. 15 (2018): e1002578. https://doi.org/10.1371/journal.pmed.1002578.

Patel, M., Lee, A.D., Clemmons, N.S., et al. "National Update on Measles Cases and Outbreaks- United States, January 1 – October 1, 2019." *Morbidity and Mortality Report.* Vol. 68 (2019): 893-896 (2019). https://www.cdc.gov/mmwr/volumes/68/wr/pdfs/mm6840e2-H.pdf

Pelčić, G., Karačić, S., Mikirtichan, G.L., et al. "Religious exception for vaccination or religious excuses for avoiding vaccination." *Croatian Medical Journal.* Vol 57 (2016): 516–521. https://www.ncbi.nlm.nih.gov/pmc/articles/PMC5141457/

Pew Research Center. "Key Findings about Americans' declining trust in government and each other." Pew Research. July 22, 2019. https://www.pewresearch.org/facttank/2019/07/22/key-findings-about-americans declining-trust-in-government-and-eachother/

———. "Public Opinions about childhood vaccines for measles, mumps, and rubella." Pew Research. February 2, 2017. https://www.pewresearch.org/science/2017/02/02/public-opinion-about-childhoodvaccines-for-measles-mumps-and-rubella/

Snyder, Howard A. *Salvation Means Creation Healed: The Ecology of Sin and Grace: Overcoming the Divorce between Earth and Heaven.* Eugene, OR: Cascade Books, 2011.

Sweet, Leonard I. *Health and Medicine in the Evangelical Tradition: Not by Might nor Power.* Valley Forge, PA: Trinity Press International, 1994.

Wakefield, A. J., et al. "Ileal-Lymphoid-Nodular Hyperplasia, Non-Specific Colitis, and Pervasive Developmental Disorder in Children." *The Lancet.* Vol. 351 (February 28, 1998): 647–41. https://www.thelancet.com/action/showPdf?pii=S0140-6736(97)11096-0.

Walton, John. *Old Testament Theology for Christians: From Ancient Context to Enduring Belief.* Downers Grove, IL: InterVarsity Press, 2017.

Williams, J. T. B., Rice, J, Cox-Martin M, et al. "Religious Vaccine Exemptions in Kindergartners: 2011-2018." Pediatrics volume 144 (2019): e20192710. https://pediatrics.aappublications.org/content/pediatrics/144/6/e20192710.full.pdf

World Health Organization. "Ten Threats to Global Health in 2019." 2019. https://www.who.int/emergencies/ten-threats-to-global-health-in-2019.

Wright, N.T. *Surprised by Hope: Rethinking Heaven, the Resurrection, and the Mission of the Church.* New York, NY: Harper Collins Publishers, 2008.

———. *Simply Good News: Why the Gospel is News and What Makes It Good.* New York, NY: Harper One Publishers, 2015.

Chapter 8

"I Was Suicidal And You Welcomed Me": Framing Suicide Prevention In Mongolia Through The Lens Of Christian Hospitality

Michael S. Bennett[1]

Abstract

Across the globe, suicidality is an observed behavior recognized by the World Health Organization as devastating and therefore an international priority. However, despite the preventable nature of suicide and the WHO's call for national suicide prevention programs to be developed in every country, a number of countries including Mongolia have yet to develop a comprehensive program that operates the suicide prevention plan at the national level. Drawing inspiration from Mongolia's traditions of hospitality and taking seriously the role of the Church within Mongolia's public (and very secular) sphere, action steps informed through the lens of Christian hospitality are offered as a possible starting place for the actual conceptualization of a national prevention plan in which the Church is proactively engaged. By creating safe spaces through suitable infrastructures, valuing the inner dimension of people's lives, and facilitating shared responsibilities, the Mongolian Church is able to step into the public sphere as a proactive contributor and participant in preventing suicide in Mongolia.

---

[1] Michael S. Bennett is presently an Intercultural Studies Ph.D. student at Asbury Theological Seminary studying the intersections of trauma studies, counseling, cultural and cognitive anthropology, theology, and Christian mission. Michael formerly obtained a Master of Divinity and a Master's in Clinical Mental Health Counseling from Pentecostal Theological Seminary. He also works as a trauma-informed mental health clinician. Michael enthusiastically welcomes dialogue and partnership with anyone interested/working in these areas, especially theories to understanding trauma through the lenses of global cultures: mbennet6@live.com.

"For I was [*suicidal*] and you welcomed me," *Jesus to his disciples*.[2]

As a result of an escalation of adolescent suicides in Mongolia at an alarming five-fold increase,[3] UNICEF has declared an urgent need for cross-sector cooperation for developing an effective and comprehensive national suicide prevention strategy.[4] In conjunction with their call to action, UNICEF implemented the training of almost 100 professionals across governmental, medical, or academic environments.[5] National suicide prevention programs aim to both reduce suicide mortality rates through the nation-wide implementation of robust strategies and to combat the stigma associated with suicide in order that those at-risk feel less discouraged from seeking professional help. Edwin S. Shneidman rightly assesses the character of such programs as being both scientific and moral.[6,7] Research into the history of Mongolia's suicide mortality reveals stigma against those at-risk who either communicate the presence of suicidal thoughts or have acted with suicidal behaviors. While there is evidence that Mongolia has at various times addressed this issue, research indicates that a comprehensive program has yet to be effectively developed and implemented.

In this paper, the impact of suicide in Mongolia will be demonstrated as requiring urgent response in the form of suicide

---

[2] While this paper will not explore the particular reference of Matthew 25:31-40 and its inherent theme of hospitality ethics, I am intentionally titling the paper with such a reference to directly frame the paper within a discussion of the Christian ethics of hospitality and its role in responding to persistent suicidality within the context of Mongolia.

[3] UNICEF, "Adolescents," *UNICEF Mongolia*, n.d., https://www.unicef.org/mongolia/adolescents.

[4] Zetty Brake, "Adolescents Need More Mental Health Services," UNICEF Mongolia (blog), (October 9, 2015), http://unicefmongolia.blogspot.com/2015/10/adolescents-need-more-mental-health.html.

[5] Ibid.

[6] Edwin S. Shneidman, "The National Suicide Prevention Program," in *Organizing the Community to Prevent Suicide* (Springfield, IL: Charles C Thomas Books, 1971), 19.

[7] Various disciplines of science have contributed to the formation of three particular approaches of suicide prevention programs: the public health model, the operational model, and the injury control model. While helpful for understanding the construction of suicide prevention programs, the scope of this paper limits further detail, so consider Granello & Granello's text for deeper insights. Darcy Haag Granello and Paul F. Granello, *Suicide: An Essential Guide for Helping Professionals and Educators* (Boston, MA: Pearson Education, Inc., 2007), 173.

prevention. While there is need to consider at depth the role of the Mongolian government in providing such a program and how it could move forward in developing and implementing it, this paper will instead concentrate on the role of the Mongolian Church in decreasing suicidality within their communities. Christopher Tadman-Robins argues why believers should be compassionate towards those at-risk and involve themselves in suicide prevention initiations: "[W]e believe in God's special concern for the weak and the oppressed, and in the context of those driven to self-destruction, we must include the abused, lonely and the marginalized in society, the poor, troubled and those with reduced future prospects."[8] Supporting this view, I propose that the Mongolian church's involvement should emulate God's hospitality towards humanity and concurrently adopt Jesuit priest Georg Sporschill's model of mission to respond to Mongolia's problem of suicide in culturally-appropriate methods.

Part I- Socio-Cultural Meanings of Issue

Global Impact of Suicide

In 2013, the World Health Organization (WHO) released its Mental Health Action Plan 2013-2020 containing four major objectives to improving global wellbeing, particularly by assessing the present global mental health status for areas of deficit. This resulted from the 65th World Health Assembly's determination in May 2012 that mental disorders presented an enormous global burden that necessitated attention and resolution.[9] Self-identified by the Director-General as "ambitious," the plan was written to address severe deficits in global mental health, which the document overviews, and challenges member-countries of the WHO to respond by employing the plan's suggestions.[10] The document describes mental health disorders, specifically major depression and schizophrenia, as greatly increasing the risk of disability and premature mortality, including death by suicide which is the "second

---

[8] Christopher Tadman-Robins, *Suicide: The Last Taboo* (Bristol, IN: Wyndham Hall Press, 2001), 89.
[9] World Health Organization, *Mental Health Action Plan 2013-2020* (Geneva, Switzerland, 2013), 6, https://apps.who.int/iris/bitstream/handle/10665/89966/9789241506021_eng.pdf?sequence=1.
[10] WHO, *MHAP 2013-2020*, 5.

most common cause of death among young people worldwide."[11] A 2018 WHO document reported a trend outlining how those with mental disorders involving psychosis may die up to 20 years earlier than mentally healthy individuals.[12] Scholars agree that while some mental health disorders often increase one's proclivity towards suicidal ideation and behaviors, the reality of this phenomenon's etiology, or causation, is also extremely complex. This complexity of the etiology of suicidality stems from compounding factors such as societal systems, community and relationship dynamics, and the individual acute stressors[13] that increase risk for suicide.[14] Such a reality is disconcerting when viewed alongside the global mortality rate of 800,000 deaths per year with at least 20 attempted suicides per single successful suicide and at least six persons directly affected by the suicide, the overwhelming impact (96,000,000 people affected) is shocking.[15] When understood that the presence of suicidal history among family and friends increases one's own risk towards distress, mental disorders, and suicidality and causes

---

[11] WHO, *MHAP 2013-2020*, 7. Additionally, certain characteristics have been found by S. Davaasambuu et al. to be commonly associated with suicidality among Mongolian adolescents: "being female, feeling lonely and worried, smoking cigarettes, drinking alcohol, and having fights at school." The research of Lee et al. supports this finding and encourages strategies to be taught that can be implemented in both home and school environments to improve the psychological distress that often accompanies suicidality. Sarantsetseg Davaasambuu et al., "Suicidal Plans and Attempts Among Adolescents in Mongolia: Urban Versus Rural Differences," *Crisis* 38, no. 5 (September 2017): 330–43, https://doi.org/10.1027/0227-5910/a000447. Heeyoung Lee et al., "Psychological Distress among Adolescents in Laos, Mongolia, Nepal, and Sri Lanka," *Asian Nursing Research* 13, no. 2 (May 2019): 147–53, https://doi.org/10.1016/j.anr.2019.04.001, 148.

[12] WHO, *Mental Health Gap Action Programme Operations Manual* (Geneva, Switzerland, 2018), 66, https://apps.who.int/iris/bitstream/handle/10665/275386/9789241514811-eng.pdf?ua=1.

[13] The WHO provides examples of societal, community/relational, and individual challenges that may comprise one's unique etiology. *Preventing Suicide: A Global Imperative* (Geneva, Switzerland: WHO Press, 2014), 10, https://apps.who.int/iris/bitstream/handle/10665/131056/9789241564878_eng.pdf;jsessionid=E77C15184CAA6E0219AB09C280E403F0?sequence=8.

[14] Granello and Granello, *Suicide*, 172. Rory C. O'Conner and Jane Pirkis, eds., "Suicide in Asia: Epidemiology, Risk Factors, and Prevention," in *The International Handbook of Suicide Prevention*, 2nd Edition (West Sussex, UK: John Wiley & Sons, Ltd., 2016), 529.

[15] WHO, *Preventing Suicide*, 13. Khan et al. provides the statistic that at least six people are affected by the successful or attempted suicides. O'Conner and Pirkis, "Suicide in Asia: Epidemiology, Risk Factors, and Prevention," 525.

deleterious effects on society, the impact is felt throughout all levels of society thereby requiring a systems approach to suicide prevention that increases protective factors at the federal, local, and individual levels. The WHO proposed that all member-countries create and employ national suicide prevention strategies, focusing especially on vulnerable groups (minorities, LGBT+, youth, etc.) within their societies, to accomplish by 2020 a 10% decrease in suicide mortality.[16]

Suicide Mortality in Mongolia

Asia has a history of not representing an accurate number of suicide occurrences resulting from unreliable surveillance, misattributing cause of death, or failure to report due to socioreligious factors (e.g. suicide is criminalized in a number of Islamic countries); and, in 2003 the WHO discovered at least 19 countries not reporting any occurrences which implies that Asia's contribution of 60% of suicides to the global rate is likely higher than what is reported.[17] Records of Mongolia's suicide mortality rate appear in different documents under both the suicide rate of 13.00 (2016) and the age-standardized rate 13.3 (2018).[18] Peng Qin et al. observed that between 2008 and 2015, Mongolia experienced a "waterfall pattern" drop in mortality rate and credited this to Mongolia implementing a policy prohibiting select pesticides after discovering their popular use in suicide-by-poisoning.[19] While this

---

[16] WHO, *MHAP 2013-2020*, 9, 17, 22.

[17] O'Conner and Pirkis, "Suicide in Asia: Epidemiology, Risk Factors, and Prevention," 525-526.

[18] Though there is also a conflicting report posted to the Sustainable Development Goals of Mongolia website that provides different rates (unlabeled) for both years as being 14.9 (2016) and 14.1 (2018), so it is uncertain if these were crude or standardized rates. Additionally, there is no indication as to where the data originated to create the suicide mortality rate graphs. Government of Mongolia, "Goal 3. Good Health and Well-Being for People," *Sustainable Development Goals of Mongolia*, 2019, http://www.sdg.gov.mn/Goal/?id=3. World Bank, "Mongolia Suicide Rate 2000-2019," Macrotrends, https://www.macrotrends.net/countries/MNG/mongolia/suicide-rate; WHO, "Suicide Rate Estimates, Age-Standardized, Estimates by Country," *Global Health Observatory Data Repository* (Western Pacific Region), July 17, 2018, http://apps.who.int/gho/data/node.main-wpro.MHSUICIDEASDR?lang=en.

[19] Suicide-by-hanging was identified along with suicide-by-poisoning as the top two methods of choice in Mongolia. Limiting access to a preferred method was suggested by WHO as being effective in decreasing suicides. Peng Qin et al., "The Waterfall Pattern of Suicide Mortality in Inner Mongolia for 2008– 2015," *Journal of*

data reveals the presence, the methods, and the precursors of complex stressors provoking suicides in Mongolia, the data does not reveal the Mongolian perception of suicide. For this reason, I am utilizing Émile Durkheim's studies in suicidology to provide insight for hypothesizing a possible perception that may reflect Mongolian sociocultural values.

In his text *Suicide: A Study in Sociology*, Durkheim offers four classifications of suicide that are based on sociocultural value-based perceptions: egoistic, altruistic, anomic, and fatalistic.[20,21] Table 1 above provides a summary description of Durkheim's classifications which are grouped according to their shared influencing social power as well as briefly offering examples which are explained below. In the discussion below, the classifications of suicide will be discussed according to their influencing social power, so egoistic and altruistic will be considered alongside each other while anomic and fatalistic are done likewise.

Egoistic suicide relates to high influence from the social power of individualism resulting in the person's isolation from others within their community thereby providing the "space" in which one would experience greater freedoms towards suicide. Alternatively, altruistic suicide occurs when one is highly influenced by their social obligations and expectations stemming from being centered to the community of origin as opposed to being highly individualized. Instead of comparing egoistic suicide to altruistic suicide, Ronald W. Maris reflectively compares the influential limitations of egoistic suicide to the limitations of anomic stating that "egoism [is] more a failure of interpersonal restraints and anomic as failure of normative restraints."[22] With this comparison based on "the failure of restraints" being centered upon the interpersonal and social, Maris suggests that Classical Western Christian positions against suicide reveal the perception that suicide results from a person

---

Affective Disorders 256, no. 1 (September 1, 2019): 331–36, https://doi.org/10.1016/j.jad.2019.05.057.

[20] Emile Durkheim, *Suicide: A Study in Sociology* (USA: The Free Press, 1951), 152-276.

[21] "Fatalistic Suicide," in *APA Dictionary of Psychology* (American Psychological Association, 2018), https://dictionary.apa.org/fatalistic-suicide.

[22] Ronald W. Maris, *Pathways to Suicide: A Survey of Self-Destructive Behaviors* (Baltimore, MD: The Johns Hopkins University Press, 1981), 239.

Classifications of Suicide

Table 1: Descriptions & Examples of Suicide as Motivated by Social Forces			
Forces	Classification	*Description*	*Examples*
Individualism	*Egoistic*	Highly individualistic, centered upon the loss/success of the individual's values, and relating to perceived/real personal failures as overwhelmingly unresolvable.	"Free Inquiry" Protestants
Individualism	*Altruistic*	Less individualistic, more centered upon social obligations/ expectations, and relating to the heroic fulfillment of duty; is perceived honorably within the community of origin.	"Kamikaze" pilots of World War II; Trobriand Islander who commits incest
Regulation	*Anomic*	Less individualistic, more centered upon social obligations/ expectations, and relating to the heroic fulfillment of duty; is perceived honorably within the community of origin.	Coast Salish & Kwakwaka'wakw Nations of Canada
Regulation	*Fatalistic*	Stemming from excessive regulation; relating to the over-regulation of social values/ expectations (typically morality-based) which oppress the hopes, passions, or futures of the individuals within such societies or communities.	Young Immigrant Women in the Netherlands of Turkish, Moroccan, & South Asian Origin

such as "thou shall not kill."[23] Durkheim explains that the presence of "free inquiry" within the Protestant tradition is compatible with the becoming too individualized that they diverge from not only their community but so also their faith and religious commandments, high influences of individualism upon Protestants while the opposite of free inquiry, e.g. staunch observance of church teachings and practices, is understood within Roman Catholicism due to the greater emphasis upon adherence to orthodoxy and orthopraxy.

Altruistic suicide, being interpreted as acts of honor and obligation when the individual experiences a situation in which the alternative brings dishonor to their community of origin, is represented in the "heroic" suicides of Kamikaze pilots in World War II as well as the "dutiful" suicides of the incestuous Trobriand Islander who must return honor to their family and cultural system.[24]

Maris earlier indicated that anomic suicide can be a result of normative restraints failing, which points out a dysfunction in the regulation of what is normative. So, for instance, normative restraints are utilized legally within international relations to decrease a government's ability to wage war according to their own discretion. Historically, the lack of normative restraints within international relations created space for imperialism and colonization to occur leading to the detriment and destruction of peoples, cultures, and lands. So, then, an example of anomic suicide can be found in the provocation of individuals to suicidality as a result of colonialism in the communities of the Coast Salish and Kwakwaka'wakw Nations in Canada.[25] These communities believe that a restoration of the pre-colonial social norms is the best prevention to suicide in their context. The opposite of anomic suicide is fatalistic suicide, which finds its etiology within the overly regulated constraints of a system upon the individuals within the system, particularly those individuals who feel their hopes, passions, futures, and lives are constricted by the regulation of their system. While an unregulated or dysregulated system creates spaces where threats enter

---

[23] Tadman-Robins, *Suicide*, 86-87.
[24] Maris, *Pathways to Suicide*, 239-240.
[25] Darien Thira, "Aboriginal Youth Suicide Prevention: A Post-Colonial Community-Based Approach," *International Journal of Child, Youth and Family Studies* 5, no. 1 (2014): 158–79, https://doi.org/10.18357/ijcyfs.thirad.512014, 162-165.

and endanger that system, overly regulated systems themselves are perceived as the danger. An example of fatalistic suicide then may be found in the suicidal behavior of young immigrant women of South Asian, Turkish, and Moroccan origin who live in the Netherlands.[26]

However, it would seem that Durkheim's classifications are not so easily applied, but instead there are possibilities of suicide etiology stemming from multiple classifications. The behaviors of a human are rarely one-dimensional but are influenced by multiple factors, so it would be reasonable for the causation of an individual's suicidal behavior to include more than one reason between the social powers of individualism and regulation. In fact, in a study of Indigenous communities in rural Alaska, it was discovered that there was no one meaning officially attributed to the behavior but instead multiple meanings were attributed and held simultaneously within the community.[27] Furthermore, there is also the influence of globalization on societies- the sometimes clashing and sometimes harmonious coexisting of global elements, values and experiences- bringing about both positive and negative changes which influence people in a variety of ways.

When considering the sociocultural values and rationale utilized by Mongolians to understand suicidal behavior, is there evidence of what the act of suicide means for Mongolians? And does Durkheim's classification of suicidal types provide insight to understanding Mongolian perspectives? Or is there too little information provided about Mongolian suicides that elicit more robust understandings within this cultural context? For example, such evidence might be found in published psychological autopsies (PA) that trace and analyze the deceased's behaviors, living environment, belongings and interview friends and family and could be used to theorize the deceased's thoughts and motivations leading up to the suicide attempt. From such

---

[26] Diana van Bergen et al., "Suicidal Behaviour of Young Immigrant Women in the Netherlands. Can We Use Durkheim's Concept of 'Fatalistic Suicide' to Explain Their High Incidence of Attempted Suicide?," *Ethnic and Racial Studies* 32, no. 2 (February 2009): 302–22, https://doi.org/10.1080/01419870802315043.

[27] Lisa Wexler, Jennifer White, and Bridie Trainor, "Why an Alternative to Suicide Prevention Gatekeeper Training Is Needed for Rural Indigenous Communities: Presenting an Empowering Community Storytelling Approach," *Critical Public Health* 25, no. 2 (March 15, 2015): 205–17, https://doi.org/10.1080/09581596.2014.904039, 208.

information, profiles of suicide victims may be constructed, studied, compared, and improved to better understand how suicide is understood and used within Mongolia.

Hypothesis about a Mongolian Perception to Suicide

The purpose of this section is to offer consideration into the perception that Mongolians may have towards suicide, because often times perception can be a determining protective or risk factor for suicide. However, I do not mean to conflate all possible perceptions into one type as a true representation, nor do I intend to posit that sociocultural perceptions can be so simple. Just as suicide's etiology is complex, so too are perceptions as cultures within the same region may rely upon unique cultural values (religion, family systems, honor/shame, individualism, etc.) that may not be shared even while the cultures may be neighbors. To support my hypothesis, I am presenting the evidence of spirituality, stigma, and the government's response.[28]

Of the estimated 3,213,000 people living in Mongolia, half are Buddhist while 40% are secular/irreligious, and the remaining 10% being comprised of shamanists, Christians, Jews, and "others."[29] Research of web-based resources uncover a varied mix of Buddhist perceptions towards suicide, ranging from ambivalence and support (because death begets the next reincarnation of life) as well as opposition (because it is "delusional" to believe that suicide resolves the person's suffering and it goes against the precept that all life is an opportunity to pursue healing and growth).[30] While academic sources have not been discovered as to the Mongolian Buddhist perception of suicide, I found a news article from a primary Mongolia news provider that shared the views of individuals randomly selected at the capital city Ulan Bator. Most of the

---

[28] There are most likely more appropriate sociocultural values that may be determinants in perception, and a Mongolian local or expatriate would have the most valid ideas concerning this as opposed to a white American who has never traveled to Mongolia. However, I humbly submit my thoughts and request that they be corrected where they are not valid. Thank you for entering into this discussion with me.

[29] "Mongolia," Online Encyclopaedia, *Encyclopædia Britannica*, August 22, 2019, https://www.britannica.com/place/Mongolia.

[30] Lee Wolfson, "Buddhist Religious Experts View Suicide and Suicide Prevention" (Suicide Prevention Resource Center, 2019), 1-2, https://theactionalliance.org/sites/default/files/2018_buddhist_perspective_final.pdf.

respondents interviewed were Buddhist or nonreligious. Respondents cited issues such as pressure from life stressors, failure to succeed in life, loss of power and freedom, stupidity or lack of intelligence, exposure to abuse from parents, not caring for children, and discarding precious life.[31] These interview responses revealed views towards suicide that reinforce stigmatization, but the idea that one is discarding precious life that was given to them appears to be congruent to Buddhist thought.

In Mongolia, the news article reported very little understanding of suicide, so it may be possible that there is not much consideration about the phenomenon.[32] The Mongolian government gives diminished attention to suicide prevention because it believes suicides are rare and inconsequential to the overall health of the nation. Consequently, I believe that there are no inherent sociocultural values that clearly demonstrate Mongolian life as supporting a perception that promotes altruistic suicide that relates to duty or honor. Instead, it seem more likely that Mongolians may perceive suicide with a mix of Durkheim's other three categories: egoistically with victims diverging from accepted norms; anomically with victims having experienced a detrimental loss of regulated resources or environment upon which they felt dependent; and fatalistically with victims experiencing or perceiving themselves so severely constricted by their society or environment that their hopes, futures, and lives were likewise constricted. A combined view reflecting the elements of egoistic and anomic suicide is reflected in a study on the suicidality of the Meng, Hui, and Han ethnic groups in Inner Mongolia. The Meng chose suicide after disconnecting from their rural cultural roots and adopting urban and materialist life; the two Hui were unreligious instead of Muslim and had relocated from their original homes.[33]

---

[31] Dulguun Bayarsaikhan, "Time to Draw Attention to Teen Suicide," *The UB Posts* (January 13, 2018), http://theubposts.com/time-to-draw-attention-to-teen-suicide/.

[32] S. Davaasambuu et al., "Suicidal Plans and Attempts," 340.

[33] The Han would be an exception, perhaps, as the suicides could have been viewed altruistically out of filial love or sacrifice. Ding Wang, Yu Ting Wang, and Xue Ya Wang, "Suicide in Three Ethnic Groups in Huhhot, Inner Mongolia," *Crisis: The Journal of Crisis Intervention and Suicide Prevention* 18, no. 3 (1997): 112–14, https://doi.org/10.1027/0227-5910.18.3.112, 113.

There may be some level of credence to a fatalistic view based upon significant predictors observed within Mongolian adolescents.[34] In their study, Davaasambuu et al. identified that an Mongolian adolescent "feeling worried" is the strongest predictor with the risky behaviors of drinking alcohol, smoking cigarettes, fighting at school, and missing classes as significant predictors along with the experience of being bullied as also being a significant predictor.[35] If one were to consider through a "trauma-informed" lens these significant predictors which suggest a higher probability of suicidality,[36] one could argue that Trauma[37] terrorizes, constricts, and immobilizes adolescents living within a system (whether nuclear family system, broader community, or their host society) that enables singular or chronic traumatic events to harm adolescents. Thus, from such a lens, the significant factors identified by Davaasambuu et al. suggest the presence of a fatalistic (or a mixed view combining fatalism) perspective of suicide which understands the choice to die-by-suicide as one granting freedom from the horrifying restrictions of a traumatizing system which cuts off adolescents from their hopes and ideal futures.

However, any understanding of egoist, anomic, fatalistic, or combined view of suicide in Mongolia is based on limited resources. I would encourage further applied research to ascertain this aspect of Mongolian suicidality. Such findings would provide beneficial

---

[34] "Significant Predictors" should be understood as "variables" or "factors" that are present within a particular context which increase the probability of a certain event occurring. Essentially, by noting the presence of such a factor, one may be able to identify the possibility of a certain outcome. In this present article, certain behaviors and experiences being present within Mongolian adolescents were identified as significantly increasing the likelihood of suicidal plans and behaviors. S. Davaasambuu et al., "Suicidal Plans and Attempts Among Adolescents in Mongolia."

[35] Ibid., 339-340.

[36] Contributor to the book, Dr. Gabrielle Carson, elucidates the connection between such significant predictors and former trauma(s) experienced by adolescents. While the text is focused on teenagers in the United States, the chapter utilizes resources which indicate that the connection between trauma and suicidality is consistent globally across cultures. Ruth Gerson and Patrick Heppell, eds., "Suicide and Self-Injury," in *Beyond PTSD: Helping and Healing Teens Exposed to Trauma*, (Washington, DC: American Psychiatric Association Publishing, 2019), 73–93.

[37] Here, I am using the capitalized "Trauma" to connote it as a "systemic entity" which is both "fed"/"emboldened" by unhealthy, detrimental, and dehumanizing systemic behaviors or "starved"/"averted" by healthy, life-giving, compassionate systemic behaviors.

data for improving suicide prevention strategies. This data would aid in determining any cultural values that may promote or encourage suicide as an appropriate response to specific circumstances (or as an inappropriate response fueling stigmatization of those known to struggle with suicidality). It would further contribute to knowledge of beliefs held by Mongolians pertaining to suicide, especially as they connect to sociocultural values. This would be beneficial especially for the Mongolian Church as believers consider their own individual and corporate engagement in national suicide prevention initiatives.

The Mongolian Government's Response to Suicide

WHO argues that "a national strategy indicates a government's clear commitment to dealing with the issue of suicide… through surveillance, means restriction, media guidelines, stigma reduction, [advocacy], training for health workers, educators, police and other gatekeepers, crisis intervention services and postvention."[38] In a January 2018 Mongolian news article, Dr. R. Enkhtuvshin, a doctor at the National Center for Mental Health of Mongolia, complained that at that time there was not yet a comprehensive suicide prevention strategy.[39] We know from Mongolia limiting access through policies to preferred methods of suicide and the creation of the mental health hotline that *something* is being developed in accordance to the WHO Action Plan's suggestions.[40,41] As alluded to earlier, one wonders whether the inconsistent response from the Mongolian government highlights the prevalence of implicit sociocultural values informing the official perception of suicidality and devaluing the provision of a fully developed and implemented comprehensive national suicide prevention strategy.[42] When considering social issues, particularly social issues involving vulnerable populations, what is the role of the Church? This

---

[38] WHO, *Preventing Suicide*, 11.
[39] Bayarsaikhan, "Time to Draw Attention to Teen Suicide."
[40] Qin et al., "Suicide Mortality in Inner Mongolia 2008-15."
[41] World Health Organization, "WHO 'Depression: Let's Talk' Campaign Calls for End to Mental Health Stigma," World Health Organization Western Pacific Region, (April 7, 2017), https://www.who.int/westernpacific/news/detail/07-04-2017-who-depression-let-s-talk-campaign-calls-for-end-to-mental-health-stigma.
[42] For instance, while Mongolia has participated at the regional and international level with the World Health Organization, effective and comprehensive national suicide prevention tactics have yet to be improved or developed into a nationwide initiative.

question is especially vital when the church is marginalized, and when the government's attention and efforts to address the prevention remain inconsistent. There is a hollow space between the marginalized church and an inconsistent government, and this space fills with those who are hurting, vulnerable to the overwhelming pressure of social powers, and at-risk for suicidality. This space is beckoning for helpers just as is the cries of the suicidal. Is it possible that the Church is to act and speak prophetically, welcoming those vulnerable to suicidality while also advocating for preventative measures? And if so, how?

WHO – Western Pacific Region (WPR) Response

In August 2005, 22 countries within the WHO-WPR met in Manila, Philippines to discuss the issue of suicide and how the WPR was going to respond.[43] From this meeting, the Suicide Trends in At-Risk Territories (START) study was created and began to be implemented in the countries who agreed to participate in the study. Mongolia participated.[44] The study's purpose was to monitor suicidality within the WPR, provide randomized-controlled interventions with suicide attempters, conduct cross-cultural psychological autopsy studies, and conduct follow-up with suicide attempters who became medically serious.[45] The WHO-WPR website's description of the study has not been updated with results to reflect the level of completion the study has been able to fulfill since its inception in 2006. However, one of the most recent documents posted from a 2012 regional meeting report, recognizes that "the urgency of the issue is severely underestimated by the public and by policy makers," which has greatly impeded a number of member-countries of the WHO-WPR to successfully create and implement effective national suicide prevention strategies.[46] This meeting's report substantiates the earlier hypothesis about Mongolia's sociocultural perception, because in this meeting Dr. Ganchuluun Ochir stated that

---

Maurizio Pompili and Roberto Tatarelli, *Evidence-Based Practice in Suicidology: A Source Book*, 1st Edition (Cambridge, MA: Hogrefe Publishing, 2010).

[43] WHO - West Pacific Region Office (WHO-WPRO), "Suicide Trends in At-Risk Territories (START)," World Health Organization Western Pacific Region Office, n.d., http://origin.wpro.who.int/mnh/START/en/.

[44] Pompili and Tatarelli, *Evidence- Based Practice*, 61.

[45] WHO-WPRO, "START."

[46] WHO-WPRO, "Seoul Forum on Suicide Prevention in the Western Pacific Region" (WHO-WPRO, 2013), 10.

"suicide prevention still largely remains out of state health policy and programs."[47] Although the WHO-WPR's website has recently called for greater initiatives to prevent suicide, highlighted the severity of living with depression and its comorbidity with chronic and noncommunicable diseases, it also directed readers to national and community resources, such as the National Center for Mental Health 24/7 helpline that provide help to those at-risk for suicide use.[48]

Part II- Theological Engagement

As I begin this section, I believe it is important to provide a few thoughts regarding my development of the following theological engagement of suicidality by the Mongolian Church. First, I should begin by explaining the limitation I experienced in locating sources sharing the details of what Mongolian believers, Christian ex-patriates, and missionaries who make up the Mongolian Church are already doing in addressing the issue of high suicidal ideation and behaviors within their friends, family, and neighbors. However, I ponder if this is not due to a lack of resources, but the lack of my being able to speak Mongolian or read Mongolian Cyrillic text. Thus, automatically, the first step in truly engaging the issue of suicide in Mongolia would be to partner with Mongolians who would be able to offer insight and direction in finding the appropriate resources or to provide their own insight regarding the experience of suicidality in Mongolia.

---

[47] Dr. Ganchuluun Ochir details the tasks that were to be completed over the following three to five years: "the conduct of a nationwide study of suicide and the setting up of a database at national level; an in depth study of social, psychological and biological risk factors that contribute to suicide; setting up of a counseling center, telephone help line services for suicide attempters, their family members, people with mental health problems; collaboration with support organizations to help suicide attempters; training of physicians including primary doctors on suicidology; public education about health and public training on appropriate use of medication is needed; and a public information campaign on suicide prevention by disseminating notes, brochures." WHO-WPRO, "Forum on Suicide," page 29 (unmarked) of the 41-page report.

[48] World Health Organization, "Calling for Stronger Efforts to Prevent Suicide," *WHO Western Pacific: Mongolia News Releases* (October 9, 2019), https://www.who.int/mongolia/news/detail/09-10-2019-press-conference-on-suicide-prevention; World Health Organization, "WHO 'Depression: Let's Talk' Campaign Calls for End to Mental Health Stigma."

Another point I wish to preface before the following engagement is the appropriateness of hospitality as the lens through which a national suicide prevention campaign could be made. David Sneath, in "Everyday Hospitality in Mongolia," provides helpful anthropological insights to understanding the role and value of hospitality in Mongolia, which he notes is different from Western roles and values but instead focuses upon a historical expression of duty tied to their nomadic roots. He writes, "Mongolian everyday hospitality does not imply acts of generosity directed toward any particular person; it is an expression of the status of the householders and their ability to fulfil a public norm."[49] It takes on the idea, "Because of where you are presently and my sovereignty here, I have a duty to show hospitality." Sneath explains that this idea is particularly applied in the context of nomadic strangers appearing at a residence (a *ger*). He also elaborates through the provision of Mongolian history that this duty was enforced with a legal expectation within Qing-era Mongol law code, the *Khalkha Jirum*, and held serious consequence for not performing the expectation.[50] So not only was this provision of hospitality done within the sovereignty of the household leader of the particular *ger*, there was also a communal accountability enacted within the *Khalka Jirum* to ensure the practice of hospitality.

With this point in mind, I would like to propose the following idea as an option in which the Mongolian Church might live out their rich heritage of Mongolian hospitality. The Mongolian church could consider itself as the host and its nation the *ger* with them bearing the responsibility of practicing hospitality as a duty to those experiencing distress from the unbalanced individualism or dysregulation that influences one to contemplate, plan, or act upon suicidality. With this, we may begin to see the development of a Mongolian public theology of suicide prevention that is rooted to Mongolian culture and tradition. With this, the Mongolian Church may participate, and in fact lead, in promoting the health and safety of its *ger*- Mongolia.

In his article, Clemens Sedmak recounts the work of Georg Sporschill, SJ, a Jesuit priest whose lifework has focused on serving

---

[49] David Sneath, "Everyday Hospitality in Mongolia: Obligation, Enaction and Projects of Governance," *L'Homme*, no. 231/232 (2019): 67–88, https://doi.org/10.2307/26838987, 72.

[50] Ibid., 77.

Romanian families and children as well as Moldovan children. Sedmak expresses that Sporschill's work contains commonsense insights that are reflective of hospitality: 1) providing suitable infrastructures, 2) valuing the inner dimension of people's lives, and 3) facilitating shared responsibilities."[51] Particular to Sedmak's telling of Sporschill's insight, I appreciate his systemic delineation of outer spaces (infrastructure), inner spaces (spiritual and religious affiliations), and shared experiences (trust and shared responsibility). Accordingly, this section of theological engagement on the topic of suicide prevention in Mongolia will utilize a framework of hospitality based on Sporschill's missional work in Romania and Moldova. In the 2012 WHO-WPR meeting, the WPR offices recommended to its region's member-countries that they should employ the assistance of the religious bodies within their communities.[52] Therefore, this section takes the opportunity to discuss the role of the Mongolian believers and their communities in the nation's suicide prevention through the practice of hospitality.

Providing Suitable Infrastructures

Sporschill's first "commonsense" insight about mission relates to the creation of space that not only exists for people to inhabit and engage but, even more importantly, is also a safe space into which people are invited, welcomed, called, and drawn.[53] This is especially vital in that the space offers to its guests that which they need. The space is both generous and discerning, seeking through engagement with guests to understand their experiences, desires, needs, and passions. It is in this created space that, in the end, both the guest and host are transformed not only through the interpersonal engagement but so also through God's presence sharing the space too. Such ideas may sound familiar if readers have formerly engaged the works of Christian Pohl, particularly in her text *Making Room* when discussing that while physical places may already be created they also need to be oriented and situated by

---

[51] Clemens Sedmak, "Mission as Kinship on the Margins," *International Bulletin of Mission Research* 42, no. 3 (July 2018): 199–210, https://doi.org/10.1177/2396939317717455, 202.

[52] WHO-WPRO, "Forum on Suicide Prevention in WPR," 11.

[53] Sedmak, "Mission as Kinship," 202.

an attitude of openness to and awareness of the other.[54] In the case of Sporschill's created infrastructure for hospitality, a house and farm was constructed and maintained with the agenda that the space would be used for others, so that others could experience hospitality.

In the same way that Sedmak identified Sporschill's space as infrastructure, the idea of infrastructure can be transferable to the larger space of a nation in which humans engage each other through policymaking and in the abstract space of legislation. How might infrastructure be constructed or reoriented for the purpose of hospitality to the vulnerable? This question can be answered many different ways and may even provide answers not suitable for what this paper seeks. How can a nation-state's infrastructure be created so that it is not just a space for people to utilize as just another segment of public, communal space but a space intentionally formed to be attentive to the needs of community members at-risk for suicide? It is here that Pohl's words ring true: "the environment also [must] have room for brokenness and deep disappointments."[55] Public spaces, both corporeal and conceptual, should not be constructed and maintained so narrowly, rigidly, and ungraciously that the broken and disappointed are relegated to the margins, the shadows of society, or where no care or attention can be effectively offered. Hospitable infrastructures are created with the welfare of people in mind, with an attitude and spirit of hospitality that challenges the community to fulfill its duties as a community and to provide attention, support, and care for those at-risk.

Jason C. Whitehead argues that a pastoral theology of belonging is necessary to combat the systemic marginalization of persons with mental illnesses, which he bases on the principle that humans are social beings.[56] Whitehead recognizes the movements of people within shared spaces, such as communities and societies, and that these movements are often influenced through powerful constructs like stigmas. A constructed stigma that pushes people out of the center of the community must be combatted by an intentionally reconstructed sense of belonging

---

[54] Christine Pohl, *Making Room: Recovering Hospitality as a Christian Tradition* (Grand Rapids, MI: Wm. B. Eerdmans Publishing Co., 1999), 150–52.

[55] Ibid., 152.

[56] Jason C. Whitehead, "Ghosts and Guests: A Pastoral Theology of Belonging For Ministry With Persons With Mental Illness," *Journal of Pastoral Care & Counseling* 70, no. 4 (December 2016): 257–65, https://doi.org/10.1177/1542305016680627.

that welcomes people from the outskirts into the center of view and relationships. The foundation of his pastoral theology of belonging is constructed with Pohl's ethic of hospitality, and he contributes to it the importance of being empathic and creative guests when relating to those suffering from mental illnesses. Whitehead then argues that Pohl's ethic must be expanded to fulfill the requirements of this pastoral theology,[57] and he offers his order of logic supporting it:

> (1) I experience God as relational, just, empathic, and hopeful; (2) we, human beings, are cooperative social animals; (3) we, as a culture, currently lift up ideologies that isolate, marginalize, stigmatize, exclude, and render certain individuals and groups invisible; (4) stigmas hurt, especially when they exclude and isolate individuals and groups, more than we might realize; (5) hospitality seems to be the current best response of communities to social isolation and loneliness; however, hospitality may not be enough; therefore, (6) a pastoral theology of belonging gives us a better set of tools to describe the identities of creative empathic guests who see the impact of structural and personal stigma and seek to be in relationship as a response.[58]

Following this rule of logic, Whitehead indicates that persons with mental illness are often stigmatized and marginalized by attitudes of individualism, meritocratic values, and hyper-rationalism. His pastoral theology of belonging, what I will argue is hospitality observed in its proactive form, acts as a counteragent to these inhospitable attitudes by

---

[57] While Whitehead argues that Pohl's ethics of hospitality should be expanded more practically and proactively, Pohl does indicate the importance of belonging and going to those who feel they do not belong by referencing Jean Vanier who inevitably had to go out from his comfortable setting in order to meet two men with learning disabilities before inviting them to live with him and establishing hospitable living spaces for people with developmental disabilities (L'Arche at Trosly-Breuil). Both his own words through his many books and his actions demonstrate that those who are lost and lonely require the gift of belonging, and Christians must commit themselves to finding the lost and lonely, inviting them in, and giving them the gift of belonging to a community. Pohl, *Making Room*, 168-169.

[58] Whitehead, *Ghosts and Guests*, 258.

informing community members, especially leaders, with humble and hospitable attitudes who prioritize the vulnerable and at-risk.[59]

Pierre Bourdieu likewise contributes vital concepts in understanding society. One of his frameworks is *habitus* and another emphasizes the power of narrative in shaping, maintaining, and revolutionizing society.[60] From his sociological observation of social spaces, Bourdieu was able to detect that symbolic struggles occur within society for the power to shape space for the benefit of certain groups, and narrative is wielded to create hierarchies usually to the benefit of current power-holders. Whitehead too identifies the role of narrative to shape and maintain social spaces, and he explains that in order to hospitably fashion a social space then a new language –*narrative*– must be adopted to better influence the attitudes of space-creators towards those who are psychologically vulnerable and at-risk. He suggests that part of this is changing how mental illness is understood and offers John Swinton's narrative-based description of mental illness, "a rupture in the stories we tell ourselves and that are told about us."[61]

So how do Mongolian believers influence the abstract infrastructures of policy and legislation of a nation-state, particularly when this is a space already created by others? Through advocacy and challenging the present narrative by offering an alternative but hospitable narrative. If Mongolian believers, as the Body of Christ, were to act as host within the infrastructure of Mongolia as a *ger*, then being and practicing the communally expected hospitality might look like advocating for the creation of a nationwide comprehensive suicide prevention program. Their hospitable advocacy could be such that the new social narrative could be introduced and championed so that the current narrative that stigmatizes the mentally ill might be replaced. If Mongolian believers desire to bring positive social change in their communities that improves the lives of at-risk persons, then they must

---

[59] Ibid., 258–59.

[60] Christian Scharen, *Fieldwork in Theology: Exploring the Social Context of God's Work in the World*, The Church and Postmodern Culture (Grand Rapids, MI: Baker Academic, 2015), 15; Pierre Bourdieu, John B. Thompson, and Gino Raymond, *Language and Symbolic Power* (Cambridge: Harvard Univ. Press, 2003), 229.

[61] John Swinton, "Time, Hospitality, and Belonging: Towards a Practical Theology of Mental Health," *Word & World*, Lecture Series, 35, no. 2 (Spring 2015): 175 quoted by Whitehead, *Ghosts and Guests,* 260.

recognize and accept the cause-effect correlation that exists between their perceptions and stigmas (narratives) and their community. The next step is to confront the inhospitable narratives that constrain their actions and that shape inhospitable social spaces that further marginalize the at-risk. To create hospitable infrastructures then, the narrative must change, the attitude must transform through grace, and the believers must proactively practice welcoming and extending belonging.[62] The vulnerable guest should not be turned away from the *ger*, but instead the host should fulfill their duty and intentionally, creatively respond to their needs of their guest within their space.

Valuing the Inner Dimension of People's Lives

In an article covering an anti-stigma awareness campaign for mental health, Dr. Shin Young-soo, the WHO Regional Director for the Western Pacific, expressed that "Depression does not discriminate. Anyone can be affected – chances are you know someone suffering from depression, and you may be suffering from it yourself. Please, talk to your loved ones today and ask them if they are okay. A simple conversation can change – and even save – a life."[63] Young-soo rightly calls upon every individual within the Western Pacific Region to recognize their personal responsibility to their loved ones and friends who may be suffering from depression, a mental disorder that increases risk towards suicidality. According to Sporschill and Glenn Virgil Lorenz, such conversations with at-risk loved ones can be especially enriching when focusing on their spirituality and areas of spirituality where they can grow. The aforementioned step of hospitality in the public space of policymaking and legislation, can utilize advocacy for better policies and inclusive narratives to replace the stigmatization of mental health illness that pushes the vulnerable to the margins of society. This present step

---

[62] For further reading to better develop a more hospitable narrative towards at-risk Mongolians, I suggest Tadman-Robins' *Suicide: The Last Taboo* for his Model of Response including "Influencing of Attitudes," page 93, and additionally Raymond D. Boisvert's "Ethics is Hospitality" for his discussion of ontological sameness vis-à-vis the theological use of *fecunditas*. Raymond D. Boisvert, "Ethics Is Hospitality," in *Reckoning with the Tradition*, ed. Michael Baur, Proceedings of the American Catholic Philosophical Association 78 (Bronx, NY: Nat. Off. of the American Catholic Philosophical Assoc, 2004), 294–96.

[63] WHO, "WHO 'Depression: Let's Talk' Campaign Calls for End to Mental Health Stigma."

suggested to the Mongolian Church begins the movement of hospitality inward from the public spaces to the internal dimensions of people's lives. In creatively and effectively practicing hospitality according to the needs of their guests, the Mongolian Church can fulfill their hospitable duty as a host by intentionally accommodating also the internal needs of their guest, namely those which interact with their guest's spiritual aspects of life.

Sedmak describes working with the inner dimension of people's lives as navigating the spiritual aspects of life. The inner dimension of Sporschill's social work was in fact spiritual work.[64] As such, to neglect examining internal matters without offering spiritual or religious perspectives on the solution, one would be neglecting the person's need for spiritual fulfillment and peace. While Sporschill is clearly connecting this with the Christian faith and providing an individual direction in understanding Christian faith, salvation, and redemption, this principle is reflected in clinical studies supporting the benefits of confessing faith broadly and consistently participating in religious rituals that build into one's sense of spiritual fulfillment and peace.[65]

In Lorenz' dissertation *Leading from the Margins*, hospitality is defined simply for the practical purposes of church leadership practice as "the warm welcome of God…[that brings] redemption, healing, and

---

[64] Sedmak, 203.

[65] Clinically significant data provides evidence that faith and spirituality provide a protective influence on at-risk individuals whether they are Muslim Malaysian teens or Muslim Hui (Wang, Wang, and Wang, "Suicide in Three Ethnic Groups"; Mansor Abu Talib and Abbas Abdollahi, "Spirituality Moderates Hopelessness, Depression, and Suicidal Behavior among Malaysian Adolescents," *Journal of Religion and Health* 56, no. 3 (June 2017): 784–95, https://doi.org/10.1007/s10943-015-0133-3), Christian African Americans (Deidre M. Anglin, Kamieka O. S. Gabriel, and Nadine J. Kaslow, "Suicide Acceptability and Religious Well-Being: A Comparative Analysis in African American Suicide Attempters and NonAttempters," *Journal of Psychology & Theology* 33, no. 2 (Summer 2005): 140–50), and Protestant, Catholic, or Jewish White Americans (Maris, *Pathways to Suicide*). In fact, some studies suggest that it is not specifically the deity being worshipped that provides protective factors for at-risk individuals, but instead the support and strength gained from the religious group's inherent social network and relational connectivity which increases their hopefulness (Randy H. Simonson, "Religiousness and Non-Hopeless Suicide Ideation," *Death Studies* 32, no. 10 (November 3, 2008): 951–60, https://doi.org/10.1080/07481180802440589; Anglin et al., 2005 references Neeleman, Wessely, and Lewis, 1998; Early, 1992; and, Stack and Wasserman, 1992).

wholeness to a person or group."⁶⁶ By practicing hospitality towards those vulnerable within the larger community, the church is acting in accordance to its core teachings of church identity. Essentially, to be a church and connected to the larger Church identity is to be a hospitable people offering a space of hospitality to others. Consequently, Lorenz indicates that a church who does not welcome the vulnerable, such as in the present case of those at-risk for suicidal ideation and behaviors, undermines the very identity and teachings of the Church.⁶⁷ Additionally, he emphasizes the importance of church leadership practicing hospitality because "delight[ing] in [hospitality], modeling it, [and] being faithful in it"⁶⁸ fosters community, and more importantly a community that practices hospitality. Therefore, if the church leadership does not practice hospitality, the church will be unable to effectively welcome and care for the vulnerable in their community. Leadership must model the message that hospitality brings –"that Jesus loves you, especially you"⁶⁹ –because this truth of the gospel can only be authenticated by received hospitality. Furthermore, Lorenz describes church leadership who practice hospitality as being "highly sensitive to others," "demonstrate[ing] empathy to a high degree," and "sens[ing] interconnectedness and mutuality with the marginalized."⁷⁰

He continues to argue that effective church leadership are those who understand "the nature of the church to be a community that reaches out to the hopeless and the helpless and acts out the love of Jesus to people everywhere, especially to the marginalized."⁷¹ He goes on to emphasize that hospitality should be prioritized towards "those in precarious physical circumstances, [and] the needy."⁷² In the context of Mongolia where both suicide and mental health is stigmatized and marginalization effectively isolates those suffering from mental health disorders, perhaps Lorenz' argument can be restated and amplified. The nature of the church is to be a community that reaches out to the

---

⁶⁶ Glenn Virgil Lorenz, "Leading from the Margins: Recovering the Christian Tradition of Hospitality in Church Leadership" (Dissertation, Wilmore, KY, Asbury Theological Seminary, 2005), 101.
⁶⁷ Ibid., 92–93.
⁶⁸ Ibid., 93.
⁶⁹ Ibid.
⁷⁰ Ibid., 103.
⁷¹ Ibid., 94.
⁷² Ibid., 99.

hopeless and the helpless. It acts out the love of Jesus to depressed and suicidal Mongolians, especially those who are actively suffering from stigmatization and isolation. In perceiving Mongolia as its *ger*, the Mongolian church as host can practice hospitality by not just being mindful of the vulnerable but by also building relationships with the vulnerable that fosters spiritual growth and transformation, healing and rejuvenation, life and vitality.

Such relationships begin with an intentionality centered upon building the relationship first and then by having conversations which encourage and strengthen those who are vulnerable. With a true and proper relationship that has no other motive than having the relationship, the appropriate trust, rapport, and friendship lays the foundation for meaningful conversations which can spiritually strengthen those who were or may still be vulnerable to suicidality. These conversations should not seek to convert and then abandon the person upon their conversion, but be conversations offering both encouraging insight and hope that is meaningful to their situation as well as offering provocative questions to nurture their spiritual curiosity.[73] Furthermore, such relationships based in hospitality which do not require or push conversion but instead nurture spiritual curiosity can be blessed by the presence of God, the true and Divine Host, who is able to give wisdom, knowledge, and understanding to both the Mongolian believer and their friend alike. In this way, demonstrating hospitality that focuses on the internal and spiritual dimensions of the at-risk person is congruent to the cultural and religious values of Mongolian believers and it involves the hospitable provision of supernatural gifts from the Divine Host according to the particular internal and spiritual needs of the at-risk person.

Facilitating Shared Responsibilities

---

[73] While this paper does not focus on the specifics of evangelism, those interested in the evangelistic understanding of this valid approach to relationships involving spiritual guidance as opposed to being conversion-oriented can consider further reading the respective texts of Rick Richardson and Bryan P. Stone which discuss evangelism through friendships along spiritual journeys and evangelizing within a pluralist society. Rick Richardson, *Reimagining Evangelism: Inviting Friends on a Spiritual Journey* (Downers Grove, IL: InterVarsity Press, 2006); and, Bryan P. Stone, *Evangelism after Pluralism: The Ethics of Christian Witness* (Grand Rapids, MI: Baker Academic, 2018).

Sporschill's final insight from his missional social work emphasizes the vitality of building trust within a community and allocating responsibility. These actions together lend to the establishment of solidarity and mutuality that is valued among those who share both the space and the responsibilities of that shared space.[74] Solidarity and mutuality are apparent themes within the cultural undertones of Mongolian hospitality, because the duty of the practice reflects that the needs of the guest become the needs of the host and remain such until the host provides resource and refreshment to the guest. For the host to not align themselves in solidarity with their guest, they break the bonds of mutuality, assume dishonor upon their *ger* and household, and endanger themselves to the consequences of demonstrating hostility to their guest. Likewise, the Mongolian believers who do not care for the vulnerable at-risk and suicidal guests of their *ger* may be viewed as demonstrating the same hostility or their silent complacency be viewed or misconstrued as stigmatized antipathy and opposition. It is for this particular reason that this paper now considers the impact of creating and maintaining shared responsibilities with those at-risk friends, family, and neighbors with whom Mongolian believers have been building spiritually enriching relationships and for whom they have advocated in public spaces. Holding shared responsibilities engages those who are at-risk with the Mongolian Church and ties them into a community of belonging. Sometimes being an effective host of the *ger* might mean creatively strengthening the bonds of commonality between host and guest by engaging in shared responsibilities.

Perry W.H. Shaw and Corneliu Constantineanu's article on equipping children to be participants in ministry[75] reflects this emphasis on facilitating shared responsibilities among each other in a shared space. In fact, they argue that the mission of God can only be accomplished when all people within the space are equally investing and participating according to their own abilities. It is only in such hospitable spaces that God's work is fulfilled because everyone is sharing their giftings by participating in the community responsibly. Their explanation of

---

[74] Sedmak, 204.

[75] Perry W.H. Shaw and Corneliu Constantineanu, "Space and Community, Engagement and Empowerment: The Missional Equipping of Children," *Transformation: An International Journal of Holistic Mission Studies* 33, no. 3 (July 2016): 208–17, https://doi.org/10.1177/0265378816633611.

how children are welcomed into the community as future contributors accentuates Sporschill's insight on the need for trust and shared responsibility: "Through the provision of opportunities for children and youth to take responsibility they are empowered to discover and exercise their gifts, and in an atmosphere of trust they are able to take initiative and gain confidence in their service, and in their role and place in God's mission."[76] In such a hospitable environment fostering trust and practicing shared responsibility, those members of the community not only learn of God's mission and grow in their own active role in God's mission, but they also experience fellowship with the God of Mission as they live and work in this mission-oriented community. Furthermore, whether a community member can contribute out of a natural gifting or by being equipped through training, that community member is empowered to bring change into that space and into their own life. Just as a high school's mission may be to prepare students to become active and contributing participants in society, the church must also operate in this world by creating spaces where all, even children, or even those deemed unable or to weak, can contribute to the space.

How does this look for at-risk community members in Mongolia? How might they act out their sense of belonging by contributing to their shared space, by fulfilling a shared duty? What are they able to give in demonstration of their belonging? And if at-risk community members in Mongolia are unsure of their giftings, how might the infrastructure of the created space give opportunity to empower or equip these at-risk members to participate in shared responsibilities and equal belonging to the community? If it is possible to construct the infrastructure of the hospitable space to welcome the depressed and at-risk into the space and then to provide them an opportunity to contribute, this counteracts their experiences living in the margins and shadows of society where they had no place, no purpose, no belonging, and no hope for change.

I wish to elaborate on Shaw and Constantineanu's observation: "a person is grown up not when they can take care of themselves, but when they can take care of others."[77] In the same way that a person is not considered "grown up" until they are caring for another, citizens of a nation cannot be truly a member of a community unless they are contributing

---

[76] Ibid., 212.
[77] Ibid., 212.

and receiving in the cycle of mutual care among the community, which should include not only those who are healthy and at the center of the community but also, and especially, those who are unhealthy and at the fringe of the community. Empowerment can restore hope in a new and better future when the formerly hopeless and helpless cannot only bring change in their own lives but also contribute to positive change in the lives around them. To build a sense of belonging as Whitehead suggests, those at-risk should not be avoided and ignored but welcomed into our shared spaces and given opportunities to participate as an equal contributor to the space.

This point is also argued by Bahtiyar Eraslan-Capan based on a study on the impact of increased social connectedness to hopelessness, which indicates that people suffering "low social connectedness and high level of hopelessness should be encouraged to voluntarily attend [activities, events, or gatherings that build social connectedness with those in their community.]"[78] Thus, if church leadership is concerned about suicide prevention, particularly in involving themselves in the discussions of spirituality with at-risk persons, they should create opportunities that would welcome at-risk persons into social gatherings. As they participate in these events and practice investing in the community by fulfilling responsibilities related to the events, at-risk persons are greatly benefited. They experience a sense of belonging as they are contributing to a common mission, and they are participating in dynamic conversations about spirituality.

As this paper has a limited scope, further theological considerations cannot be further discussed; however, I highly suggest deeper engagement with theological themes of hope[79] and empowerment.[80] Not only are these themes frequently and

---

[78] Bahtiyar Eraslan-Capan, "Social Connectedness and Flourishing: The Mediating Role of Hopelessness," *Universal Journal of Educational Research* 4, no. 5 (May 2016): 938, https://doi.org/10.13189/ujer.2016.040501.

[79] Edward C. Chang, "Hope and Hopelessness as Predictors of Suicide Ideation in Hungarian College Students," *Death Studies* 41, no. 7 (August 9, 2017): 455–60, https://doi.org/10.1080/07481187.2017.1299255; Eraslan-Capan, "Social Connectedness and Flourishing."

[80] Wexler, White, and Trainor, "Why an Alternative to Suicide Prevention Gatekeeper Training Is Needed for Rural Indigenous Communities"; Cynthia Grant, Elizabeth D. Ballard, and Jennifer H. Olson-Madden, "An Empowerment

robustly discussed by theologians across theological disciplines and denominational expressions, but also both of these themes appear frequently in clinical studies on suicidality as indicators predicting the risk of suicidal thoughts and behaviors.

Theology's Role in Moving Forward

Strong personal relationships, personal belief systems, and positive coping strategies have all been identified by the WHO as imperative to suicide prevention due to their influence as protective factors for at-risk persons.[81] These three protective factors easily assist in framing how theology can guide the Church forward in addressing the issue of suicides within the community and participating as actively hospitable community members who attempt into foster the protective factors in at-risk persons the members may meet in public. Additionally, the three kinds of strategies provided by the WHO[82] in their identifying suicide prevention as a global imperative also help illustrate how the Church can be involved. Even while continuing to use the framework offered by Sporschill, the "universal" prevention strategies can guide the Church in creating hospitable spaces through advocacy, raising awareness, and promoting safe and responsible environments and media. The "indicated" prevention strategies target at-risk *individuals* which can then be incorporated into Sporschill's emphasis of having hospitable conversations that engage spirituality and faith in hopes of establishing faith as a protective factor. Meanwhile, the "selective" prevention strategies demonstrate ways in which trust and shared responsibilities can be practiced within communities of belonging which form within the created and shared hospitable spaces. Accordingly, if found appropriate, below are brief suggestions for where Mongolian

---

Approach to Family Caregiver Involvement in Suicide Prevention: Implications for Practice," *The Family Journal* 23, no. 3 (July 2015): 295–304, https://doi.org/10.1177/1066480715572962; Thira, "Aboriginal Youth Suicide Prevention"; Adele Cox et al., "Using Participatory Action Research to Prevent Suicide in Aboriginal and Torres Strait Islander Communities," *Australian Journal of Primary Health* 20, no. 4 (2014): 345, https://doi.org/10.1071/PY14043; Komla Tsey et al., "Empowerment-Based Research Methods: A 10-Year Approach to Enhancing Indigenous Social and Emotional Wellbeing," *Australasian Psychiatry* 15, no. 1 (February 2007): S34–38, https://doi.org/10.1080/10398560701701163.

[81] WHO, *Preventing Suicide*, 10.
[82] Ibid.

believers could consider starting their work of hospitality for suicide prevention.

Creating and Ministering in Hospitable Spaces

As discussed earlier, the Mongolian church can participate in creating spaces that are tangible in both the physical and political realms. Part of creating hospitable spaces may also have more to do with identifying the space as already conducive for hospitality, such as the earlier suggestion in considering Mongolia as the *ger* of Mongolian believers. To do this, believers will be required to confront their stigmas towards suicidality and replace them with hospitable attitudes towards the at-risk and vulnerable members of society. With this shift in narrative and *habitus*, believers can begin by modifying the physical space where the church meets, whether it be an official church building, a rented space, or a public/private venue. Understanding the collective and individual forces that provoke individuals towards suicide, the Church can best prepare or cater the created spaces so that they are most appropriate, do not cause harm, promote maximum flourishing, etc. Believers can also frequent popular public spaces as well as seek ways to transform unhealthy spaces through community initiatives. Additionally, it is important that the church create and improve spaces in accordance to suggestions provided in government-based suicide prevention initiatives.

To be effectively hospitable in creating spaces within the political realm (infrastructure), believers should adopt the practice of advocacy.[83] I propose that hospitality and empowerment can be integrated at the community-level through the mode of advocacy and care for "neighbor." Just as one may practice hospitality within the home by ensuring they have resources that can be used to generously care for guests, community members can practice hospitality by building personal knowledge (a resource) about mental disorders, adverse life stressors, and suicide. This will empower them to both advocate and give special attention and care to those at-risk instead of perpetuating the stigma.

Following Sporschill's example, once such a hospitable space has been established and is being maintained in the spirit, ethics, and

---

[83] WHO, *MhGAP Operations Manual*, 48, 68.

practices of hospitality, church leaders and church members have created a safe environment in which dynamic conversations about spirituality and faith can flourish without fear of judgment, ridicule, condemnation, and rejection. By opening the door to these conversations and welcoming those at-risk to engage them, this action directly challenges the usual behaviors informed by suicide stigma. Additionally, as those at-risk increasingly frequent the church's created spaces, they can be invited to participate in social events hosted by the church that include community-building activities and opportunities to serve and contribute to the community from them personal strengths. This would nurture within those at-risk an improved sense of belonging and personal ownership in the community. As such, the church gifts to those at-risk protective factors which they may not have had originally.

Conclusion

Biosvert ends his article on hospitality ethics with fitting wisdom from Jacques Derrida: "the manner in which we relate to ourselves and to others, to others as our own or as foreigners, *ethics is hospitality*; ethics is so thoroughly coextensive with the experience of hospitality."[84] This quote encapsulates the priority of creating hospitable spaces to the vitality of a community, which requires attention, consideration, and acceptance of those that stigma demands to be unworthy of consideration. If any shared space, whether it be a physical space or an abstract, policy- and legislature-based infrastructure, is to be created hospitably- that is, *ethically*- then the government and church alike must go to, listen to, and learn from those impacted by mental illness or emotional distress that causes them to be at-risk for suicidality. Otherwise, to not do this, the government and the church would effectively be identifying these at-risk individuals as foreigners instead of as their own community members. Sporschill's example offers a framework for understanding theologically the practices of hospitality that can transform a community, and recent WHO and Mongolian Government documents reflect increased attention to the issue of suicide. The doors for change have been long

---

[84] Jacques Derrida, *On Cosmopolitanism and Forgiveness*, translated by Mark Dooley and Michael Hughes (London: Routledge, 2001) quoted by Raymond D. Boisvert, "Ethics Is Hospitality," in *Reckoning with the Tradition*, ed. Michael Baur, Proceedings of the American Catholic Philosophical Association 78 (Bronx, NY: Nat. Off. of the American Catholic Philosophical Assoc, 2004), 298.

open, and it is time that the church enter the community emboldened by the spirit of hospitality and welcome the community's vulnerable into a shared space of care and belonging.

Works Cited

Anglin, Deidre M., Kamieka O. S. Gabriel, and Nadine J. Kaslow. "Suicide Acceptability and Religious Well-Being: A Comparative Analysis in African American Suicide Attempters and NonAttempters." *Journal of Psychology & Theology* 33, no. 2 (Summer 2005): 140–50.

Bergen, Diana van, Johannes H. Smit, Anton J.L.M. van Balkom, and Sawitri Saharso. "Suicidal Behaviour of Young Immigrant Women in the Netherlands. Can We Use Durkheim's Concept of 'Fatalistic Suicide' to Explain Their High Incidence of Attempted Suicide?" *Ethnic and Racial Studies* 32, no. 2 (February 2009): 302–22. https://doi.org/10.1080/01419870802315043.

Boisvert, Raymond D. "Ethics Is Hospitality." In *Reckoning with the Tradition*, edited by Michael Baur, 289–300. Proceedings of the American Catholic Philosophical Association 78. Bronx, NY: Nat. Off. of the American Catholic Philosophical Assoc, 2004.

Bourdieu, Pierre, John B. Thompson, and Gino Raymond. *Language and Symbolic Power*. Cambridge: Harvard Univ. Press, 2003.

Chang, Edward C. "Hope and Hopelessness as Predictors of Suicide Ideation in Hungarian College Students." *Death Studies* 41, no. 7 (August 9, 2017): 455–60. https://doi.org/10.1080/07481187.2017.1299255.

Cox, Adele, Pat Dudgeon, Christopher Holland, Kerrie Kelly, Clair Scrine, and Roz Walker. "Using Participatory Action Research to Prevent Suicide in Aboriginal and Torres Strait Islander Communities." *Australian Journal of Primary Health* 20, no. 4 (2014): 345. https://doi.org/10.1071/PY14043.

Davaasambuu, Sarantsetseg, Suvd Batbaatar, Susan Witte, Phillip Hamid, Maria A. Oquendo, Marjorie Kleinman, Michael Olivares, and Madelyn Gould. "Suicidal Plans and Attempts Among Adolescents in Mongolia: Urban Versus Rural Differences." *Crisis* 38, no. 5 (September 2017): 330–43. https://doi.org/10.1027/0227-5910/a000447.

Dulguun Bayarsaikhan. "Time to Draw Attention to Teen Suicide." *The UB Posts*, January 13, 2018. http://theubposts.com/time-to-draw-attention-to-teen-suicide/.

Durkheim, Emile. *Suicide: A Study in Sociology*. USA: The Free Press, 1951.

Edwin S. Shneidman. "The National Suicide Prevention Program." In *Organizing the Community to Prevent Suicide*, 19–29. Springfield, IL: Charles C Thomas Books, 1971.

Eraslan-Capan, Bahtiyar. "Social Connectedness and Flourishing: The Mediating Role of Hopelessness." *Universal Journal of Educational Research* 4, no. 5 (May 2016): 933–40. https://doi.org/10.13189/ujer.2016.040501.

"Fatalistic Suicide." In *APA Dictionary of Psychology*. American Psychological Association, 2018. https://dictionary.apa.org/fatalistic-suicide.

Gerson, Ruth, and Patrick Heppell, eds. "Suicide and Self-Injury." In *Beyond PTSD: Helping and Healing Teens Exposed to Trauma*, 73–93. Washington, DC: American Psychiatric Association Publishing, 2019.

Government of Mongolia. "Goal 3. Good Health and Well-Being for People." Sustainable Development Goals of Mongolia, 2019. http://www.sdg.gov.mn/Goal/?id=3.

Granello, Darcy Haag, and Paul F. Granello. *Suicide: An Essential Guide for Helping Professionals and Educators*. Boston, MA: Pearson Education, Inc., 2007.

Grant, Cynthia, Elizabeth D. Ballard, and Jennifer H. Olson-Madden. "An Empowerment Approach to Family Caregiver Involvement in Suicide Prevention: Implications for Practice." *The Family Journal* 23, no. 3 (July 2015): 295–304. https://doi.org/10.1177/1066480715572962.

Lee, Heeyoung, Eun Young Lee, Brian Greene, and Young-jeon Shin. "Psychological Distress among Adolescents in Laos, Mongolia, Nepal, and Sri Lanka." *Asian Nursing Research* 13, no. 2 (May 2019): 147–53. https://doi.org/10.1016/j.anr.2019.04.001.

Lee Wolfson. "Buddhist Religious Experts View Suicide and Suicide Prevention." Suicide Prevention Resource Center, 2019. https://theactionalliance.org/sites/default/files/2018_buddhist_perspective_final.pdf.

Lorenz, Glenn Virgil. "Leading from the Margins: Recovering the Christian Tradition of Hospitality in Church Leadership." Dissertation, Asbury Theological Seminary, 2005.

Maris, Ronald W. *Pathways to Suicide: A Survey of Self-Destructive Behaviors*. Baltimore, MD: The Johns Hopkins University Press, 1981.

Encyclopædia Britannica. "Mongolia." Online Encyclopaedia, August 22, 2019. https://www.britannica.com/place/Mongolia.

O'Conner, Rory C., and Jane Pirkis, eds. "Suicide in Asia: Epidemiology, Risk Factors, and Prevention." In *The International Handbook of Suicide Prevention*, 2nd Edition. West Sussex, UK: John Wiley & Sons, Ltd., 2016.

Pohl, Christine. *Making Room: Recovering Hospitality as a Christian Tradition*. Grand Rapids, MI: Wm. B. Eerdmans Publishing Co., 1999.

Pompili, Maurizio, and Roberto Tatarelli. *Evidence-Based Practice in Suicidology: A Source Book*. Cambridge, MA: Hogrefe Publishing, 2010.

Qin, Peng, Maolin Du, Shubi Wang, Xingguang Zhang, Yanling Wang, Tao Yan, Lehui Li, et al. "The Waterfall Pattern of Suicide Mortality in Inner Mongolia for 2008– 2015." *Journal of Affective Disorders* 256, no. 1 (September 1, 2019): 331–36. https://doi.org/10.1016/j.jad.2019.05.057.

Richardson, Rick. *Reimagining Evangelism: Inviting Friends on a Spiritual Journey*. Downers Grove, IL: InterVarsity Press, 2006.

Scharen, Christian. *Fieldwork in Theology: Exploring the Social Context of God's Work in the World*. The Church and Postmodern Culture. Grand Rapids, MI: Baker Academic, 2015.

Sedmak, Clemens. "Mission as Kinship on the Margins." *International Bulletin of Mission Research* 42, no. 3 (July 2018): 199–210. https://doi.org/10.1177/2396939317717455.

Shaw, Perry WH, and Corneliu Constantineanu. "Space and Community, Engagement and Empowerment: The Missional Equipping of Children." *Transformation: An International Journal of Holistic Mission Studies* 33, no. 3 (July 2016): 208–17. https://doi.org/10.1177/0265378816633611.

Simonson, Randy H. "Religiousness and Non-Hopeless Suicide Ideation." *Death Studies* 32, no. 10 (November 3, 2008): 951–60. https://doi.org/10.1080/07481180802440589.

Sneath, David. "Everyday Hospitality in Mongolia: Obligation, Enaction and Projects of Governance." *L'Homme*, no. 231/232 (2019): 67–88. https://doi.org/10.2307/26838987.

Stone, Bryan P. *Evangelism after Pluralism: The Ethics of Christian Witness*. Grand Rapids, MI: Baker Academic, 2018.

Swinton, John. "Time, Hospitality, and Belonging: Towards a Practical Theology of Mental Health." *Word & World*, 35, no. 2 (Spring 2015): 171–81.

Tadman-Robins, Christopher. *Suicide: The Last Taboo*. Bristol, IN: Wyndham Hall Press, 2001.

Talib, Mansor Abu, and Abbas Abdollahi. "Spirituality Moderates Hopelessness, Depression, and Suicidal Behavior among Malaysian Adolescents." *Journal of Religion and Health* 56, no. 3 (June 2017): 784–95. https://doi.org/10.1007/s10943-015-0133-3.

Thira, Darien. "Aboriginal Youth Suicide Prevention: A Post-Colonial Community-Based Approach." *International Journal of Child, Youth and Family Studies* 5, no. 1 (2014): 158–79. https://doi.org/10.18357/ijcyfs.thirad.512014.

Tsey, Komla, Andrew Wilson, Melissa Haswell-Elkins, Mary Whiteside, Janya McCalman, Yvonne Cadet-James, and Mark Wenitong. "Empowerment-Based Research Methods: A 10-Year Approach to Enhancing Indigenous Social and Emotional Wellbeing." *Australasian Psychiatry* 15, no. 1_suppl (February 2007): S34–38. https://doi.org/10.1080/10398560701701163.

UNICEF. "Adolescents." UNICEF Mongolia, n.d. https://www.unicef.org/mongolia/adolescents.

Wang, Ding, Yu Ting Wang, and Xue Ya Wang. "Suicide in Three Ethnic Groups in Huhhot, Inner Mongolia." *Crisis: The Journal of Crisis Intervention and Suicide Prevention* 18, no. 3 (1997): 112–14. https://doi.org/10.1027/0227-5910.18.3.112.

Wexler, Lisa, Jennifer White, and Bridie Trainor. "Why an Alternative to Suicide Prevention Gatekeeper Training Is Needed for Rural Indigenous Communities: Presenting an Empowering Community Storytelling Approach." *Critical Public Health* 25, no. 2 (March 15, 2015): 205–17. https://doi.org/10.1080/09581596.2014.904039.

Whitehead, Jason C. "Ghosts and Guests: A Pastoral Theology of Belonging For Ministry With Persons With Mental Illness." *Journal of Pastoral Care & Counseling.* 70, no. 4 (December 2016): 257–65. https://doi.org/10.1177/1542305016680627.

World Bank. "Mongolia Suicide Rate 2000-2019." Macrotrends, n.d. https://www.macrotrends.net/countries/MNG/mongolia/suicide-rate.

World Health Organization - West Pacific Region Office. "Seoul Forum on Suicide Prevention in the Western Pacific Region." WHO-WPRO, 2013. http://origin.wpro.who.int/mnh/documents/docs/Meeting_Report_Seoul_Forum_on_Suicide_Prevention_full_version.pdf.

———. "Suicide Trends in At-Risk Territories (START)." World Health Organization Western Pacific Region Office, n.d. http://origin.wpro.who.int/mnh/START/en/.

———. "Calling for Stronger Efforts to Prevent Suicide." *WHO Western Pacific: Mongolia News Releases,* October 9, 2019. https://www.who.int/mongolia/news/detail/09-10-2019-press-conference-on-suicide-prevention.

———. *Mental Health Action Plan* 2013-2020. Geneva, Switzerland, 2013. https://apps.who.int/iris/bitstream/handle/10665/89966/9789241506021_eng.pdf?sequence=1.

———. *Mental Health Gap Action Programme Operations Manual.* Geneva, Switzerland, 2018. https://apps.who.int/iris/bitstream/handle/10665/275386/9789241514811-eng.pdf?ua=1.

———. "Preventing Suicide: A Global Imperative." Geneva, Switzerland: WHO Press, 2014. https://apps.who.int/iris/bitstream/handle/10665/275386/9789241514811-eng.pdf?ua=1.

———."Suicide Rate Estimates, Age-Standardized, Estimates by Country." Global Health Observatory Data Repository (Western Pacific Region), July 17, 2018. http://apps.who.int/gho/data/node.main-wpro.MHSUICIDEASDR?lang=en.

———. "WHO 'Depression: Let's Talk' Campaign Calls for End to Mental Health Stigma." World Health Organization Western Pacific Region, April 7, 2017. https://www.who.int/westernpacific/news/detail/07-04-2017-who-depression-let-s-talk-campaign-calls-for-end-to-mental-health-stigma.

Zetty Brake. "Adolescents Need More Mental Health Services." *UNICEF Mongolia* (blog), October 9, 2015. http://unicefmongolia. blogspot.com/2015/10/adolescents-need-more-mental-health. html.

Chapter 9
Toward A Public Ecclesiology For The Evangelical Church: Embodying Our Biblical Identity

Michael Schlatt[1]

Abstract

*Churches are meant to have a positive impact on surrounding communities and the world in the midst of the public realities that confront them daily. But how should this calling be fulfilled? And how is the church doing? With reflections that target the evangelical church in the American context but could be applied more broadly, this essay seeks to recognize room for improvement in the contemporary church's public posture and to provide suggestions for a helpful reorientation. Specifically, adopting a theology of **faithful presence** will better position the church to have a more positive impact on public realities, and one of the primary ways of embodying this posture is through the adoption of a robust public ecclesiology, rich in the biblical images of the church, such as the people of God, the body of Christ and a community of witnesses. Implications and practical matters concerning such an ecclesiology are explored in conclusion.*

---

[1] Michael Schlatt received MDiv and ThM [Intercultural Studies] degrees from Asbury Theological Seminary in 2020. Following a career in technology research, he now desires to serve the church through theological education, with a heart for leaders with little access to resources. Currently, he resides in Wilmore, Kentucky with his wife Katie, and three kids, David, Benjamin, and Anna.

Introduction

A recent sitcom on NBC named *Perfect Harmony* brilliantly places together a retired Ivy League music professor with a rag-tag group of small-town Kentucky churchgoers. Hilarity ensues as values and customs clash, but mutual understanding also emerges as each of the characters are portrayed as flawed but lovable and sympathetic. In one particular episode, the professor witnesses a day in the life of this little church faithfully providing for its members and the wider community, through babysitting for a single mother looking for work, the preparation of a community meal to celebrate local firefighters, and support for families needing spiritual guidance. Throughout the day, this professor wrestles with the value of the church, citing as evidence the wider church's history of abuses. The story culminates as the agnostic professor, after witnessing this normal day in the life of this little church, makes a profound statement: "I don't believe in *the* church, but I do believe in *your* church."[2]

Churches are meant to have a positive impact on the community and the world in the midst of the public realities that confront them daily. Congregations are meant to function in a way that reveals the beauty of the gospel and the goodness of God. But how should we, as members of the church, go about fulfilling that calling? And how are we doing? In short, I believe there is room for great improvement in our posture toward the wider public. And I seek to provide suggestions in this essay for moving forward in becoming the church I believe God has for us to be. My reflections will be primarily targeted to my own corner of the faith, the evangelical church in the American context, but I believe these suggestions will benefit global evangelicalism and the wider church as well.

Specifically, I contend that adopting a theology and posture of *faithful presence* will better position the church to have a more positive impact on public realities. I further contend that one of the primary ways of embodying this posture is by allowing God to transform us,

---

[2] *Perfect Harmony*, Season 1, episode 8, "Any Given Monday," directed by Natalia Anderson, aired on NBC, 2019, accessed April 4, 2020, http://www.hulu.com/perfect-harmony/.

individually and corporately, through sustained meditation upon a public ecclesiology, rich in biblical images of the church.

In this essay, I first provide evidence of confusion and inadequacy in the American evangelical church's response to the complexities of the 21st century, globalized world. I will then explore the theology of *faithful presence* as a way forward to improve the church's public orientation. Finally, I will begin to construct an evangelical public ecclesiology based on three biblical images of the church and finish with implications and practical matters.

Unsettling Realities

In the midst of the impeachment of President Donald Trump at the end of 2019, *Christianity Today's* editor-in-chief Mark Galli posted an editorial that called for American evangelicals to advocate for the removal of the president and to break their unwavering political alliance with the Trump administration. He writes

> If we don't reverse course now, will anyone take anything we say about justice and righteousness with any seriousness for decades to come? Can we say with a straight face that abortion is a great evil that cannot be tolerated and, with the same straight face, say that the bent and broken character of our nation's leader doesn't really matter in the end?[3]

The editorial, interestingly enough, largely quoted from an opinion piece that called for the impeachment and removal of President Bill Clinton for what the author considered similar moral offenses: "the words that we applied to Mr. Clinton 20 years ago apply almost perfectly to our current president."[4]

The editorial caused a firestorm of responses, both positive and negative, revealing the polarization of politics within the evangelical community and the alignment of American Christianity with political

---

[3] Mark Galli. "Trump Should Be Removed from Office," *Christianity Today*. December 2019. Last accessed April 4, 2020: https://www.christianitytoday.com/ct/2019/december-web-only/trump-should-be-removed-from-office.html.

[4] Ibid.

powers, a reality Scot McKnight calls "statism" in his reflections on the response to *CT*'s editorial position.[5] These and similar commentaries have raised concerns that something might be flawed in the public posture of the evangelical church and its emphasis on grasping political power, at least in the American context. The response of division and vitriol to the opinions expressed by Galli are further evidence of this possibility.

Even if you disagree with the assessment of Galli and McKnight, there are other disconcerting trends and perceptions concerning the church in America and its relationship to the wider public. Barna Research group did a survey in 2011 which probed the perceptions of people in America concerning the positive ways churches contribute to their local community. Those surveyed generally say that the church has a positive influence on society. The numbers show "that three-quarters of U.S. adults believe the presence of a church is 'very' (53%) or 'somewhat' positive (25%) for their community."[6] Pew Forum similarly shows that surveyed adults see religion, in general, as a force for good in America.[7]

However, there is an ambiguity about what that influence could or should actually look like. The Barna findings show that despite their positive feelings toward churches, many adults are unclear as to how churches could actually best serve their communities. One-fifth of adults (21%) did not venture a single response as to how churches could contribute positively. Among the unchurched, defined as those who have not attended a church in the last six months, fully one-third are not certain how congregations could be beneficial."[8] Though public perception is generally positive concerning the church, a significant percentage of people have trouble identifying concrete, positive effects of the church on the wider community. What does this say about the church's public witness? Is it possible that the church's remaining positive

---

[5] Ibid.

[6] Barna Group, "Do Churches Contribute to Their Communities?" Barna Group, last modified 2011, https://www.barna.com/research/do-churches-contribute-to-theircommunities/ (accessed Dec. 2019).

[7] Pew Research Center, "Americans Have Positive Views About Religion's Role in Society, but Want It Out of Politics." Pew Research Center, last modified Nov. 15 2019, https://www.pewforum.org/wpcontent/uploads/sites/7/2019/11/PF_11.15.19_trust.in_.religion_FULL.REPORT.pdf (accessed Dec. 2019): 20.

[8] Barna, "Do Churches Contribute."

favor is still held afloat by residual but waning effects of christendom in our country?

A third set of troubling evidence comes from the rate of millenials leaving the church and not returning like previous generations. David Kinnaman and Aly Hawkins, in their book *You Lost Me*, capitalize on several years of Barna research to explore the reasons this younger generation is becoming increasingly unengaged with the church. Though no single issue was cited by a majority of those leaving the church, five themes were discerned in the data. The perception, whether actually true or not, is that the church is *overprotective, shallow, anti-science, repressive, exclusive,* and *doubtless*.[9]

All three of these unsettling realities can be traced back to the practices of the church's engagement with the surrounding culture and public realities. Indeed, Kinnaman and Hawkins show that one of the primary reasons that the younger generation is so unengaged is because the generation gap they are experiencing is greater than in previous generations, due to the changes in our culture and world occurring so rapidly. Because congregations are not recognizing these changes and taking them seriously, they are experiencing decline in cultural influence and losing members.[10] Even though political matters were not significant in the study by Kinnaman and Hawkins, a different study of young adults has shown that disagreement on political issues is becoming a significant reason for leaving church as well, increasing from 18% to 25% from 2007 to 2017.[11]

Given this unsettling set of evidence of unhelpful engagement of public realities by the church, what then is a starting point for a course correction? The rest of this essay seeks to answer this question by first reviewing an important development of thinking on the subject and then suggesting an ecclesial theology that better positions the church to form a publicly-oriented people.

---

[9] David Kinnaman and Aly Hawkins, *You Lost Me : Why Young Christians Are Leaving Church-- and Rethinking Faith* (Grand Rapids, MI: Baker Books, 2011), 92-3.

[10] Ibid., 38.

[11] This was calculated from two Lifeway Research studies from 2007 and 2017 the results of which can be found at https://lifewayresearch.com/2019/01/15/most-teenagers-drop-out-of-church-as-young-adults/ and https://lifewayresearch.com/2007/08/07/reasons-18-to-22-year-olds-drop-out-of-church/.

Faithful Presence

In 2010 James Davison Hunter penned an important book titled *To Change the World*. Here, he describes two fundamental challenges to the mission of the church in our late-modern age which he calls *difference and dissolution*.[12] For Hunter, the challenge of *difference* is caused by the pluralism that is pervading the world in which people with differing worldviews, communal understandings and religious ideas are co-mingling at unprecedented rates. The presence of multiple communities in such proximity leads to the weakening of the plausibility structure of each of the individual communities. To consistently maintain and embody a worldview from any one of those communities now requires more intentional use of the personal will than previously required in more homogeneous environments.[13]

The second challenge is what Hunter calls *dissolution*, which is a divorce occurring in our perception of daily life between our words and "our world." Put another way, there is now increasingly a skepticism that words that are said do not actually have much of anything to do with reality out there. This skepticism can be traced to shifts in postmodern philosophical currents that have played out in the Western academy in the last century and to the popular embodiment of those philosophical currents in mass media and culture.[14]

In response to the waning influence of the church in wider culture, prominent leaders from a variety of political and ecclesial persuasions have turned to coercive power through secular political structures, a move Hunter chronicles in painful detail. Though Hunter primarily emphasizes the Christian Right, he also challenges a similar grasping of power in the Christian Left and the Neo-Anabaptist movement that, in his view, unhelpfully defines itself, albeit in contrast, by those same structures.[15] Regardless of origin or orientation, Hunter shows that this pursuit of political power proves ineffective for producing actual lasting

---

[12] James Davison Hunter, *To Change the World: The Irony, Tragedy, and Possibility of Christianity in the Late Modern World* (Oxford: Oxford University Press, 2010), 200.

[13] Ibid., 200-4.

[14] Ibid., 205-10.

[15] See Hunter's chapters on the Christian Right (II.3), Christian Left (II.4) and the Neo-Anabaptists (II.5).

cultural change.[16] Each of the three unsettling realities from the previous section of this essay should be seen, at least in part, as symptoms of the failure of the church to adapt to our rapidly changing world. This narrowed emphasis on the pursuit of political power, which plays out primarily in the form of electing senior political leaders who promise to enforce Christian values, is simply not a helpful posture for the church to positively contribute to our world.

In stark contrast to the current orientation of much of the church, Hunter says that the answer to the challenges of *difference* and *dissolution* is simple, though certainly not easy: local enactment and incarnation of believers and communities grounded in what Hunter calls a theology of *faithful presence*. In the midst of skepticism of the validity of words, incarnational presence is required. In the midst of weakened plausibility structures, an even more intentional enactment by the believing community is required. This posture of embodied presence is modeled by and fundamentally grounded in the incarnation of Jesus Christ. And his followers, individually and corporately as the church, are called to follow suit.

Hunter describes his theology of *faithful presence* in three moves. In the first move, Hunter shows the character of God as one who is present to us and with us. This presence fundamentally includes a commitment to us as his people which, for Hunter, has at least four important attributes.[17] First, God *pursues us*, as evidenced by the chosenness of Israel, the prophets' pronouncements of God drawing the people back and ultimately in the Incarnation. Second, God *identifies with us*, as one who "knows our frame" (Ps. 103:14) but further as one who became like us, but without sin, and moving in compassion while bodily present to those in need. Third, God's presence and commitment are demonstrated in *the life he offers*, evidenced by the shalom found in the Edenic garden and the New Jerusalem and the calls of the writers, prophets, and Jesus himself as "the bread of life." Fourth, this commitment to the life he offers is rooted in *sacrificial love*, as most fundamentally demonstrated at Calvary. The purpose of God's presence and commitment has always

---

[16] Ibid., 101-10. Analysis of these power dynamics would benefit the topic of this essay, but unfortunately space limits its inclusion.
[17] Ibid., 241-3.

been for the purpose of restoring relationship with us. This pursuit is not for instrumental purposes, but merely out of love and affection for us.[18]

Hunter's second move is to show that our only fitting response to God's presence is to be present to him in return. This response occurs in the corporate and individual disciplines of sacraments, intercession, devotions, prayer, study, and others, ultimately acknowledging individually, but together as the church, that there is no other God and that we desire his will and kingdom.[19] And, just in the same way that he pursues us out of love and affection, we are not to pursue him for instrumental purposes but simply because he is worthy to be adored.

Hunter's final move is to declare that "[o]nly by being fully present to God as a worshiping community and as adoring followers can we be faithfully present in the world."[20] Though he does not precisely say how this transition is to occur, he describes the results as occurring primarily in three areas.

First, we become faithfully present to one another. In this presence, we are to imitate the commitments of God: to "pursue each other, identify with each other, and direct our lives toward the flourishing of each other through sacrificial love."[21] Hunter calls for this engagement to occur inside and outside the community of faith, a challenge to increase the bonds of existing relationships within the church and to similarly reach out to the stranger, citing Levitical holiness laws and Jesus' memorable parable of Matthew 25.[22] The stranger remains different, so the challenge of *difference* remains, but just as God seeks us out as strangers, so we are to do so for others.

Second, one way of serving those around us is to be faithfully present to the tasks that we have before us to do. Citing Colossians 3, Hunter bids us that "whatever you do, work at it with all your heart, as working for the Lord, not for men" in all of our tasks. The framing of our tasks as "for the Lord" dignifies the tasks as in themselves bringing

---

[18] Ibid., 243.
[19] Ibid., 244.
[20] Ibid.
[21] Ibid.
[22] Ibid., 245.

honor to God, produces a willingness to bring skill and quality to them, and keeps them from becoming idols.[23]

Finally, we are to be faithfully present within our spheres of social influence. The power that is inherent to the social structures in which we find ourselves must not be used thoughtlessly, but rather to, as much as possible, "do what we can to create conditions in the structures of social life we inhabit that are conducive to the flourishing of all."[24] Though instances of direct opposition in unjust circumstances are sometimes necessary, most often this presence is a "lived-version of the shalom of God within every place and every sphere where Christians are present."[25]

These three movements of the theology of *faithful presence* provide a helpful conceptual and theological framework for facing the challenges of *difference* and *dissolution*, but what could or should this look like in the daily life of a given local church community?

Five years after the release of Hunter's book, David Fitch wrote *Faithful Presence*, desiring to extend Hunter's line of thinking. Here, he provides a conceptual model for a missional, public-facing church and then effectively describes seven core disciplines that a church should be performing in order to embody the theology of *faithful presence*.

Fitch's model for navigating the spaces between what happens in the church and what happens in the world makes concrete Hunter's theology. For Fitch, the difference between the church and the world is not spatial, but is best understood in temporal terms:

> The difference between the church and the world therefore is not...between where God is and where he is not. There is no in here and out there when it comes to the church...Instead, the church in essence experiences God's presence visibly now, ahead of the time when God shall visibly reign among the whole world. The difference between the church and the world then is just a matter of timing. The church experiences

---

[23] Ibid., 246-7.
[24] Ibid., 247.
[25] Ibid., 248.

the kingdom ahead of time. The rest of the world is heading there; they just don't know it yet.[26]

The understanding of the boundaries of the church as primarily temporal has implications for the final movement of Hunter's theology of *faithful presence*: being present to the world.

In Fitch's description of *how* this public movement occurs, he forms a conceptual model he calls "the disciplines on the move" with three spaces in it: the close circle, the dotted circle and the half circle. The close circle is the intimate space among committed believers that sacramentally centers around each of the disciplines described in the book. This space is not closed to others but is primarily one in which the gathered people are substantially submitted to one another and to Christ in a supernatural closeness. Here, Jesus is host.[27]

The dotted circle is the space generally occupied by the same participants as above, but more intentionally located in a neighborhood setting and with greater openness to others outside the community to join in and witness God's work in the community. Here, the Christian is the host.[28]

The half circle refers to the spaces believers visit throughout their days as guests bringing the presence of God with them and discerning God's presence already at work. Here, the Christian is the guest.[29] Fitch understands the location of the church ultimately as a way of life functioning in all three spaces.

The frequent result in these three spaces together is a reordering of our world through God's presence. "Where the presence of the Lord is, there is always a reordering of life: forgiveness, reconciliation, peace and renewal. This is his kingdom."[30] This reordering is the goal of the disciplines he recommends.

---

[26] David E. Fitch, *Faithful Presence : Seven Disciplines That Shape the Church for Mission* (Downers Grove, IL: IVP Books, 2016), 39.
[27] Ibid.
[28] Ibid., 40.
[29] Ibid.
[30] Ibid., 140.

Fitch does an admirable job turning Hunter's recommendations into concrete practices. His three-space model is helpful for understanding the "spaces" between the church and the world and how to live as embodied individuals and communities within those spaces. The limitation of Fitch's description, however, is that he provides no direct definition of the church, implying that it is a community of people practicing the disciplines he recommends in commitment to one another and God. While this is true, it is a definition based on the actions of the community, rather than a more foundational and fundamental identity.

If Hunter and Fitch are correct in their recommendations, which I believe they largely are, how do we as the church learn to be the kind of people who embody this posture of *faithful presence*? How do we grow, individually and corporately, into an incarnational, enacting community for the sake of others as both authors invite us to do?

I believe that one key answer to this question, one that is largely missing from their analyses, is that we need to better understand our identity as the church. In other words, we need a more robust ecclesiology. The remainder of this essay is meant to begin to construct a theology of the church in order to provide a vehicle for the formation of individuals and communities that embody the call to *faithful presence* by Hunter and Fitch.

Building Blocks

Before beginning construction, I would like to describe the building blocks that I plan to use. First, as mentioned earlier, my own context of the American evangelical church is primarily in view here, so I begin from the perspective of evangelicalism. Though David Bebbington's definition of the movement from 1989 has been critiqued from a post modern perspective as overemphasizing belief and not properly considering affections,[31] his four marks remain a helpful starting point for this discussion. For Bebbington, the core doctrines that have

---

[31] See Amanda Porterfield. "Bebbington's Approach to Evangelical Christianity as a Pioneering Effort in Lived Religion." *Fides et Historia* 47 (1) (2015): 58–62.

united a diverse group of global churches and denominations include the following: conversion, biblicism, activism, and cross-centeredness.[32]

That the nature of the church is not included in Bebbington's four marks of evangelicalism provides generous space for diversity in how the church is understood within the movement's boundaries. Conversely however, any definition or description of the church should follow from or at least align with the four marks that make up that boundary.

Despite biblicism being a core mark of the evangelical movement, Howard Snyder observes that "Scripture is a distinctively remote source in much evangelical ecclesiology…To the degree that Scripture is a factor, it is mediated primarily through the Protestant/Catholic and free church traditions. In neither case, however, is Scripture determinative of ecclesiology."[33] In light of this observation, Snyder powerfully constructs an ecological model, describing the church as the household of God with three core aspects: worship, fellowship and witness.[34] He begins by establishing the organic nature of the church through the invocation of several rich images from the Bible[35] and then emphasizes the understanding of the church as the household of God and body of Christ to make his construction.[36] Any evangelical ecclesiology should begin with the BIble, as Snyder masterfully demonstrates. But which parts of the Bible should be emphasized for such a construction?

Avery Dulles, in his foundational text on ecclesiology, *Models of the Church*, begins by describing the importance of images in any description of the church. Ultimately, the church, as a divine/human identity, is a mystery and cannot be described using "clear and univocal

---

[32] Mark Noll, "Defining Evangelicalism" in *Global Evangelicalism: Theology, History & Culture in Regional Perspective*. Edited by Donald M. Lewis and Richard V. Pierard (Downers Grove, IL: IVP Academic, 2014), 20-1.

[33] See Howard Snyder, "The Marks of the Evangelical Church" in E*vangelical Ecclesiology : Reality or Illusion*? Edited by John g. Stackhouse (Grand Rapids: Baker Academic, 2003), 97. He then goes on to show the inadequacies of using the traditional four marks of the church and helpfully expands those marks using biblical evidence to tell "the other half of the story" concerning the church.

[34] Howard A. Snyder, *Radical Renewal: The Problem of Wineskins Today* (Wilmore: First Fruits Press, 2015), 161.

[35] Ibid., 9.

[36] Ibid., 158-60.

concepts."[37] Instead, the Bible exclusively uses vivid, multivalent images to describe the church, a tradition that has since been followed by theologians and preachers throughout its history.[38] And for good reason:

> In the religious sphere, images function as symbols. That is to say, they speak to man existentially and find an echo in the inarticulate depths of his psyche. Such images communicate through their evocative power. They convey a latent meaning that is apprehended in a nonconceptual, even a subliminal, way. Symbols transform the horizons of man's life, integrate his perception of reality, alter his scale of values, reorient his loyalties, attachments, and aspirations in a manner far exceeding the powers of abstract conceptual thought. Religious images, as used in the Bible and Christian preaching, focus our experience in a new way. They have an aesthetic appeal, and are apprehended not simply by the mind but by the imagination, the heart, or, more properly, the whole man.[39]

It seems that God has wired us in such a way that these sorts of images affect us as whole people, reaching us at the multiple levels of mind, body, spirit, imaginations, desires, and habits. Dulles continues by showing the communal effects of these evocative images:

> Any large and continuing society that depends on the loyalty and commitment of its members requires symbolism to hold it together…[These symbols] suggest attitudes and courses of action; they intensify confidence and devotion. To some extent they are self-fulfilling; they make the Church become what they suggest the Church is.[40]

There is a power to, and a corresponding responsibility for, the images that we use to describe ourselves individually and communally.

---

[37] Avery Dulles, *Models of the Church*. Unabridged (New York: Doubleday, a division of Random House, Inc., 2013), 9-10.
[38] Ibid., 11.
[39] Ibid., 12.
[40] Ibid.

Richard Beaton similarly suggests that when discussing and describing the church, it must be done with care, because the "overarching models, or metaphors, have the power to shape and transform."[41] He then advocates for a reconsideration of the main metaphors found in the New Testament which provide entry into rich theological and sociological worlds beyond the plain understanding of the image. He takes this further, appealing to McLuhan's understanding that any message is shaped by the medium through which it's conveyed, and thus in a sense, the medium is the message.[42] Applied to the church, this advises us to take seriously the metaphors we identify with because they will directly affect how we organize, perform our communal rituals, and understand and posture ourselves toward others and the public realities we share.[43]

Beaton prefers the image of the people of God, which will be explored in the following section. Other images can and should supplement this understanding, but any image used should emphasize the "corporate, social aspects of belonging to this people" which is in stark contrast to "a loose collection of autonomous individuals."[44] This is especially important in the hyper-individualistic ethos of American culture, which has significantly found its way into the church.

In his *Cultural Liturgies* series, James K. A. Smith provides a look at transformation that he calls liturgical anthropology. In this approach, Smith emphasizes the centrality of desire and imagination in the process of formation.[45] He argues,

> it is because I imagine the world (and my place in it) in certain ways that I am oriented by fundamental loves and longings. It is because I "picture" the world as this kind of place, this

---

[41] R. Beaton "Reimagining the Church: Evangelical Ecclesiology" in *Evangelical Ecclesiology: Reality or Illusion?* Edited by John g. Stackhouse (Grand Rapids: Baker Academic, 2003), 219.

[42] Lesslie Newbigin has similarly argued that the church itself is the plausibility structure for the gospel: "the only hermeneutic of the gospel, is a congregation of men and women who believe it and live by it." See Lesslie Newbigin, *The Gospel in a Pluralist Society* (Grand Rapids, MI: Eerdmans 1989), 225.

[43] Ibid., 222.

[44] Ibid.

[45] James K. A. Smith, *Imagining the Kingdom : How Worship Works. Cultural Liturgies* (Grand Rapids: Baker Academic, 2013), 124.

kind of "environment," that I then picture "the good life" in a certain way that draws me toward it and thus construes my obligations and responsibilities accordingly.[46]

For Smith, this idea of "the good life" can be thought of as one's "ideal picture of human flourishing," or the configuration of life for yourself and others worth desiring.[47] Because we have been molded to imagine this "good life" in a certain way, we become people who then desire it. Imagination drives desire, but this desire bears fruit in action that is primarily from "an acquired habitual disposition."[48] Because this molding emphasizes the imagination, symbolic and vivid images uniquely provide the vehicles for influencing action. Thus, images, not abstract concepts or even models, provide the best fodder for this process, so any evangelical ecclesiology should not only start with the Bible, but focus on biblical images of the church for its construction.

In addition to the formation that occurs through our senses, there is another dynamic at work that helps form the "acquired habitual disposition" just mentioned. Smith reveals this force to be one that forms a congregation and the individuals within it, one that engages our whole selves through bodily, communal practice. Referencing terminology from the sociologist Pierre Bourdieu, he describes this formational force by using the concept of *habitus*.

Smith describes *habitus* as "the habitual way we construct our world," which primarily consists of unconscious dispositions and actions that are *inscribed* in us through the communal dispositions that surround us.[49] These dispositions, or *embodied know-how*, are *carried* in a community and are transferred through a community's practices. These practices have an *irreducible logic* to them that defies theoretical description[50] much like the mysterious nature of the church itself. I believe that this reality is particularly important when trying to describe a public ecclesiology because the church's public orientation must be

---

[46] Ibid., 124-5.
[47] James K. A. Smith, *Desiring the Kingdom: Worship, Worldview, and Cultural Formation. Cultural Liturgies* Vol. 1 (Grand Rapids: Baker Academic, 2009), 26.
[48] Smith, *Imagining the Kingdom*, 141.
[49] Ibid., 81.
[50] Ibid., 80.

centrally concerned with embodiment, practices, and actions at the individual and communal levels.

That a given congregation's *habitus* is a fundamental building block for public ecclesiology also shows an important limitation inherent to any construction made through logic and theological concepts employed in an essay like this. A congregation's public ecclesiology must be passed down in practices, postures, and rituals in addition to conceptual teaching and learning. In other words, the responsibility of individual and communal formation cannot be fully contained in a rational theology but must also be embedded in the local discipleship and the shared practices of a given community.

Now that I have established a context, described the building block of biblical image, and provided a caveat of the limitations of theoretical analyses for communal formation, I am now ready to explore images that will serve as the foundation of this public ecclesiology.

Biblical Images of the Church

It is puzzling that the evangelical church has often not included much of the biblical imagery of the church in its own ecclesial definition and understanding, given the rich possibilities. One survey of the biblical data describes eight primary pictures of the church: a household or family, a people, a bride, a priesthood, a temple, a vine and an olive tree, a flock, and a body.[51] In addition, three primary designations of the individuals that reside in those communities can be found: disciples, witnesses, and believers.[52]

Any fully-orbed ecclesiological description should consider all of the above images, but the emphasis of this essay is to suggest a *public* ecclesiology for the church, so the images that provide metaphorical space to describe the interaction between the church and the public will

---

[51] Christopher J. H. Wright. "The Whole Church--A Brief Biblical Survey." *Evangelical Review of Theology* 34, no. 1 (2010): 21-28.
[52] Ibid., 20-1.

take priority.[53] With this consideration, I see three that are most helpful: the people of God, the body of Christ, and a community of witnesses.

The People of God

The first biblical image of the church to be explored is the people of God. According to Beaton, this image should be primary for several reasons: it provides continuity with the Jewish conception of people of God; it challenges individualism; it embraces the unity and catholicity dimensions of our understanding of the church; and it emphasizes God's choice to have a people bear his name, as was made clear in the Old Testament.[54] Ultimately, this image forces us into an awareness of the history and narrative of the people of God throughout the scriptures, including interaction with God and the surrounding peoples. This image further provides continuity between the Old Testament and the New as God continues his plan of redemption of his people.

This image also encompasses an eschatological depth that situates the current moment firmly between the past and the future. Any self-understanding requires knowledge of the communal past, including Israel's history and that of the early church. By identifying with the people of God, we must deal with the complex history of our ancestors. Framed this way, Bible study becomes a genealogical exploration of the family into which we have been adopted, for good and for ill. However, we also get to enjoy the favor and commitment that God shows to his people (Deut. 31:6) and can draw inspiration from the great cloud of witnesses that have gone before us in the faith (Heb. 12:1). Our self-understanding also requires knowledge of our promised future, including the final consummation of the kingdom of God in Christ's return. Our confidence in the hope of resurrection for the people of God

---

[53] This emphasis is justified by other descriptions of the church as fundamentally publicly-oriented. George Hunsberger points out that this public nature of the church and the gospel is built into the original words used to denote those concepts. The word *ekklesia* draws from the idea of civic meeting. The core word for the gospel, *kerygma*, is closely related in line with herald or one who publicly announces on behalf of another with the force of their authority. The word used for worship, *leitourgia*, is publicly-oriented and is more rightly to be understood as a "work for the people." See George R. Hunsberger, "The Missional Voice and Posture of Public Theologizing," *Missiology* 34, no. 1 (2006): 17.

[54] Beaton, Reimagining the Church, 220.

frees us from pragmatic grabs of power and allows us to be present to our neighbors and our world with little to lose. These considerations taken directly from scriptural stories and history well align with the biblicism and cross-centeredness marks of evangelicalism.

There is a further important aspect of this image: God's presence was to be a central feature for God's people. George Vandervelde suggests "an ecclesiology of God's dwelling with and in the Christ-community" as an important description of the church.[55] He cites New Testament evidence to make his point. For instance, in 1 Cor. 3:16, when Paul asks "Don't you know that you yourselves are God's temple and that God's Spirit dwells in your midst?", the *you* is plural and the *temple* is singular.[56] This dwelling of the Spirit as God's presence is to happen for individual believers, but also together at the communal level. Peter's living stones built into a single spiritual house in 1 Pet. 2:5 is further evidence of God's desire to dwell among his people.[57]

Indeed, Moses understood the importance of this dynamic when he pleaded for God's continued accompaniment with the people: "If your Presence does not go with us, do not send us up from here. How will anyone know that you are pleased with me and with your people unless you go with us? What else will distinguish me and your people from all the other people on the face of the earth?" (Ex. 33:15-16).

It is important to notice how this image of the people of God with God's presence as a central concern fits the first move of Hunter's theology of *faithful presence*. We are to be a people of the Presence!

The Body of Christ

A second biblical image of the church to be explored is the body of Christ. This description is found exclusively in Paul's writings and provides a multivalent metaphor for understanding the identity of the church. There are at least two aspects important to this study.

---

[55] George Vandervelde, "The Challenge of Evangelical Ecclesiology," *Evangelical Review of Theology* 27, no. 1 (January 2003): 12.
[56] Ibid., 16.
[57] Ibid.

First, the body is an organic entity that grows and matures as interdependent parts work together. Paul uses the image of the body in two distinct ways. First, Paul's reference to the church as the body in 1 Cor. 12:12 emphasizes the interconnected nature of the members.

Snyder's ecological model emphasizes that the health of the whole is dependent on the health of the individual members and that equilibrium should be sought between the members and their interdependent activities.[58] Robert Mulholland provides a formational perspective: "Paul implies that our spiritual journey, while it is unique to each of us as an individual member of the body of Christ, is not an isolated pilgrimage but is part of a sort of caravan with the diverse members of the body."[59] The second way Paul uses the image of the body is demonstrated in Eph. 4 emphasizing the body's collective reliance on and growth into the head of the body, Jesus Christ.[60] In the two ways we see Paul use the body image, symbolic space is opened up for holding together the commands to love God, the head, and love one another, the other members of the body (Mark 12:30-31).

The second important aspect is the embodied nature of the church. Some scholars contend that the image of the church as a body is only helpful to understand the internal structure of the faith community because it does not contain a public orientation,[61] but I would disagree. This image is fundamental for a public ecclesiology because it makes clear that the church must essentially be embodied. Perhaps it is straining Paul's metaphor, but it cannot be avoided that the image of a body implies a physical presence to others around it in our created world. And so, there is an internal importance to the body, which is emphasized by Paul in his direction about the internal fellowship and worship of the church, but there is an inevitable embodied and enacted reality into which the church is called to live. This has important implications for the way the church postures itself amidst the public realities that surround it.

---

[58] Snyder, *Radical Renewal*, 158.

[59] M. Robert Mulholland and R. Ruth Barton, *Invitation to a Journey: A Road Map for Spiritual Formation*. Revised and Expanded (Downers Grove, IL: IVP Books, 2016), 60.

[60] Ibid., 158.

[61] See Timothy George, "Toward an Evangelical Ecclesiology," *Evangelical Review of Theology* 41, no. 2 (April 2017): 104.

It is important to notice how this image of the body of Christ fits the second move of Hunter's theology of *faithful presence*. We are to be an interdependent people who seek to be present to God together!

A Community of Witnesses

The images of the church in the Bible reflect a dual reality, showing the importance of individuals and the gathered community. For instance, Paul emphasizes the community together when speaking of the church as a body, but precisely for the sake of showing the value of each of the individual members. From the three biblical images of the individual members of the body mentioned earlier, the image of the church as a community of witnesses will serve as the third and final image for our consideration.

Michael Green argues that "nothing but transformed lives will be able to intrigue and attract a generation that is bored with religion and cynical of pious talk."[62] He further describes the church as presented in Acts: "They were not all preachers, but they were all witnesses. And they expected every Christian to have something to say about Jesus and the difference that Jesus makes to life."[63]

This expectation of the early church was the same as Jesus' own commission in Acts 1:8: "But you will receive power when the Holy Spirit comes on you; and you will be my witnesses in Jerusalem, and in all Judea and Samaria, and to the ends of the earth." This came as a response to the disciples' question about whether Jesus was going to establish his earthly reign. They were asking about ruling and reigning, but Jesus directed them to witnessing instead. It is also important to note that witnesses are in the plural in this command. There is an implied togetherness to the witnessing that is to occur.

But what does a witness do? A witness shares from his or her own experience and does not try to convince, but rather points to the reality to which he or she is witnessing. Volf observes the characteristics of one who faithfully witnesses to the wisdom of God to others. For

---

[62] Michael Green, *Thirty Years That Changed the World: The Book of Acts for Today* (Grand Rapids, MI: W.B. Eerdmans, 2004), 40.

[63] Ibid., 94.

him, this witness is not one who imposes, but is self giving; not one who sells, but recognizes the gospel as a gift; not merely a teacher, but one who embodies and demonstrates; and finally not a midwife who helps cultivate what is already within, but rather points to the wisdom from without: that is Christ![64] A final important aspect to remember: witnesses do not have control over the use of their testimonies. But rather, the responsibility of the witness is to testify faithfully. Whether the reality to which the witness points is received from that faithful testimony is then the responsibility of the other and the Holy Spirit. This sacrifice of control well aligns with the cross-centeredness mark of evangelicalism.

It is important to notice how this image of a community of witnesses fits the third move of Hunter's theology of *faithful presence*. We are to be witnesses of the presence of God in our midst for the sake of others!

Implications

In summary, the images of the people of God, the body of Christ, and a community of witnesses, taken together, provide the imagination forming weight helpful for transforming the community's desires, thinking, and habits as previously described by Dulles and Smith. They provide a foundation of symbolic space that is specific enough to suggest helpful practices within a community to embody it, but flexible enough to allow significant variations in practice based on context, while remaining faithful to the underlying biblical witness.

In addition, each of these images corresponds with Hunter's three moves in his theology of *faithful presence*. The image of the church as the people of God, with an emphasis on God's presence, corresponds with Hunter's first move, God being present and committed to his people. The image of the church as the body of Christ echoes Hunter's second move which is the response of the faith community to be present to God together. The image of the witness aligns with Hunter's third move which is the further response of the individuals in the church to be present to each other, to others and to the tasks before them.

---

[64] Miroslav Volf, *A Public Faith: How Followers of Christ Should Serve the Common Good* (Ada: Brazos Press. 2011), 106-7.

Finally, it is important to note that these three images do not assume or require a particular place in a contemporary political order to be relevant. At the same time, location still matters significantly in terms of how the images are to be embodied. Specifically, the people of God image can be applied to any political situation because the community's identity is based on their relationship with God, not their position in the surrounding society. In fact, the Bible and the church throughout its history both witness to the people of God functioning within vastly different circumstances and social locations, providing ample stories for use in reflection for helping local churches construct their own identity within their own context. Similarly, the body image emphasizes Christ as the head and the one providing and sustaining the rest of the body working together in mutual interdependence. However, a body still exists within a context that must be considered. And finally, the very nature of a witness is to give up power when faithfully telling what has been experienced and allowing the hearers freedom to respond as they will. Because these images do not require secular political power, they help us understand the freedom that we have to be faithfully present in whatever circumstance and with whatever authority we find ourselves having in a given moment.

Responding to the Unsettling Evidence

Given the unsettling realities referenced at the beginning of this essay, what difference will this theology make? I will take each in turn.

First, faithfully present individuals and churches avoid grasping for secular, political power and subsequently the division and fallout that pursuit inevitably garners. The people of God, with a rich heritage of taking care of the poor and being empowered by the presence of God, have little need for secular power to impact culture. Electing the political leaders who will enforce our values will not alone provide positive change. Leaning into our identity together as witnesses to what God is doing among us and reaching out from that place of abundance will prove powerful at the level we have the most impact: in our local communities and specific places in which we have relational influence.

Second, faithfully present individuals and churches make concrete differences in our local communities cutting through any perceived confusion about the helpfulness of the church. The witnessing community, following their leader Jesus, embodies power in sacrifice and positively impacts the relational sphere of influence that is provided to each individual as well as the community as a whole. If these acts of service are to follow in the rich heritage of God's commands to his people, they will naturally be seen as unambiguously good.

Third, faithfully present individuals and churches have real and relevant discussions and are not afraid to wade into the complexities of modern life. When we understand ourselves as the people of God, including the complex history of the relationship of God's people with the surrounding cultures, we need not have fear of engaging with the world. Jesus is holding all things together (Col. 1:17) and remains committed to his people as he has demonstrated throughout the history of Israel and the church. This is precisely the type of engagement that younger generations are rightly hungering for.

Altogether, faithfully present individuals and churches enact and embody their identities providing holistic answers and real responses to the challenges of difference and dissolution in our time.

Getting Practical

In his recent article, "Making Public Theology Operational," Frederike van Oorschot explores the relationship between public theology and the church with much of his analysis centering on the *explicit* and *implicit* functions of church. This analysis provides a helpful way of understanding the practical outworking of the ecclesiology discussed in this essay.

According to van Oorschot's survey, the explicit function of the church can be understood in terms of advocacy and public social teaching and critique.[65] Put succinctly, "the explicit function of the church can be described as the churches' public commentary on societal issues. Church representatives take up issues discussed in civil society or political debates and comment on them publicly according to their

---

[65] Frederike van Oorschot, "'Making Public Theology Operational': Public Theology and the Church," *International Journal of Public Theology* 13, no. 2 (2019), 206-8.

beliefs."[66] In some contexts, this may be a viable expression of positive outworking of the church's influence where clergy are publicly recognized as authoritative. This is becoming decreasingly so, in especially post-Christian and post-Christendom Western contexts, making the implicit function of the church all the more important and relative.

The implicit function of the church, according to van Oorschot's survey, includes three important aspects. First, the church provides a place to learn about ethics. This is grounded in the reality of the dual nature of the church as an institution that is to be both loyal to and critical to surrounding society.[67] This provides a setting to helpfully wade into contextual ethical complexities, together as a community of faith. Our dual citizenship with the kingdom of God and our surrounding society provides space for having difficult conversations, working through ethical dilemmas and wrestling with doubt. This may look like affinity groups and Sunday School classes where complex issues are freely discussed, or Alpha courses where seekers may find safe places to express honest thoughts about their spiritual and moral journeys.

Closely associated with this ethical learning, is the shaping of the individual believer. According to van Oorschot, referencing Max Stackhouse, "every change in society is based on changes in personal beliefs. Inside Christian communities personal beliefs are deeply influenced by teaching, preaching and sacraments. Given that believers shape their surroundings…the sanctification of individuals offers a unique potential for changing society."[68] To the teaching, preaching and sacraments, I would add prayer, times of singing together, confession, small group discussions, and service together. Additionally, I would recommend that a theme consistently present in these activities would be the identity images discussed earlier in this essay. As the church, individual and collectively, we need to be constantly reminded that we are the people of God, the body of Christ and a community of witnesses. These images should become part of the regular vernacular of the members of our faith communities and that begins with the intentional inclusion of these words, images and related practices in our activities and gatherings.

---

[66] Ibid., 208.
[67] Ibid.
[68] Ibid., 210.

The third implicit function of the church is embedded in its very structure. "The church implies a normative approach to the coexistence of the people beyond the church,"[69] which means that how the members of the church relate with one another and how the church hierarchy itself is structured is to be a model for the wider community. The three images emphasized in this essay seriously impact this reality. For instance, take the understanding of the church as the body of Christ with its unity and diversity and radical care for one another. The enactment of this identity provides a model for our wider society which should be working toward the reconciliation of alienated neighbors and the bridging of societal divides so prevalent in our daily lives. The way a given church approaches leadership, empowerment of members of the community, decision-making processes, and the nature of public gatherings should all be critically considered in light of the central images of the church discussed here.

Conclusion

In this essay, I first tried to show the confusion and inadequacy of the church's engagement of the wider culture as evidenced by political posturing, confusion about the church's role in society, and the increasing alienation of young people from the church. I then reviewed the suggestions of James Hunter and David Fitch and their presentations of the theology of *faithful presence* as a new way of engaging the public realities in which we live. Next, I showed the power and importance of images in our formation and began the construction of a public ecclesiology based on three particular images of the church found in the Bible: the people of God, the body of Christ, and a community of witnesses. I then allowed those images to provide the imaginative foundation for the church to embody the theology of *faithful presence*. Finally, I explored the implicit and explicit functions of the church to show the ways in which these identificational images may influence the advocacy coming from the church, the formation of believers in the church, and the structure of the church itself. In the end, we need to be constantly reminded of our identity in the activities and very structure of our local church communities.

---

[69] Ibid., 211.

Ten years after Hunter's call to be faithfully present, and five years after Fitch's call to concrete practices of that presence, I believe the church in America is still at a crossroads. Will we continue with the same paradigms leading to the same outcome of waning influence and further confusion about our purpose in light of surrounding public realities? Or will we do the hard work of learning to embody our identities as the people of God, the body of Christ, and a community of witnesses, in a posture of *faithful presence*? Let us continue to remind ourselves frequently who we are and whose we are as we continue this journey of grace in light of the hope-filled future to come.

Works Cited

Barna Group. "Do Churches Contribute to Their Communities?" Last modified 2011. Accessed Dec. 2019, https://www.barna.com/research/do-churches-contribute-to-theircommunities/.

___. "Christians at Work, Part 3: The Church's Role." 2012. Accessed Dec. 2019, https://www.barna.com/research/church-vocation/.

Beaton, R. "Reimagining the Church: Evangelical Ecclesiology" in *Evangelical Ecclesiology : Reality or Illusion?* Edited by John G. Stackhouse. Grand Rapids, MI: Baker Academic. 2003.

Dulles, Avery. *Models of the Church.* Unabridged. New York: Image, 2013.

Fitch, David E. *Faithful Presence: Seven Disciplines That Shape the Church for Mission.* Downers Grove, IL: IVP Books, 2016.

Green, Michael. *Thirty Years That Changed the World : The Book of Acts for Today.* Grand Rapids, MI: W.B. Eerdmans, 2004.

Galli, Mark. "Trump Should Be Removed from Office" *Christianity Today.* December 2019. Last accessed April 4, 2020: https://www.christianitytoday.com/ct/2019/december-web-only/trump-should-be-removed-from-office.html.

George, Timothy. "Toward an Evangelical Ecclesiology." *Evangelical Review of Theology* 41 (2) (April 2017): 100–118.

Hunsberger, George R. "The Missional Voice and Posture of Public Theologizing." *Missiology* 34 (1) (2006): 15–28.

Hunter, James Davison. *To Change the World: The Irony, Tragedy, and Possibility of Christianity in the Late Modern World.* Oxford: Oxford University Press, 2010.

Kinnaman, David, and Aly Hawkins. *You Lost Me: Why Young Christians Are Leaving Church-- and Rethinking Faith.* Grand Rapids, MI: Baker Books, 2011.

Noll, Mark. "Defining Evangelicalism" in *Global Evangelicalism: Theology, History & Culture in Regional Perspective*. Edited by Donald M. Lewis and Richard V. Pierard. Downers Grove, IL: IVP Academic, 2014.

McKnight, Scot. "Christianity Tomorrow." *Christianity Today Blog Forum: Jesus Creed*. January 2020. Last accessed April 4, 2020: https://www.christianitytoday.com/scot-mcknight/2020/january/christianity-tomorrow.html.

Mulholland, M. Robert, and R. Ruth Barton. *Invitation to a Journey: A Road Map for Spiritual Formation*. Revised and Expanded. Downers Grove, IL: IVP Books, 2016.

Newbigin, Lesslie. *The Gospel in a Pluralist Society*. Grand Rapids, MI: Eerdmans. 1989.

Perfect Harmony, Season 1, episode 8, "Any Given Monday." Directed by Natalia Anderson. Aired on NBC, 2019. Accessed April 4, 2020, http://www.hulu.com/perfect-harmony/.

Pew Research Center. "2016 Campaign: Strong Interest, Widespread Dissatisfaction." Last modified July 1 2016. Accessed Dec. 2019, https://www.peoplepress.org/2016/07/07/2016-campaign-strong-interest-widespread-dissatisfaction/.

___. "Americans Have Positive Views About Religion's Role in Society, but Want It Out of Politics." Last modified Nov. 15 2019. Accessed Dec. 2019, https://www.pewforum.org/wpcontent/uploads/sites/7/2019/11/PF_11.15.19_trust.in_.religion_FULL.REPORT.pdf.

Porterfield, Amanda. "Bebbington's Approach to Evangelical Christianity as a Pioneering Effort in Lived Religion." *Fides et Historia* 47 (1) (2015): 58–62.

Smith, James K. A. *Desiring the Kingdom : Worship, Worldview, and Cultural Formation. Cultural Liturgies*: Vol. 1. Grand Rapids, MI: Baker Academic, 2009.

___. *Imagining the Kingdom : How Worship Works. Cultural Liturgies:* Vol. 2. Grand Rapids: Baker Academic, 2013.

Snyder, Howard A. *Radical Renewal : The Problem of Wineskins Today.* Wilmore: First Fruits Press, 2015.

___. "The Marks of the Evangelical Church" in *Evangelical Ecclesiology : Reality or Illusion?* Edited by John G. Stackhouse. Grand Rapids, MI: Baker Academic, 2003.

van Oorschot, Frederike. "'Making Public Theology Operational': Public Theology and the Church." *International Journal of Public Theology* 13, (2) (2019): 203–26.

Vandervelde, George. "The Challenge of Evangelical Ecclesiology." *Evangelical Review of Theology* 27, (1) (January 2003): 4–26.

Volf, Miroslav. *A Public Faith : How Followers of Christ Should Serve the Common Good.* Ada, MI: Brazos Press. 2011.

Wright, Christopher J. H "The Whole Church--A Brief Biblical Survey." *Evangelical Review of Theology* 34 (1) (2010): 14–28.

Conclusion
Amanda Allen

Coediting a public theology book in the middle of a global pandemic is a very odd experience. On the one hand, every essay in this book feels so distant, written for a different context—almost a different world. I clearly remember sitting, as the teaching intern, in Okesson's *Public Theology for Global Development* class last fall, enjoying the rich and deep theological discussions around such issues as poverty alleviation, healthcare, and embodiment. Reading through the class's final papers, which have grown into the chapter submissions you now read, I appreciated how well these authors wrestled with a myriad of everyday issues like food, technology, and land rights, and I looked forward to helping them turn those final papers into solid chapters of this book. Then the spring of 2020 came, and with it a global pandemic from the spread of a novel corona virus, COVID-19. Living in this once-in-a-hundred year event that has drastically changed the physical, economic, and cultural landscape of a globalized world has made me wonder if what we pondered, debated, discussed, and wrote before it all began has any bearing on this strange new world.

On the other hand, as seen in both the desolation of quarantined cities and the potency of protests against longstanding social ills, public theology is being written on the very streets of global cities and playing out in real time in all media outlets, from a 24-hour news cycle to first-hand videos posted on social media. The role of the State, individual rights and responsibilities as citizens, freedom in the midst of a public health crisis, police brutality, election year pressure, and systemic racism, for example, are just some of the prominent public issues boiling in a pressure cooker of an America under quarantine. So now, more than any other moment of my life, I see the necessity of those past conversations to help us lean into the complicated, difficult, and thick issues of a world rocked by change, rejecting the temptation to reduce any of this messiness into simplistically rendered memes, soundbites, or 280 character tweets.

Supreme Court Justice Oliver Wendell Holmes Jr. is attributed as saying: "For the simplicity that lies this side of complexity, I would not give a fig, but for the simplicity that lies on the other side of complexity, I would give my life,"[1] and we should still take his 19th century quip seriously as a warning against naïve reductionism within the public realm. Yet with both the proclivity of Americans to "boil down" complicated issues into straightforward responses, the conflation of the public realm with the political,[2] and the necessity of transmitting events, ideas, and ideologies in short bursts of information to reach a wider audience, public conversations around important issues are often overly simplistic. American evangelicals are not immune to this cultural trait for, as Offutt et al remind us, we "have inherited an uneasy dichotomy between private beliefs and public facts. They have relegated God to the former and left the realms of politics, economics, and technology deprived of theological input."[3] Thus, the sacred is private, the secular is public, and this legacy of theological division has left us ill equipped to confront the complexities of modern life through the tools of our faith.

Public theology, as Okesson reminded us in the introduction of this volume, is a discourse that grew in the grey areas between private and public realms. Even though theology has always had public expression through the embodiment of Christians as the living members of the body of Christ as we, in our daily lives, dwell in and move through the public realm, it has rarely penetrated the discourse of public life. So public theologians are not looking to simply unmake the dichotomies of public/private and secular/sacred (holdovers from the era of Enlightenment), they also seek to help people build healthy forms of being theologically more present in their everyday lives of work, school, shopping, social

---

[1] Jon Kolko, "Simplicity on the Other Side of Complexity," *Jon Kolko Blog* (January 11, 2016), accessed August 10, 2020, http://www.jonkolko.com/writingSimplicityComplexity.php.

[2] James Davidson Hunter, *To Change the World: The Irony, Tragedy, and Possibility of Christianity in the Late Modern World* (Oxford: Oxford University Press, 2010), 105.

[3] Stephen Offutt, et al., *Advocating for Justice: An Evangelical Vision for Transforming Systems and Structures* (Grand Rapids, MI: Baker Academic, 2016) 15.

media, and all the other areas of public life. This requires not a reduction of complexity but an increase of it.

Public theologians are skilled at "turning the crystal,"[4] which is a way of meditatively studying complex problems or issues. When held up to a light and turned, a crystal's various facets are brought into focus and reflect light in different ways, allowing an observer to see the way its different facets interconnectedly gleam on the surface while also seeing deeper into the stone, all without disregarding the crystal's full essence. Similarly, "turning the crystal" of an issue allows the light of theological doctrines to highlight different aspects of a specific issue that might otherwise go unseen while simultaneously preventing a reduction of the complexity of its whole. Thus, public theologians problematize an issue, expanding it beyond a simple linear cause-and-effect equation to illuminate its true intricacies and enabling us to see its relationship to the interlocking web of contact points that make up our globalized world. While public theologians have historically engaged such issues as secularization and political theory, what excites me about this book is how our authors have "turned the crystal" of issues in everyday life.

Navigating the Complicated Realities of Our Common Life

The title of our volume, *Navigating Complexity in Our World: Public Theologies for Everyday Life*, highlights the importance of public theology engaging the regular lives of normal people. Locating their conversations in their lived experiences, our authors ask questions about the daily rhythms of life and in doing so, they showcase the normalcy of public theology and how it can dynamically impact individual choices and concerns. Written by and for the everyperson, these chapters give us opportunities to see the world in a new and fresh way. Furthermore, the commonplace, as we see below, is not only "allowed" but is ripe fodder for a public theologian's engagement with the world, even though it has too often been overlooked.

For example, what can be more commonplace than food? Yet through the chapters of Sadie Sasser and Graham Hoppstock-Mattson,

---

[4] Steven C. Bahls, "Turning the Crystal," (Speeches and Statements: Augustana College, 2003): 1-2, accessed March 2, 2020, http://digitalcommons.augustana.edu/presidentsstatements/3.

we discover how very deep and complicated this topic really is. In her work, Sasser uses the US corn industry to explore the connections between poverty, obesity, and the commodification of calorie-dense, highly processed foods. She pays particular attention to the systems in place that complicate and perpetuate food deserts and obesity among the poor and presents the lackluster ways in which current theological discussions respond. She then responds herself by looking at the eternal truth of the Incarnation in relation to food, the body, and care for others. Thus, we views how God sees the body as good, how he has special heart for those in poverty, and that the church can respond to him by advocating for the voiceless, being good stewards of our resources, and recognizing and changing unjust systems.

Hoppstock-Mattson adds to this topic by exploring how globalization, and its reactionary opposite, naïvely localized nationalism, has disrupted food and place, dislocating both and turning them into mere images, or non-entities, of what they were. Public theology responds to this by exploring how food, when seen as a full representative of the other, reintegrates the eater into a social location of hospitality and imbues the act of eating with what it means to be truly alive in Christ. In other words, food grounds us in our unique places and relationships: with others, the created order, and the Creator. From these authors' work, when more deeply contemplated through the lenses that public theology provides, we discover how even such a routine, commonplace thing as food leads us to deeper connections with the world around us and to our Almighty God.

Furthermore, public theology allows, even encourages, the everyperson to engage their everyday world using the resources their faith has given them. The discipline of public theology is not only done by and for the priest, pastor, or professor, but also by and for the everyperson who lives their lives in the common places and spaces we all share. We see the importance of the everyperson in the ways the authors of this book discuss human responsibility toward caring for creation and the land through the lenses of public theology.

Kyeo Re Lee, for example, examines the role key women have played in shaping Taiwan's response to pollution. She notes how their ecofamilism, rather than ecofeminism, extends the Confucian expectation of women's care for the home to include the whole of creation as a universal household. She then contends that their perpetual giving up of self, as an ideal in Confucian society, is another form of oppression because women themselves are lost in service and sacrifice for the good of others. Lee offers the theological themes of salvation, incarnation, and Trinity as alterative motivators for creation care, saying that sacrifice is incomplete without the love of God. Women's self-identity is not found in who they marry or what they can do for the world, but from being in relationship with the triune God. When thus situated in the Gospel, their lives of public service are marked with self-flourishing as an outpouring of love to God, rather than self-deprivation. Importantly, her work also highlights the important (though often still-hidden) role women play in public life.

Benjamin Foss, like Lee, engages creation care through public theology, and like, Lee, focuses his chapter on the redemption of broken relationships and the work that everyperson can do in their daily lives to affect change. He takes a different tack, though, by arguing against using stewardship, and the image of God in humanity at creation, as a justification for the Western mechanistic view of the world. Instead, he says, we must understand stewardship as a means to cultivate the interconnectedness of life in our shared world. Conversion thus includes turning away from ourselves and towards loving the world as Christ did, and we obey and embody the second great commandment "love thy neighbor as thyself" through listening to and sacrificing for the sake of others, who are, in truth, not Other at all but our ecological neighbors. Furthermore, stepping into the prescriptive stream of public theology, Foss shows us how a good theological understanding of restoration urges us to love our neighbors by taking reparative ecological action through disseminating proper information, caring for and aiding those most impacted by diminishing ecological resources, choosing sustainable options that impact supply and demand, and living lives that take the current ecological crisis seriously. These two chapters show us how the discipline of public theology can radically shape the ways everyperson lives and loves and interacts with their world.

The relationship between humankind and creation is then expanded with Dwight Mutonono's work as he explores a public theology of land and its political and religious implications for Zimbabwe. He begins by explaining how land is never far from the Zimbabwean people, where the relationship between people and land transcends time and religiously ties ancestors to those living on the land in the present age. Political forces, both during and after decolonialization, have coopted this narrative so that chiefs are powerful patrons and gatekeepers of traditional ancestral land and religion, but are also expected to ensure that their clients, the rural populace, vote for a specific political party. In this conversation, land is more than land: it is also a symbolic mythos turned into a means of political control with everyperson trapped in these forces. Tying in historical and current ebbs and flows of migration with the religious history of the area, Mutonono responds to this myth by recounting Christianity's African ties, discussing the possibilities of certain ancestors themselves being followers of Christ, and finding commonality within the biblical and African traditional perspective on land: God owns the land as people move across its surface, and the land is made to benefit all people. He ends by advocating for chiefs to be custodians of their people and land (rather than political pawns), and for deeper theological engagement with land from non-Western perspectives.

Mutonono's work highlights the importance of everyperson using the tools of public theology to interrogate political narratives that seek to polarize the population and sway power, as well as to stand against allowing a mythos to coopt history for the purpose of political gain. Furthermore, all three of these authors, writing from and to three very different regions of the world, show how public theology is a theological discipline that can speak to everyone everywhere about anything. This is public theology's face looking outward.

One of the discipline's other strengths is its ability to face inward, to speak to the Church as much as speaking from the Church to the world. Stemming from their missiological roots, each chapter of this publication included a conversation about how the Church, both universal and local, can be agents of change at the intersection of public and private life. However, the four following chapters I summarize emphasize how public theology can particularly help the Church navigate the complex realities of contemporary life. Two authors, Jacob Tenney and Samuel Hood, address privacy and vaccinations, respectively, which are at the forefront of modern life but have traditionally rested outside the walls (and are often theologically overlooked) by the evangelical church. Two other authors, Michael Bennett and Michael Schlatt, discuss suicide and the role of the church, respectively, which are more commonly included in traditional theological discourse, but are here approached from within a new context and with fresh eyes.

Tenney's work raises significant questions about rights to privacy and the relationship between a private life and a public faith for individual Christians and for the Church. He begins by exploring the current conversation around the right to privacy, saying that modern life prioritizes efficiency over much else, resulting in governments and goliaths of the technological age commodifying personal information and the individual's online presence. Bringing the conversation to a question of power, Tenney says that without a public theology of privacy, the technologically powerful will invade and exploit the technologically weak (i.e., individual persons) for their own profit. Tracing the rise of, and tension between, private and public spheres in Western history, he explores the development of the theoretical and legal concept of a right to privacy. He then notes the importance of theologically viewing privacy not through the lens of protecting one's own self, but of respecting other people's intimacies to mitigate exploitation and the influence of unjust power usage. Tenney's theological conversation is located in the themes of freedom, power, and modesty, and he calls the Church to recalibrate the private sphere toward rest, retreat, solitude, intimacy, and perfect love within a public Kingdom of God, but only if it roots such privacy in the freedom, respect, and love for other persons.

While Tenney addresses the theologically unusual topic of technological privacy, Hood steps into the complicated world of public health with a chapter on how the evangelical Church may more critically engage the issue of vaccine hesitancy. Distinguishing between the anti-vaccination movement and vaccine hesitancy, Hood examines the sentiment surrounding this hesitancy and the conflicting narratives that undermine confidence in both vaccines and medical institutions. Addressing the trend of religiously affiliated parents refusing to vaccinate their children, he teases out the important distinction that evangelicals root their vaccination choices in the conversation of parental choice and freedom, rather than in any specific theological belief. In response, Hood presents a public theology of creation and new creation that redresses three underlying myths behind evangelical vaccine hesitancy. First, human institutions are seen as an imperfect but nonetheless integral aspect of the design of the world and a means through which God can work. Second, sickness and disease are a product of the Fall, and human work within the created order can mitigate some of the Fall's effects. Finally, the vision of the new creation gives the Church a means for actively participating with God as healing agents in the world. Hood ends his chapter by speaking directly to the evangelical Church, offering practical ways in which a local church, rooted in public theology, might shepherd its congregants toward a deeper engagement with issues of public health, and in particular vaccine hesitancy. Tenney and Hood show us how public theology aids the Church in addressing issues at the forefront of our modern life, yet that have often been theologically overlooked.

Writing from a new perspective, Bennett employs his expertise in mental health counseling to create a public theology of hospitality that aids the Mongolian Church in addressing a long-standing theological issue, suicide. Using a Durkheimian sociocultural matrix of suicide, Bennett begins by interrogating the *meaning* of the act of suicide in the Mongolian context. There, the mentally ill are stigmatized or invisible, and he hypothesizes that those who are suicidal see the act as an avenue to freedom from the restrictions of a system of trauma that shatters hope for a better future. Considering the marginalized status of the Church in Mongolia, Bennett then says the Church has an opportunity to step into the traditional role of host and haven to the distressed and emotionally wandering peoples (suffering from mental illness) who seek refuge from inhospitable, isolating elements that might otherwise pull them toward suicide. Using a missional model of hospitality that addresses outer and inner spaces and shared experiences, Bennett highlights how the Mongolian Church could use a public theology of hospitality to challenge and change the stigmatization around mental illness and the meaning of suicide. As local churches create hospitable spaces for and build authentic relationships with those on the margin in need of refuge, it can also spur the nation itself on to build a national program of suicide prevention. In writing his chapter, Bennett not only exemplifies how public theology can help the Church, no matter where, respond to significant societal issues like mental health, he also shows how social science best practices can inform Church responses.

Conclusion | 283

Intentionally kept last as a reflection of the role of the Church in the public sphere, our final chapter issues a call to the evangelical Church to have a richer engagement with the public realities of the world through a public ecclesiology of *faithful presence*. Schlatt begins by exploring the rather thin presence of American evangelical churches in the public sphere and the way Christian leaders (of all political persuasions) reacted to the Church's waning influence in the wider culture by employing coercive power usage to achieve political agendas. Schlatt then explores James Davidson Hunter and David Fitch's public theologies of *faithful presence*, where the Church's public actions should stem first from abiding in the presence of God and so be willing hosts to bring people into the real presence of God and be a worshipping community. Then the Church moves to serving the world through her congregants bringing the presence of God as guests who embody God's presence through living every day in submission to God. Importantly, Schlatt notes that neither author fully explores the nature of the church itself, and so develops a public ecclesiology of *faithful presence* using Hunter and Fitch's biblical images of the people of God, the body of Christ, and a community of witnesses. These images should guide the way the Church approaches the public sphere by changing the way it postures itself as an embodiment of *faithful presence*, influencing the way it advocates for justice, disciples and forms believers, and informs the way the Church structures itself. Schlatt's chapter reminds us how important it is to continually do the hard work of ecclesiology for our continually changing contexts, and all four authors show how public theology can speak to the Church itself as a public institution.

What excites me about this book is how well each of our authors have engaged the regular, everyday lives of normal people in very different contexts through theological lenses and from their unique perspectives. Written by and for everyperson, their chapters give us opportunities to see the world differently, asking questions about the daily rhythms of life and showcasing the normalcy of public theology. They speak to the things we all think about and that shape our world: how we can and should see our neighbor, what we can do as individuals and as a Church to respond to injustices in the world, and how we can serve others through small and large actions, both inside and outside the Church, to the glory of God.

They also show us, despite the rhetoric of earlier ages, how theology has always been located within time and space, written from a specific context. All theology is particular, even as it reaches beyond its initial context in ripples and waves to touch the realities of God in the universality of human life. So, a chapter on obesity and food deserts in America can help those around the world working toward food security to articulate the importance of feeding the body through a theology of the Incarnation. A chapter written very specifically for Taiwanese women working in creation care can also speak the Gospel to all who serve the greater good, reminding us that that our truest identity is found in relationship with the triune God, and only from that relationship can self-flourishing in the midst of sacrifice occur. And a chapter urging the Mongolian Church to embrace its marginalization as an opportunity to be a host and refuge for the mentally ill and stigmatized provides the American Church with articulations of how to meet the needs of this same population in their own midst. Thus, we see how public theology for everyday life can, in fact, be a roadmap to navigate the complexities of a globalized world.

What's Next?

So, where do we go from here? The authors of this volume have taken the time to think deeply about their lived experiences, asking hard questions of the faith and not being content with simple answers. They have examined a myriad of forces pushing and pulling on the threads of the webs that make up contemporary public life and so are able to articulate the simplicity on the other side of complexity. Their work illuminates how simple narratives have rich and deep undercurrents of unseen ideologies, how complex normalcy really is, and how the tools of our Christian faith can help us navigate the complex currents of a globalized world. Yet, importantly, they do not stop there.

You may have noticed that the chapters in this volume go beyond simple description; they all have prescriptive elements as well. This is partly because they are all fostered in the same school of thought: that public theology has a "bent toward praxis," as Okesson wrote in the introduction. Theologian Miroslav Volf reminds us that Christianity is not to be idle in the world, but is in fact to be the shaper of the everydayness of life; work, education, commerce, social organizations, church, and all other mundanity are to be sculpted by the story of God in the world.[5] The chapters in this volume give us glimpses of how our rich faith, can inform our public engagement and open us to wider possibilities of healthy praxis.

However, more work is needed. Primarily, the world needs more everyday people from different backgrounds, contexts, and socioeconomic statuses to be thinking, doing, and publishing public theology. Within an everchanging, globalized world, we need a diverse group of everyday public theologians who are willing to do the hard work of asking tough questions about seemingly commonplace things and who will not be satisfied with the simplicity on the near side of complexity. Similarly, we need a diverse group of everypersons to examine and illuminate the Church's own presuppositions and undercurrents (in all contexts) and allow the light of God to shine in hidden places and blind spots. How else can we see all the facets or the true depths of the important public conversations that are rocking the world today? By refusing an easy reductionism of our own lives and the issues we grapple with, and by taking the time to abide in the richness of living in a globalized world, public theology enables us to navigate the complexities of everyday life with surety and hope.

Amanda L. Allen,
August 2020

---

5 Miroslav Volf, *A Public Faith: How Followers of Christ Should Serve the Common Good* (Grand Rapids, MI: Brazos Press): 16-17.